What Families Say about
· · · · · · · · · · · · · · *The Truth about College Admission* ·

"I read *The Truth about College Admission* in March while our high school senior was waiting to hear from her choices. This puts me about two years too late. I winced at where I got it wrong and felt lucky where I got it right. Barnard and Clark have combined their considerable experience to craft a guide that is witty and wise, profound and practical, funny and full of heart. They keep the focus on the essential questions in an effort to convert the college experience into something bold and wonderful—a celebration of family. This book will be my gift for friends who have children starting their college adventure." **—MICHAEL K-D.**, parent, Saint Paul, MN

"Who knew a college admission book could be so enjoyable *and* provide pertinent information? This is exactly what I found. Barnard and Clark's perspective, mixing facts with humor, helped reduce my own stress and gave me a much-needed reality check. *The Truth about College Admission* is an outstanding resource for families, as it thoughtfully addresses the journey of college admission from beginning to move-in day." **—TINSLEY H.**, parent, Peachtree Corners, GA

"We could tell our sixteen-year-old was anxious about the college admission process. So we determined to make it a fun family activity: we agreed to meet once a week on Saturdays over cookies and tea to chat, ask questions, and explore ideas. What had been a dreaded topic became an enjoyable activity that she directed. We learned more in that first family conversation than we had over the previous several months of what seemed to her to be painful cross-examinations. This book is a godsend." **—PAUL M.**, parent, Pasadena, CA

"Barnard and Clark's writing effortlessly blends wisdom and wit, honesty and insight. It has truly saved our family's sanity during our college admission adventure." **—GAIL and LOREN S.**, parents, Atlanta, GA

"Every family approaching college applications should be armed with *The Truth about College Admission*. It begins with aligning expectations and establishing a game plan for success. Each chapter follows the process from discovery, to applications and responses, and provides questions and realignment exercises for each engagement. This book helped us make sense of the process and understand the results. It was the soothing balm we all needed." **—LINDA S.**, parent, New York, NY

"During the college admission process, we were overwhelmed by all the 'noise' out there. I longed for guidance that would lead us in a way that felt more thoughtful and conscious. Then I found this book. It gave us permission to trust our own instincts and know that we don't have to get caught up in hiring expensive college consultants and comparing our child's journey to all her peers. Because we had this book as a resource, my family has learned to step back, take a deep breath, and ask questions about what's really important to us. This book is my new go-to gift for the parent of every junior and senior in high school!" **—KASEY M.**, parent, Wilton, NH

What Professionals Say about
· · · · · · · · · · · · · *The Truth about College Admission* · · · · · · · · · · · · ·

"At last, a book about the college admission process that doesn't promise secret tips for admission (hint—there are none!) but instead provides advice from two respected and experienced professionals. If families are looking for how to manage the college admission process in an ethical, thoughtful, student-centered way, this book provides an important road map written in a way that even the most reluctant student will find engaging." —**THYRA L. BRIGGS,** Vice President for Admission and Financial Aid, Harvey Mudd College

"I love this book. It's packed with sensible advice and some wonderful questions. I highly recommend it." —**ETHAN SAWYER,** College Essay Guy

"The world of college admission has changed significantly since the pandemic. Students and families who seek to understand the nuances of applying to and paying for college in today's environment should read this important book, written by two leading experts in the profession." —**ANGEL B. PÉREZ,** Chief Executive Officer, National Association for College Admission Counseling

"Barnard and Clark make a stressful decision more sane, understandable, and educationally useful. This book is needed because misinformation and a cacophony of noise about college admission are hurting students." —**JEROME A. LUCIDO,** Executive Director, University of Southern California Center for Enrollment Research, Policy, and Practice

"Barnard and Clark offer calm, thoughtful advice to lessen the stress felt by many college-bound families. This book is full of applicable, timely, and practical tools to help navigate the complex college admission process. I fully recommend this book for anyone who is starting or has been through this exciting journey." —**DIANE CAMPBELL,** Director of College Counseling, Liberty Common High School

"In a field that is sometimes viewed as nearly as much art as science and often fraught with misinformation, Barnard and Clark provide expertise that is accurate, useful, and empathetic to the needs of applicants and their families. The book is a terrific resource for students and parents." —**GARY S. MAY,** Chancellor, University of California at Davis

"A must-read for families embarking on the college search process! Barnard and Clark provide a step-by-step guide filled with professional insight, myth-busting realities, and practical tips for students and families not just to survive but to thrive throughout the college search process." —**LISA KEEGAN,** Vice President for Enrollment Management, Bucknell University

"We have allowed admission selectivity to become a proxy for quality when it comes to how we assess colleges and universities. Barnard and Clark help us remember that talented students and incredible universities, of all levels of selectivity, find their way to each other every year. The right combination of student and college can be transformative for both! This book is a much-needed resource for families." —**GARY CLARK,** Director of Undergraduate Admission, University of California at Los Angeles

The Truth about College Admission

The Truth about
COLLEGE
ADMISSION

· ·

A FAMILY GUIDE
TO GETTING IN AND STAYING TOGETHER

· ·

SECOND EDITION

Brennan Barnard
and Rick Clark

JOHNS HOPKINS UNIVERSITY PRESS

Baltimore

Johns Hopkins University Press
2715 North Charles Street
Baltimore, Maryland 21218
www.press.jhu.edu

Library of Congress Cataloging-in-Publication Data

Names: Barnard, Brennan E., 1974– author. | Clark, Rick, 1974– author.
Title: The truth about college admission : a family guide to getting in and staying
    together / Brennan Barnard and Rick Clark.
Description: Second edition. | Baltimore : Johns Hopkins University Press, [2023] |
    Includes bibliographical references and index.
Identifiers: LCCN 2022061228 | ISBN 9781421447483 (paperback) |
    ISBN 9781421447490 (ebook)
Subjects: LCSH: Universities and colleges—United States—Admission. |
    College choice—United States.
Classification: LCC LB2351.2 .B37 2023 | DDC 378.1/610973—dc23/eng/20221221
LC record available at https://lccn.loc.gov/2022061228

A catalog record for this book is available from the British Library.

Special discounts are available for bulk purchases of this book. For more information, please contact
Special Sales at specialsales@jh.edu.

*For our friend Denis Gainty, whose joyful curiosity and
dedication to always asking "why?"
lives on in connection and spirit*

Contents

Preface

Uncertainty. If the past few years have taught us anything, it is that we must expect the unexpected. Life is uncertain and unpredictable, and so is college admission. The first edition of this book was published in fall of 2019, only months before the global pandemic changed everything. The landscape in college admission soon looked different in terms of testing, searching, visiting, applying, and attending. What did not change was the central message that we put forward in the first edition, and that is the power of family and unity. If anything, the disruption reinforced the importance of community and mutual support.

In this second edition, we acknowledge the recent changes in the admission experience, but more importantly we affirm the reality that change is inevitable and that we can control what we can control. By the time this new edition is published, parts of it may be outdated. Will artificial intelligence play a greater role in admission? Will the cost of college and the financial aid landscape look different? Will the US Department of Justice or courts of law here or abroad have dictated policy changes in how colleges assess applicants? What else can we not predict? In fall 2019 we certainly did not anticipate that six months later we would be Zooming to work from our dining room table.

This book is about what we do know: that family matters and that how you approach conversations and decisions in your family has long-term implications. In many homes around our nation, the discussion surrounding college begins in elementary school. With one eye on their own children, parents are also looking around their community. At work, on the soccer field, and at dinner parties, stories of high school seniors "getting in" to or "getting rejected" by one college or another fuel a growing consternation.

By the time middle school rolls around, the stakes seem high. "Which classes do 'we' need to take?" "Should our daughter volunteer in an orphanage abroad or attend a computing camp this summer?" "Is it true that Eagle Scouts have a better chance of being admitted to an Ivy League school?"

Loving parents simply want their kids to have choices and to live a happy, successful life. However, with understandably high hopes and expectations, parents often hinge future success on their children being admitted to a small subset of top-ranked, selective colleges.

Entering and progressing through high school with this mentality can create a pressure cooker for families that leads to fixation and constant comparisons: of the number of Advanced Placement courses taken, of grades made, test scores earned, and awards won—all in the name of "standing out" or "being enough" on college applications. Left unchecked over time, and especially in students' last two years of high school, this emphasis can create fissures in a family when the single focus becomes "getting in." *The Truth about College Admission* is meant to help you stay together as a family through this experience.

This book was written to put the college search and admission experience in perspective for your family. It challenges the common narrative that college admission is a rite of passage to fret or fear and reclaims the opportunity many students and families often miss, namely, that the admission experience provides growth, discovery, and excitement for the future. This book refutes some claims routinely made by the media: that there are only 25 great institutions of higher education in our nation, that many students have no chance of getting into a "good school," and that they must follow a secret formula through high school to unlock success.

In this book, students and their families will find insights and tips but no tricks; analogies help to frame why and how admission decisions are made, but we make no promises or offer any guarantees of acceptance to particular schools. No shortage of how-to books out there claim to uncover the "secret" to getting into college. The guidebook you now hold is one for the rest of us—parents and students who are intent on putting family first by engaging in real, healthy, balanced conversations. We will bring you smiles and some laughs and, more importantly, encourage students to think deeply about why they are going to college. Answering *why* naturally leads them to *where* they should visit, apply, and ultimately go, in order to grow, learn, and thrive in and beyond their college years.

Most books on this subject are written by visiting journalists glancing in from the outside or by former short-term staff members at competitive private colleges who are peddling a tell-all or by parents purporting to be experts because their child was admitted to an Ivy League school. These narratives feed the anxiety around the college admission conversation by perpetuating the myth that there are tricks, insider information, and foolproof ways to avoid pitfalls in college admission known only to the self-proclaimed experts. They claim to have a corner on the market of "winning essays" or to know the perfect combination of extracurricular activities to get a scholarship or a coveted spot at a highly selective university. Families are barraged with solicitations from consultants and independent agents who charge exorbitant fees for a "5-star essay" and a promise to "open the doors to the nation's best colleges." The truth, though, is that there is no blueprint for successful applications or a clear-cut pathway to a specific school. Ultimately, the secret is that there is no secret, but there can be sanity, levity, and unity.

Our guidebook is honest. It grew out of our combined four decades of work in the admission field, advising students and families in schools and communities. Using that experience, we explain why nobody can ensure you a spot at selective colleges, and we describe how institutional priorities and school missions influence admission decisions. Rather than laying out a *strategy* that can breed anxiety in families, *The Truth about College Admission* debunks the myth that there is a script for "standing out" and instead reframes the discussion about the landscape of American higher education. Punctuated with quotes from other veteran admission professionals, insight from thoughtful college leaders, and reflections from parents and students throughout our nation, this book provides anecdotes and perspective, questions and encouragement, options and hope that will help your family thrive—not just survive—during the college search and selection *experience*.

Authors' Note: As educators and admission professionals, we believe strongly in the power of higher education as a public good and a vehicle for transforming lives and benefiting both individuals and society, but we also acknowledge that college is not for everyone. This book is written for students and families who have decided that pursuing a college degree is both valuable and important. We focus our recommendations on traditional college-age students who are seeking four-year degrees. Our intention is to provide a guide for navigating college admission that is healthier and broader than what we commonly see.

We use the words *family* and *parents* as catchall terms in framing our recommendations. We are aware, of course, that families come in all shapes and sizes, so "parents" could well encompass guardians, grandparents, or other trusted adults who are supporting young people through this experience. We want to honor the power of family as representing connection and community in helping students dream and plan for their future. Our hope is that this guide will serve as a structure and resource for anyone embarking on the college search and application journey.

How to Use This Book

This book is designed to be a companion guide for families making their way together through the college admission experience. It is intended to be a progressive resource that you can follow and refer to throughout your college search and application journey.

This guide is filled with both a contextual exploration of college admission and pragmatic resources and exercises that you can use along the way. Divided into four parts, it is designed to prompt questions and facilitate conversations. The first part sets the stage for your college search. We provide suggestions for how best to approach the experience and what to expect from colleges and from one another as a family. Chapter 1 asks the important foundational question of *why* you are going to college and is followed in chapter 2 by a review of the current landscape in admission and how colleges search for students. We explain the big marketing budgets of schools and unpack the strategies they have for recruiting students. Chapter 3 explores some of the issues—or wedges, as we term them—that often drive families apart if not approached intentionally and thoughtfully.

After setting the stage, we dive into the practical aspects of the college admission experience in part II. Chapter 4 explores the realities of paying for college by providing the basic knowledge you will need to understand costs, financial aid, and other issues of affordability. Chapter 5 incorporates contextual material from the preceding chapters to help you build a balanced list of schools to apply to. We discuss the concept of *reach*, *target*, and *likely* schools while making the case that being admitted to a school in any of these categories would be a great option. We explore in detail the notion of *match* and explain why the "right" school is not about where it ranks but rather about where a student is going to learn, grow, build a network, thrive inside and outside the classroom, and launch into life after college. Next, chapter 6 discusses how to go about visiting colleges, whether in person or online. We recommend questions to ask, people to meet, and ways to maximize your time and reflect on what you've learned in your evolving college search. We relate anecdotes and provide tips for parents and students so that they can avoid conflict and division. The chapter closes with quotes from parents and students about their experiences visiting a variety of colleges.

In the third part, chapters 7, 8, 9, and 10 explore what colleges are looking for and how they make their admission decisions, while addressing some of the pitfalls and best practices in applying to college. We explain the different application plans (and their typical deadlines) that schools offer. We take readers behind the scenes in college admission offices with discussions of formulaic review, holistic review, and institutional priorities. You will understand the ruminations and deliberations of admission committees as they arrive at decisions in filling their classes. We provide nuance and context for what happens after you submit your application. Who are these people on the other end? What takes them so long to make a decision? We include anecdotes and insight from admission deans and counselors. We delve into each decision a student might receive: admit, deny, defer, or wait-list. What does each one mean? What should you do next, if anything?

In the last part, chapters 11, 12, and 13 provide practical guidance for making a final college choice that honors a mix of emotion and pragmatism. We propose a decision-making process that is grounded in honesty about desires, future, finances, and more. We also examine the decision-making time frame, which is often tight, and discuss how to do preparatory soul searching and research before admission decisions and financial aid packages arrive. We focus on the critical need to "celebrate your success," together as a family, with each college acceptance. Lastly, acknowledging that this is a bittersweet time for parents, we explore the notion of transitioning from parent to partner. We close with letters written to students and parents separately about how to make the most of this experience and to appreciate the role of family.

Just as the college admission experience is not to be approached passively, neither is this book. Our goal throughout is to help you remain together, to provide perspective, and to challenge you to consider questions that will promote introspection and unity. At the end of each chapter, you will find a Try This exercise that invites you to practice what you have just learned. This is followed by questions to reflect on and discuss in a Talk about This section. Next, a Check In prompts you to confer as family: Are you all on the same page? If not, what do you need to do, discuss, or learn to get there? Finally, in Extra Credit you will find additional resources to explore and exercises to try.

Our hope is that your family will take the time to try the exercises and have the discussions, which are designed to make your experience meaningful, uniting, and successful. The chapters are arranged progressively, but families will benefit from returning to chapters for reference through the admission journey. So, lean in, check in, and stay together as you experience this amazing adventure as a family.

PART I

CHAPTER 1

Why Are You Going to College?

We thought we had all the answers.
It was the questions we had wrong.
"11 O'CLOCK TICK TOCK" BY U2

A family with generations of graduates from Georgia Tech had a daughter who had been denied admission. Her parents came to the admission office to appeal the decision. The father began, earnestly and restrained, "I just don't understand. She has all As. She is at the top of her class. Her test scores are great. When I got into Tech, I was not half as prepared as she is now. My test scores were average, and I'd never taken an Advanced Placement class in my life." As he described the activities his daughter had participated in and the praise her teachers and coaches regularly lavished on her, his hands started to clench. Periodically, he would bite his lower lip slightly and glance anxiously at his wife.

Meanwhile, the mother's head was down. Even though her brown hair was hiding much of her face, I (Rick) could tell her eyes were softly shut, perhaps in hopes she was anywhere but in my office right then. Their daughter was just staring straight ahead and shaking her head slowly. Then, for the first time, the father paused.

Momentary silence, a pregnant pause. Speaking again, he raised his voice, not quite yelling, and knocked his clenched fist on the table, "I just don't understand! This is not fair! It's not right! She's worked her whole life for this. You all must have made a mistake."

As he talked, I was thinking of the thousands of other talented applicants we had considered, many of whom had nearly perfect grades and SAT/ACT scores. I was thinking of the hundreds of students who had received the Girl Scout Gold Award or attained a black belt in tae kwon do or who had earned their pilot's license or been captain of both the volleyball and tennis teams. In my mind I was recalling how many students we did not admit—based on the number of spots available in that year's incoming class—who would clearly do well academically and socially on any campus in the country.

Now, this family was looking to me for an answer, but what could I really offer? What would be genuine, accurate, and helpful when what I wanted to say was "I see your point"? I was definitely not going to contest that she was a bright student with excellent grades and impressive involvement outside the classroom. There was nothing *wrong* with her essays or short-answer questions. The recommendations from her teacher and school counselor were glowing. Honestly, as with most of our applicants, I could make a case for admitting her— and in looking at the notes in her file, I saw that a member of our admission staff had done just that. Would she succeed in the classroom? Absolutely. Was she the type of student we would like to have on campus? Without question. It was clear from her application that she would continue to contribute significantly beyond the classroom. Like so many parents, this father was demanding to know exactly why she was denied. He wanted me to point to test scores or grades or to the number of clubs she had been part of and tell him they were "not good enough" or "not high enough."

The reality was that, numerically, we had admitted some students with lower scores or lower grades or less involvement. We had done so based on our undergraduate admission goals—that is, institutional fit/match, geographic region, curricular interest, or specific academic, personal, or extracurricular background.

When we talk about holistic admission review to prospective families, we mean that there is no numeric formula—there is no *one* thing. College admission at selective schools is a human process, and as such, it is all things human—subjective and imperfect. In the recruitment phase, families find it reassuring to hear that admission officers use professional judgment, pay close attention to context, and do not base decisions on a single number. When a student is denied, however, they want a quantifiable rationale and are ineffably frustrated by a holistic review process. For this young woman, that was where we sat, and the decision was not going to change.

"You know," her father continued, "she has been offered merit scholarships elsewhere and was admitted to honors colleges at several universities. But you're saying she's not good enough." His daughter winced at this, and his wife let out an audible sigh. He then pulled out several acceptance and scholarship letters from other colleges from the manila folder in front of him. As he pointed to financial aid figures and phrases like "invite you," "congratulations again," and "we hope you'll join," I finally interjected, because this was where their focus should be. Right in front of them was hope: letter after letter of choices, opportunity, excitement, support, and invitation. She had amazing options from great schools expressing how excited they would be to have her on campus. Carefully, I explained that Georgia Tech was no longer an option. Our decision had been made. Our class was full. Eventually, we moved on to have a lengthy but healthy discussion about the other schools and what she hoped to experience and accomplish in college and beyond. Over the course of the next 45 minutes, incredibly, the conversation turned into a warm, productive, and enjoyable conversation that ended with an awkward (though appreciated) quasi-group hug.

> **When we talk about holistic admission review, we mean there is no numeric formula—there is no *one* thing.**

The truth, however, is that the conversation should have taken place months, or even years, before at home.

PEOPLE LOVE THEIR KIDS

Unfortunately, each year after decisions are released, admission offices around the country get hundreds of phone calls and emails from people threatening to write their alma mater out of their will, claiming bias or conspiracy, or informing us that we have ruined family vacation or winter holidays—or life altogether. How does that all feel? Terrible. But thankfully, we know where it comes from.

Regardless of the industry, it is human nature for people to question, examine, shake their head in disapproval, and express vehement opinions. One good example of this is sports, where coaches are constantly second-guessed by fans about the play they called or the player they didn't start. We have all heard this type of Monday-morning chatter on the radio or at the office or coffee shop: "If I were the coach . . ." or "How could he think that was going to work against that defense!" Similar criticism is also leveled at accountants, town councils, tech CEOs, baristas, airline gate agents, and chefs. As people, we are perpetually assessing, analyzing, and looking for ways that things could be improved or done differently. Thankfully so—because that questioning leads to better bridges, more efficient devices, safer car seats, and better-tasting food.

There is no question that the rising cost of tuition, increasing debt loads, issues of mental health, and declining admit rates at our nation's most well-known public and private colleges are legitimate concerns that contribute to consternation, speculation, and frustration. The press, politicians, and pundits in community coffee shops and high school bleachers attribute the stress and anxiety over selective college admission to these macro-issues. The reality, though, is that while these concerns are legitimate, the core of the admission experience is deeply personal and relational. If there is one fundamental truth we have come to appreciate in this field, it is this: people love their kids.

> The admission experience is deeply and uniquely personal and relational.

With children of our own and more than 40 years combined of working in college admission and counseling, we are still annually reminded of the palpable power of the basic human truth that people love their kids. While this truth is obvious, it is also central to understanding the college admission experience.

People love their kids. This is why a mother will call an admission office, pretending to be her daughter in hopes of receiving a password or an admission decision. It is why a father will show up in the admission office at 7:50 a.m. on the day after his son was wait-listed. It is why we regularly hear statements like "*We* are taking the SAT next weekend" or "*Our* first choice is Boston College." *People love their kids.* As a parent, you have been holding them up since they were born, and even now that they are young adults, you are figuratively doing the same. When they were little, you could literally pick them up above your head, spin them around, and hold them close as they smiled and giggled with joy. They trusted you implicitly. They were safe and happy.

As they grew up, you spent countless hours idling in carpool lines; you caught up on neighborhood news while waiting for a 30-second leg of a three-hour swim meet; you helped sell cookies or wrapping paper or hams for team, club, or school fundraisers. When COVID-19 upended life, one of your first thoughts was "How will this impact my child?" You have traveled hundreds or maybe thousands of miles to visit family, attend tournaments, or enjoy a long weekend at the beach or in the mountains. But fundamentally nothing has changed over the years. Sure, they weigh more now; they eat more and put product in their hair. But you are still holding them up—and through all of that change, you have not wavered in your desire for their trust, happiness, safety, and excitement, because your love is constant.

If you are a student reading this, you need to be reminded of this fact. The admission experience can make your mom or dad or other adults in your life go a little wacky at times. Maddening, swirling, repetitive questions about whether you have finished an application essay or know about a deadline or have checked out the brochure they put on your bed last Wednesday may feel like pestering. It can sound like nagging. In reality, it is just 17 years of love in disguise.

The truth is the college admission experience is all about family.
Reprinted with the permission of Adam Zyglis.

EXPERIENCING ADMISSION

There are few experiences short of death, disease, injury or divorce that have as much potential for trauma for American families as the college admissions process. The first great rite of passage for young humans once was killing a wild animal. That was replaced by getting married, or getting a job. These days it is getting into college. —Jay Mathews, *Washington Post*

You could dismiss this statement as hyperbolic journalism, but the angst surrounding college admission is both palpable and growing, as the most selective schools around the nation become even more competitive. Fundamentally, much of the anxiety about college admission comes down to a principal concept of economics: supply and demand. Phenomenally talented students from around the world are applying to a similar subset of schools with relatively fixed undergraduate population sizes. That you cannot control. What you can control is your approach. You can improve and seek perspective. You can have confidence in yourself. The reality is that the college admission experience is just that, an experience—not simply a means to a specific end but rather an opportunity for your family to learn and grow closer. Ultimately, the decisions and conversations your family should be most concerned with are the ones that occur in rooms you enter every day (your living room, your classroom)—the ones you can control—not those occurring in college admission offices hundreds of miles away.

> **Your vision should not be of *which* campus you will walk onto but rather *how* you will walk through the admission experience— together as a family.**

There are high-priced educational consultants who will assure you they can predict the probability of your admission to certain schools. They will claim to polish essays or boost test scores to "guarantee" your admittance. These promises, however, if taken at face value, would be time, money, and hope misspent. The truth is there is no "sure pathway to Pomona College" or "Dartmouth with distinction formula" to follow. Because this is the case, your vision should not be all about *which* campus you will walk onto but instead *how* you will walk through this entire admission experience—together. Many students and their families focus on getting into one particular school or small set of schools. We hope you will instead see that the real goal is being admitted to several schools you are genuinely excited about while staying close as a family. The image of success is not ultimately wearing a particular school's sweatshirt or putting a specific college's bumper sticker on your car. As you go through the admission experience, your family's commitment should be the same as it's always been—to support, encourage, share, trust, and lift one another up.

―――――

The college search is an exciting time for students and families. I so wish students could see that they are in the driver's seat when it comes to where they go to college. I realize that they don't always feel like this is the case, but students have the opportunity to <u>choose</u> to which colleges or universities they submit applications. And students then have the opportunity to <u>choose</u> at which college or university they enroll from among their admission offers. —Rachelle Hernandez, Vice Provost for Student Affairs, Johns Hopkins University

―――――

COLLEGE SEARCH REDESIGNED

Every summer colleges around the country reevaluate and redesign their "road piece." This is the ubiquitous eight-page brochure colleges use to market themselves when traveling to high schools and college fairs throughout the year. You have likely seen these showing up in your mailbox or in-box too. After a while they become extremely predictable:

Page 1: A picture of the football team winning. It is a sunny day, and the school's star player is running triumphantly toward the end zone. The scoreboard shows (perhaps was photoshopped to show) the home team winning 47–0. Bonus points if the shot includes a vanquished opponent on the ground with grass in his facemask or bent over with hands on knees in despair.

Page 2: Three students of different ethnicities sitting under a tree with a professor. One is wearing a college-branded shirt, another has a worn backpack casually slung to the side. The professor always strikes an important balance: youthful energy with sage wisdom, casual professorial fashion without being unkempt, and always at the perfect distance from students to connote caring without being creepy. You'll notice too that the students have the perfect combination of facial expression and body language to demonstrate they are simultaneously engaged yet pensive.

Page 3: A shot of a student standing on something high—possibly near a statue or a grassy bluff overlooking the ocean. The angle perfectly captures the school's logo on her sleeve or hat and her gaze of curiosity as she clearly contemplates life's limitless possibilities. No brochure is complete without a three-to-four-word, verb-led challenge: *Change Your World, Dream Big—Live Bigger, Lead the Way*, or *Create the Future*. (What you don't see are the countless sticky notes and lunch meetings spent coming up with that tagline, which invariably will be moderately adopted around campus and then phased out in a few years.)

Rounding out the brochure are some cool infographics with admission deadlines, web addresses, GPA ranges, application totals, admit rates, and, of course, rankings.

The rankings an institution chooses to advertise vary widely. There are the classics: Top 50 Public Universities, Top 100 Colleges in the Nation, and Best Value Schools. The variety of rankings also allows schools to creatively boast of less conventional accolades: "We have the best food selection!" "Our bench-to-student ratio is the lowest in the Midwest!" "We have the third-highest squirrel-to-student ratio in our conference!" "We play the widest variety of music from the lampposts on the quad!" And the list goes on. More on this in chapter 2.

At one of Georgia Tech's annual meetings to discuss brochure design, I (Rick) suggested that we remove the rankings information. Upon hearing this, our editor tilted her head slightly to the left and backward as her eyebrows furrowed. Understanding international body language for "What?!" I went on to say that we had already removed it from our daily presentation as well.

There is a ranking for everything.
Each logo is printed with the permission of the respective ranking organization.

"But that's the first thing people look for," she protested. "I see them on campus flipping through to find the rankings." Once she realized that I was not going to respond, she put her palms flat on the table and asked, "OK. Well, if not the rankings, then what do we lead with?"

It is simple really. We need to start with *why* a student would want to come to Georgia Tech. *What* makes us different? *Who* are we as a community and an institution? We can't just tout rankings and statistics and expect students and families to connect. We need to combat stereotypes of Georgia Tech (engineering only, urban jungle, lab-coated students in dark basements peering closely at beakers filled with colored liquid) and help students work through the noise of all the schools they are hearing from.

Ultimately that is your challenge as an applicant and as a family. You are going to have to work harder than scanning a particular rankings list or blindly putting stock in a school that claims to be the best at something. Cutting through the cacophony of college recruitment is not easy because the truth is that we who represent colleges don't do a great job of differentiating ourselves in the materials we send out, the presentations we give, and the websites we build. Look at enough brochures, and all schools start looking the same. Cover up the name of the college on a brochure you have lying around. You will find it hard to tell the difference between a small private college in the middle of Ohio and a flagship public university in the Pacific

Northwest. As you flip through the pages, each one paints compelling pictures of opportunities to make friends, conduct research, study abroad, work with faculty, receive an internship, and more.

Colleges do this on campus tours as well. They intentionally find the most involved students to talk about all of the amazing research they've done, trips they've taken, and jobs offers they have received. While relaying their incredible experiences, they will intersperse equally impressive anecdotes about friends or roommates studying abroad or creating companies—all the while somehow remaining impervious to the 90-degree heat. We have been on campus tours all over our country in recent years, and these student ambassadors are amazing. And they are real people, too, not cyborgs or pretend archetypes or conglomerates of multiple top students. Most adults walk away from these visits shaking their heads in amazement over their tour guide's brilliance, while silently questioning their own life accomplishments. (We will provide you with tips for maximizing your time on campus visits and good questions to ask while you are there in chapter 6.)

If every school seems perfect on its brochure, website, and guided tour, how do you find a college that is a good match for you? Where do you *start*? You start exactly where Georgia Tech *restarted* its brochure design process—by looking inward instead of outward and by asking questions. You start by asking the most critical question, *Why am I going to college?*

YOUR CORNERSTONE QUESTION

In constructing a building, the most important part of the project is not the blueprint or the location or even the style but rather the laying of the cornerstone—also known as the foundation stone. If the cornerstone is not set correctly, the integrity of the entire building will be compromised. Everything orients around this integral piece. Choosing the right location for the building, carefully selecting the materials, and understanding the associated costs are all important, but none of that will matter in the end if you don't properly set the cornerstone. When it comes to your college search, asking the right questions is your cornerstone.

We get it. The list of annoying questions a high school student hears can be long. "Did you finish that paper?" "Can I borrow your sweatshirt?" "Are you ready for school?" We are sure you can think of many other questions you commonly hear from parents, siblings, coaches, friends, or a boss. But the most frequent, most repeated, and most frustrating—and perhaps the one question all of them eventually ask you—is "Where do you want to go to college?"

While exhausting because of its prevalence, the real problem with this question of *where* is not the frequency with which it's asked but the fact that it's asked prematurely. On some level, this is to be expected because much of life in high school points in that direction. Your curriculum (or even the name of your school) may include "college preparatory." Advanced Placement, International Baccalaureate, and the opportunity to take university-level courses through dual enrollment all contribute to making college a pervasive topic of conversation for a high school student. Even the activities you love and joined for fun become mixed up in the equation: "Keep doing that. It will look great on your college application." "Definitely volunteer too. Colleges want to see that." Because you are surrounded by these programs and perspectives, college becomes assumed. It is perceived as inevitable—a foregone conclusion. As a result, far too many students arrive at college without having stepped off the hamster wheel to ask the cornerstone question, the one that is at root a family question: *Why are you going to college?*

Why is a lot more complicated and nuanced than *where*. *Where* is easy. It requires only a name and typically lacks much thought: "University of X." Done. In contrast, *why* forces introspection and leads to a host of additional questions about your future college experience.

- Why would you invest so much money in a college education?

- Why are you wanting to work hard academically beyond high school to earn a college degree?

- Why are you going to leave all of your friends and the comfort of the known to move 500 miles away, sleep in a single bed, and share a 300-square-foot room with a stranger?

- Why are you willing to eat coffee grounds to stay awake and study until 3:00 a.m. for an exam on differential equations or British literature?

Why is more layered because it leads to big questions like *Who are you?* and *Who do you want to be in the future?* Let's start, though, a little more simply.

- What types of people do you hope to meet, connect with, and learn from in college?

- What opportunities do you want this experience to provide in the future?

- How and in what setting do you best learn?

- How far away from home are you willing to go for college?

- What type of people bring out your best?

- How much can you—and should you—pay for this opportunity?

- What is most important to you as you leave high school and look ahead to your next chapter in life?

Anyone who has been married more than a few years—and certainly anyone who has been married more than once—will say that you have to love yourself, know yourself, and understand yourself before you can possibly commit to a lifetime of loving another person. College is no different. You cannot answer "*Where* are you going to college?" until you first answer "*Why* are you going?" Answering *why* will lead you to *where*. "I'm looking at this university because it has an excellent major in what I want to study" or ". . . because I can build a strong network there" or ". . . because going to school in that city will let me pursue my passion for X while in college."

WHY IS YOUR CORNERSTONE

Let asking *why* be your cornerstone. Let it be your foundation for the entire college experience. *Why* must be asked first, because it gives direction to *where*. Asking *why* puts rankings into perspective. It puts the dollars in a return-on-investment chart into perspective. It puts into perspective your parents' desire for a second-generation Bobcat,

Panther, or another ferocious mascot (and they've got a picture of you in a onesie as a baby to prove it). At the end of the day, *where* should not be answered with "because I look good in those colors" or "because they are conference champs" or "because my parents went there" or "because they are number six." Seriously, when was the last time you heard someone celebrating, "We're number six! We're number six!"

> You cannot answer "*Where* are you going to college?" until you first answer "*Why* are you going?"

Ask anyone who has been to college, and if they are being honest, they can recount memories not pictured in any college's brochure. A dark, cold day in November of their first year when they sat on a too-firm mattress in their residence hall listening to a song that reminded them of high school friends or their hometown. Eating mediocre and creatively repurposed food for the eighth straight week, doing laundry alone at midnight, leaving the library bleary-eyed and over-caffeinated. Social media will convince you that college is a never-ending string of sunny days filled with groups of smiling friends going to class outside. At some point, every first-year student has the same questions rattle around in their head: "Why am I here? Did I make the right choice? Why does everyone else seem to be doing well while I am struggling?" Everyone has that day. Everyone has those lonely walks, isolated thoughts, and inevitable doubts. Everyone.

If you skip over *why* and jump straight to *where*, your answers will not have a firm foundation. The cornerstone to your entire college search and selection experience will not be properly and securely set. If that is the case, that cold November day will be even more disconcerting. You will not be able to reassure yourself that you made the right choice if you never asked yourself *why* or if your answers were not truly yours. Class sizes, number of squirrels, championship teams, family legacy, and inspiring slogans are not the materials you want to use as you start building toward *your* college experience.

We cannot help you decrease the number of people who will inevitably ask you *where* you want to go to college. But we can promise that the question will be far less annoying if you have the confidence of knowing *why* certain schools are on your mind or on your college list. *Why* will lead you to *where*. Don't skip a step. Crawl before you walk. Lay that cornerstone first.

⚡ *Try This*

Here is what we know. The incessant, ubiquitous query "Where do you want to go to college?" will continue to come your way. So the next time you're asked by a well-intentioned relative or family friend, redirect the conversation to *why*, and then ask a few questions of your own.

1. **Ask** them *why* they went to college. You will find that friends and family can provide you with some more questions to ask yourself before you begin considering *where*.

2. **Redirect** the conversation. Ask them to look back and consider how they would go about their college experience differently.

3. **Challenge** them to recommend colleges and universities they think would make sense for you, after listening to your reasons for *why* you are going to college.

🗨 Talk about This

1. *Why* do you want to go to college? For parents—why do you want your child to go to college?

2. Which schools are currently on your list to visit or apply to? Does your *where* still match your *why*? If not, discuss the reasons these schools appear.

3. After reading this chapter, what do you think will be your biggest challenge individually and as a family in the college admission experience?

👍 **CHECK IN.** After reading this chapter, are you still on the same page as a family? If you are not all-in together, what do you need to do, discuss, or learn to get there?

☆ Extra Credit

Take some time to watch Simon Sinek's TED Talk "Start with Why." We believe his presentation will help you think more deeply about your admission experience and, ultimately, what you really want to get out of a college education.

While it is always helpful for others to ask you questions, sometimes we learn the most from the questions we pause to ask ourselves. Scan the QR code in the upper corner to access some self-reflective questions about your interests, strengths, and hopes.

CHAPTER 2

Remapping the Admission Landscape

And the people in the houses / All went to the university,
Where they were put in boxes / And they came out all the same.
"LITTLE BOXES" BY MALVINA REYNOLDS

We have discussed the importance of asking yourself, perhaps for the first time, "*Why* am I going college?" before ever considering *where* that may actually be. We asked you to consider questions about the type of people you want to spend your time with, the experiences you hope to have in a campus community, and the ideal classroom environment that allows you to learn and engage. We also implored you to put family first—to remain committed to unity, trust, support, and encouragement.

Now that you have set your foundation for approaching the college experience, you are ready to build on it. What better way to learn how to take logical next steps than to take a quiz? Do not worry. This will not be graded. There are no prizes for correct responses or penalties for wrong ones, so no googling answers or asking Alexa or Siri. Pencils ready?

1. Approximately how many colleges and universities are there in the United States (including private, public, community colleges, two-year schools, four-year universities, technical, arts, comprehensive, etc.)?
   ☐ 1,000
   ☐ 2,800
   ☐ 4,000
   ☐ 6,500

2. Approximately how many four-year colleges and universities are there in the United States?
   ☐ 460
   ☐ 1,000
   ☐ 1,597
   ☐ 2,700

3. Of the four-year colleges and universities, how many admit less than one-third of applicants (that is, their admit rate is less than 33.3 percent)?
   ☐ 100
   ☐ 425
   ☐ 550
   ☐ 1,200

We will reveal the answers later in the chapter, but first, a story.

A few years ago, my (Rick's) family went to take holiday pictures in Piedmont Park, Atlanta's equivalent to Central Park. Before I say more, let me first apologize on behalf of parents everywhere for subjecting their kids to holiday pictures. If you have been asked to wear "that new shirt" and "sit casually" while smiling or certainly if you and your siblings were ever dragged to a beach, wearing jeans, no shoes, and untucked white button-downs, I am truly sorry.

At the time, our daughter, Elizabeth, was three and our son, AJ, was six. Piedmont Park is beautiful, but the geese can be aggressive. Elizabeth was wearing an off-white dress (a terrible decision in hindsight), so my biggest concern, I thought, was keeping her clothes clean—until we lost track of AJ. As my wife and the photographer walked briskly one way to scout out the next location for a picture, AJ took off down a trail in the opposite direction.

Andrew "AJ" Clark, age six, Piedmont Park, Atlanta, Georgia.

After following the trail for about five minutes, we came around a bend to find him six feet up and eight feet out on a magnolia branch. Wearing khaki pants, a light-blue button-down shirt, and a navy sweater vest, he was sitting in a meditational pose: legs crossed, eyes gently closed, arms outstretched, with index fingers touching thumbs. I saw his left eye open ever so slightly, and he said in the deepest voice a six-year-old can muster, "Look beyond what you see!" My first thought was "Wow. This kid is kind of weird," followed by "But he may also be a prophet, which would be interesting and potentially lucrative."

As any scholar of film will know, he was referencing one of the real gems of American movie history, *The Lion King 1½*. In one scene, Rafiki, the wise old baboon, challenges Timon to look beyond what he sees in order to find "hakuna matata": a life of no worries. While we cannot promise you that exactly, there is still much to learn from this sage advice.

LOOK BEYOND WHAT YOU SEE

It is tougher than you would think to look beyond what you see as you consider colleges, but it's absolutely critical. Consider these statistics:

- More than 200 American universities with undergraduate populations above 20,000 (IPEDS Data Retrieval Center 2020)

- More than 1,300 colleges with undergraduate populations under 1,000 (IPEDS Data Retrieval Center 2020)

- Approximately 930 public community colleges (Statista 2022)

- Average admit rate of Big Ten Conference (a.k.a. Big 14):
  57 percent (IPEDS Data Retrieval Center 2021–2022)

- Average admit rate of Southeastern Conference: 60 percent (IPEDS 2021–2022)

- Median admit rate of Pacific-12 Conference: 59 percent (IPEDS Data Retrieval Center 2021–2022)

- More than 100 historically Black colleges and universities (IPEDS Data Retrieval Center 2020)

- Nearly 250 four-year colleges and universities in California (Statista 2021)

- 40 colleges and universities in Arkansas (Arkansas Division of Higher Education)

- Nearly 260,000 undergraduates enrolled in schools of the Atlantic Coast Conference (IPEDS Data Retrieval Center 2020–2021)

- Over 1,400 colleges with undergraduate populations between 1,000 and 5,000 (IPEDS Data Retrieval Center 2020)

- Nearly 300 US colleges and universities that start with the letter *B* (IPEDS Data Retrieval Center 2020)

- Approximately 63,000 total undergraduates at the eight Ivy League schools (IPEDS Data Retrieval Center 2020–2021)

- Nearly 57,000 undergraduates attending Texas A&M–College Station (IPEDS Data Retrieval Center 2021)

In our experience, the students who end up the most disappointed by the college admission experience are those with a fixed and limited mindset—those who are trapped and myopic about the idea of one school, one kind of school, or one definition of "good" or "best." Conversely, students who finish their senior year feeling satisfied and confident in their college choice are often not the ones who got into their top choice or had a completely smooth admission experience. Instead, they acted like students during the college admission experience: they thought deeply, committed to a dynamic mindset, and were willing to question information and to test their assumptions along the way.

The prospect of a college education should be filled with possibility, hope, and joy—and so should the experience to get there. Attitude is everything, so start by internalizing that it really, truly is all going to work out. The great strength of our higher education system is its incredible diversity. As you embark on this journey, suspend your preconceived notions about what "the right" school is and open your mind to the countless number of incredible options out there for your student. You'll be amazed at the possibilities, and you'll discover some hope and joy along the way. —Jenny Rickard, President and CEO, Common Application

Now back to our quiz. Ready for the answers?

1. Question: How many colleges and universities of all kinds are there in the United States?

   Answer: ~4,000 (National Center for Education Statistics 2022)

2. Question: How many four-year colleges and universities are there in the United States?

   Answer: ~2,700 (National Center for Education Statistics 2022)

3. Question: How many four-year colleges in the country admit less than one-third of applicants?

   Answer: ~100 (*U.S. News and World Report* n.d.)

Having asked these same three questions to audiences at presentations and panels all over the country, we are guessing you underestimated in your answers to questions 1 and 2 and overestimated in your answer to question 3. You may also find it surprising to learn that only around 65 colleges and universities offer admission to less than 20 percent of applicants (*U.S. News and World Report* n.d.), a number that includes military institutes and specialized art and music schools. In fact, despite the post-COVID narrative that getting into college is increasingly difficult, the average acceptance rate at four-year schools has consistently remained above 60 percent. Each summer, the National Association for College Admission Counseling (NACAC) publishes its College Openings Update list. In most years, hundreds of schools are still accepting applications in the last few months before the new academic year begins.

.What does this mean for you? It means that getting into most colleges and universities around our country is not the real challenge for students who are doing well in high school. Instead it underscores the fact that hundreds of academically excellent and financially affordable colleges are looking to admit talented students who will not only succeed inside the classroom but also contribute meaningfully to the campus community. As the executive director for educational content and policy at NACAC, David Hawkins works alongside hundreds of admission and counseling professionals each year. He offers this sound advice about finding the right *fit*: "Getting into college is not an end unto itself; it's not a 'skins game' of seeing how many colleges you can get accepted to. It's about taking your first steps as an adult, and laying the foundation for the rest of your life. In that light, it doesn't make sense to choose colleges on any basis *other* than what's right for you."

> Hundreds of academically excellent and affordable colleges are looking to admit and enroll talented students.

Later in the book, we will discuss how schools make admission decisions, but for now you need to understand this fact: most schools are simply *looking to admit and enroll* good students.

Write down the first five colleges that come to your mind.

- What do they have in common?

- Are the majority of them in the same geographic area?

- Are they all private schools or public universities?

- How did you hear about them?

- Do most belong to the same athletic conference?

Compare your list of five schools with those of other family members, and ask friends or classmates to do this exercise.

- Do you find a lot of overlap between your list and those of people you know well?

- What does the comparison tell you about how you are currently thinking about college?

THE VALUE OF PERSPECTIVE

The truth is that too many students and families have a narrow or simply dated view of the higher education landscape. Our goal throughout this book is to illustrate just how vast it really is, to demonstrate that your choices are extensive, and then to help you determine which of the many schools are good matches for you.

Think about where you live. How many colleges and universities in your state can you name? The next time you take a road trip, keep an eye on the exit signs for universities. They are everywhere: schools bearing the names of cheeses (Colby College, American University), universities designed by or honoring presidents (University of Virginia, George Washington University, Lincoln University), schools with multiple directions in their name (Northeastern University, Northwestern University, Nova Southeastern University). Walk the halls of your high school during the fall, and you will likely see posters from colleges all over the country and the world.

Maintaining an open mind and looking beyond what you see is your job in the college search and admission experience. Regardless of where you live, this can be difficult. Students from your high school often go to one of a few colleges after they graduate. You see the same college teams playing sports on TV and the same college decals on cars in your high school's parking lot. Naturally, your frame of reference is limited.

The good news is that colleges will broaden your perspective if you let them. They make it incredibly easy to remember just how many choices you have. Remember those recruitment brochures from chapter 1? Beginning your sophomore year and ramping up your junior year, these will start appearing in your mailbox and email in-box.

COLLEGE SEARCH: A TWO-WAY STREET

The college admission process is a two-way street. That's right. You are not the only one searching for a good college match. Universities are doing this too. In fact, there is an entire industry around "search" because it is big business.

Here is how it works. When you register for standardized tests—PSAT, SAT, Pre-ACT, ACT, TOEFL (Test of English as a Foreign Language), or AP (Advanced Placement)—you'll have the option, by checking a box, of permitting the test maker to share your information with universities.

Colleges and universities contract with the College Board (maker of the SAT) or ACT to access databases and purchase names and contact information. This allows them to build what are known as "search campaigns" to identify high school students who seem to be good matches. They are able to narrow their search by multiple factors.

> Universities are searching for a good college match too—and the search for students is big business.

Search has expanded in recent years, partly as a result of limited standardized testing during the pandemic. Other companies in the college admission space are eager to sell student information to colleges seeking leads for prospective applicants. Surveys you can complete at your high school or online, college software programs, and companies that integrate search into their portfolio of products (such as Niche, Cappex, and College Bound Selection Service) collect your data and contract with colleges to share it. You should always be aware of how your personal information will be used. We feature testing companies in the hypothetical case study below, but this case study would apply as well to other providers of search data.

A CASE STUDY OF SEARCH

"Example College" is a private school of 6,500 students located in the Northeast. Recently, Example College was thrilled to receive a $20 million gift to enhance its Chemistry Department. The college's president announced plans to build a new facility and endow a chaired professorship. The donor also specified that she would like to see a 25 percent increase in females majoring in chemistry over the next five years.

Translation: For Example's vice president of enrollment management or the dean/director of admission, bolstering enrollment and improving gender equity in the Chemistry Department has just become an institutional priority, or IP. (Later in the book, we discuss how IPs affect admission decisions; they also influence recruitment budgets, travel, programming, communications efforts, and search buys.)

To work toward this enrollment goal, Example College will first determine the number of "prospects" it already has in its customer relationship management system. See the figure below; this is the traditional admission funnel. As you see, the funnel begins broadly with prospects and narrows through the stages of admission (inquiries, applicants, admits, confirms, enrolled).

At Example College, admission officers analyze the academic and demographic (geographic, gender, ethnic, etc.) profile of their current students and then devise a search strategy to help them meet the new target. After they determine how many additional female students they will need to enroll in chemistry each year, they are ready to access the databases of the College Board and ACT to purchase student names.

To narrow the funnel, step by step, schools select criteria for the type of students they want to communicate with and encourage to apply. This is known as a "search purchase." A sound search strategy will marry a school's IPs with its recruitment budget. Purchase rates

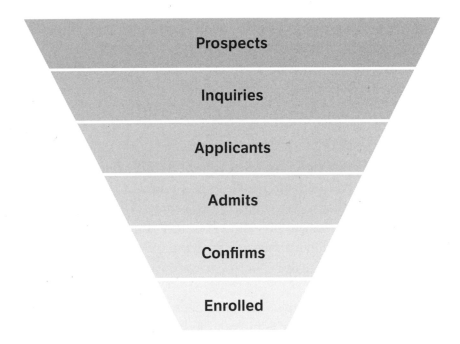

The traditional enrollment funnel.

have been increasing post-pandemic; for this case study we estimate a rate of $0.50 per student name for both ACT and the College Board.

Here is how Example College refines its search, where each parameter that's added filters the purchase toward a finer number:

Contact Information: mailing address, cell phone number, and email (assuming a student has provided each one)—2 million names, or $1,000,000

Graduation Year: sophomores, juniors, seniors—1,600,000 names, or $800,000

Major: chemistry—200,000 names, or $100,000

Geography: all New England and Middle Atlantic states (in this section you can also buy according to zip code, radius from a city, or individual state, nation, county, etc.)—60,000 names, or $30,000

Gender: female—25,000 names, or $12,500

Ethnicity: all—25,000 names, or $12,500

High School GPA: B+ or above (self-reported by the student and identified on a scale of A–D including plus and minus)—18,000 names, or $9,000

Test Scores: This is a little more complicated. PSAT and SAT scores are released in increments of 50. If the current SAT average of Example College students is 1320, the college will likely buy slightly lower scores. This is especially likely when purchasing names of sophomores and juniors, because statistics show that students raise their scores, on average, when they retake standardized tests. Example College will want to start recruiting these prospects early. The college could set the PSAT/SAT score at 1250+ and the ACT at 26+. Alternatively, the college might set a range with a floor and ceiling.* For the SAT/PSAT, let's say Example College sets a range at 1250–1400; for the ACT, at 26–30—15,000 names, or $7,500

---

*Buying names of students with no upper limit on test scores versus within a range of scores can be a philosophical or a practical decision. Schools need to ask themselves whether they are in a market position to compete for students in the highest score bands. It can also be a monetary decision based on their search budget.

After entering the search criteria above, Example College would end up paying $7,500 for 15,000 names of potential female chemistry majors from the Northeast toward meeting its new IP. There was a time when a university would have to wait weeks to receive this data. That delay was gradually reduced to days, and now the time between making a search purchase and receiving the data for contacting prospects is essentially instantaneous.

Because there are multiple administrations of standardized tests every year, most schools will purchase and receive names either after each administration or after a season of administrations (summer, fall, winter, spring). They also have the option of submitting a recurrent search or standing order that ensures they receive new names of qualifying students once they become available from ACT or the College Board. In other words, Example College will be investing additional money later that year and in the years to come in order to achieve its five-year target. Keep in mind too that Example College has yet to pay to produce and mail marketing materials geared toward female chemistry majors. As you can see, the costs add up quickly.

> Searches extend well beyond purchasing the contact information of standardized-test takers.

Example College may be hypothetical, but the search industry is a very real business. Our case study presumes that, unlike hundreds of schools nationally, Example College is not outsourcing its search purchase strategy to a firm that specializes in such services. Quotes for that kind of work start around $50,000 and reach into the hundreds of thousands of dollars on an annual basis. To provide you additional perspective on the scope of the search industry, for many years Ed Gillis, former vice president of enrollment at the University of Miami, published a search summary report in conjunction with the Harvard Summer Institute on Admission. College and university names were redacted and some data were aggregated, but the report quantified the number of student names that participating schools were buying. The average number of unique names bought by colleges was around 150,000, or $63,000 at $0.42 each. The top of the range was over 500,000, or $210,000. Odds are that some schools not participating in Gillis's survey were, and likely still are, conducting searches well above that mark. We have not even touched on the complexity and cost of purchasing and mailing information to the ever-growing international market of students who are considering attending college in the United States. In recent years, more than one million students from abroad have come to the United States to pursue their under-graduate education (Fast Facts 2021).

Adding to the financial investment that colleges make in recruiting students is the fact that searches extend beyond standardized testing. Until being acquired by ACT, the National Research Center for College and University Admissions (NRCCUA) was an organization of educational data research that administered surveys to high school students. Many colleges also bought names from NRCCUA in order to contact younger students—those who had not yet taken standardized tests. After spending millions of dollars to purchase NRCCUA, ACT will now administer those surveys to high schoolers and develop and sell lists of student names and contact information.

After the COVID pandemic upended the testing market and threatened the secure positions of ACT and the College Board, colleges became even more concerned with identifying a variety of sources from which to acquire student contact information. As a result, not only have schools had to spend even more money in searching for a larger number of prospects, but also the number of new players in the student search space has exploded. I (Rick) cannot go two days without receiving a solicitation email from a company offering to fix all of our recruitment and enrollment challenges.

We told you that search was a big and complicated business.

TAKEAWAY LESSONS

The case of Example College should help you understand why all those brochures are coming to you and how schools are searching for you. While it may be interesting (or moderately disconcerting) to understand the amount of money and effort that colleges are expending to find you, the real lesson is that you should emulate their approach to college search.

1. *Think like a dean.* Look again at the admission funnel. Any dean or director of admission would love to buy the exact number of enrollees for their class each year. If they could determine exactly who would be interested enough to apply, be qualified for admission, be able to pay

tuition, choose to attend, succeed on campus, graduate on time, and give back to the school as alumni, they could save tens, maybe hundreds, of thousands of dollars. But that is not how it works. Colleges must cast a wide net. They start by thinking about their goals and entering into conversations with students by telling them about their programs, inviting them to visit campus, and connecting them with current students, staff, and faculty. They do not begin with *exactly* who will make up their next class but begin instead with the type of students they are trying to recruit. As a sophomore or junior in high school, you should be doing the same thing. The odds are that your list of prospective colleges is too narrow right now. This means you are likely starting too far down in your own admission funnel. We want to challenge you to start broad, at the top. You will learn how to do this in chapter 5.

2. *Check that box.* When you take standardized tests (PSAT, Pre-ACT, SAT, ACT, etc.) or when a survey is distributed in your high school for the purposes of college recruitment, we recommend that you opt in to share your contact information. Yes, this means you will be inundated with recruitment mail and email. However, in our view, one of the biggest problems students and families face is a narrow perspective, one that misses much of the landscape and fails to consider the multitude of college options. Providing your contact information protects against that. Colleges are checking boxes as they craft their search purchase strategy. Opting in is your choice, of course, but we encourage you to do so. You paid to take the test, right? Receiving recruitment materials is a benefit you can receive for that registration fee. Check that box.

3. *Segment your search.* When colleges receive their search order of names, they then determine the appropriate communication flow based on the target student's profile. For instance, if Example College knows that female chemistry majors on its campus are most commonly from New Jersey with a 1300–1400 score on the SAT, Example will likely choose *not* to mail extensively to this demographic that's already enrolling. Instead, the college may push those names into an email-only campaign. Conversely, if Example finds it tougher to enroll students from Massachusetts, it may segment that population for a tailored campaign.

You should be doing the exact same thing with your search. We recommend that once brochures start showing up, set up three boxes.

Label one box "considering"; this does not mean you will definitely apply but simply that someone in the family believes that the brochures put in this box are from schools that align with your answers to *why* you are going to college. Label box two "for a friend." Colleges will be the first to tell you that search is imperfect. While they need to buy names to expand their applicant pool and meet their IPs, many of their inquiries (see the admission funnel) do not come from their search purchase. They come instead from students who visit campus or who complete interest forms online. Frequently, these students were referred by alumni, neighbors, or friends. When you receive information from a school that does not fit with your answers to *why* you are going to college, think about someone you know who may be interested and pass these brochures along to them. Lastly, label box three "recycle," and don't be lazy about using it. Let's work together to save the world one college brochure at a time! In fact, if you take nothing else away from this section, it is this: RECYCLE.

> **Thousands of schools are spending tens of thousands of dollars to recruit you.**

You will also be getting a lot of email. A lot. We strongly recommend that you open an email account that's just for your college search. Whether you decide to let any family members access this account is up to you. Create subfolders in the account—such as "consider," "visit," and "apply"—and perhaps subfolders for each individual college. The good news about email is that you can forward it to a friend, unsubscribe, or mark it as junk. While it may be boring, you should choose a straightforward email address, such as firstname.lastname17@gmail.com or something to that effect. We have both had to send emails to addresses like inittowinit@hotmail.com and studdawg@gmail.com. Some colleges compile an internal list at year's end of amusingly inappropriate email addresses from their applicant pool. You do not want to be on that list. To recap: Recycle and don't be on that list.

4. *Work the funnel.* If you receive mail or email from a school you are interested in hearing more from, you need to take action. Often the materials you receive in the mail include a QR code to scan or a URL to follow. When you do this, colleges will update your record to reflect that interest. In fact, though it might seem a bit like "big brother," some colleges will track how much you engage with different pages on their website. Don't click through just to "game" admission, but

do explore the programs and opportunities at each college in depth. Demonstrating your interest in these ways frequently means you will be invited to attend recruitment events, be sent more details about your interests, and be asked to engage with the campus community. You are now moving down the funnel from prospect to inquiry. Work. The. Funnel.

We hope that you now have a broader perspective on the landscape of higher education in our nation: thousands of schools spending tens of thousands of dollars to recruit you. In fact, according to a survey of colleges conducted by the enrollment consulting firm Ruffalo Noel Levitz (2022), the median cost for a four-year private institution to recruit a student in 2022 was $2,795, which amounts to a 32 percent increase from 2020 and further illustrates the significant expenditures by colleges to recruit students through a variety of sources.

Ultimately, your family's job is to keep that broad perspective. You have lots of options. Do not limit yourself by starting at the bottom of the funnel.

💡 *Try This*

Pick up a copy of the illustrated book *Zoom* by Istvan Banyai. Keep it with you as you go through your college search experience. Here is why: On the first page of the book, you see a picture of a bunch of red triangles. The next page zooms out to show that those triangles are actually a rooster that's being watched through a window by two children. Zooming out even more on the next page, you see that the children are actually toys in a set that a little girl is playing with. Page after page zooms out from the original scene. Ultimately, you realize this is all occurring on the cover of a magazine held by a boy sitting on the deck of a cruise ship, which in turn is but a minuscule point in an ad for a cruise line mounted on the side of a bus. Too many students and families get stuck on page 1 of *Zoom*, metaphorically. Their list of five colleges never changes. Effectively, they are seeing only the same red triangles. We are encouraging you to pull back and adjust your lens. A college search done well—a college search done as a family—means you cross schools off, add new ones, and continually compare, revisit, and revise. In the chapters to come, we provide you with tools for allocating time and asking the right questions to ensure you are communicating together effectively. For now we simply urge you to see the broader landscape, to zoom back, to look beyond what you see. Choices. Many, many choices. Your job is not to lose sight of that.

Try This (Bonus)

Our friend Jeff Kurtzman, director of college counseling at the Fountain Valley School, has his entire junior class listen to the song "Little Boxes." (Written and composed by Malvina Reynolds, it was popularized by Pete Seeger, although we are partial to the version by Walk Off the Earth.) This song, originally a political satire about suburbia, is a creative way to frame the college search and admission experience. We encourage you to listen to this (somewhat campy) song together and discuss how it may inform your perspective in the college admission experience.

Talk about This

1. What do you think will be the biggest challenge or obstacle to keeping an open mind as you go through the college search and application experience? Why?

2. List five factors in your family/school/community that could contribute to a narrow approach to finding colleges.

3. After reading this chapter, what are you most excited for in the college search and application experience? Why?

4. Based on what you've read so far, what has changed about your list of colleges? Write down one or two reasons why each school is of interest to you.

CHECK IN. After reading this chapter, are you still on the same page as a family? If you are not all-in together, what do you need to do, discuss, or learn to get there?

☆ Extra Credit

Less Stress High School's website (www.lesshighschoolstress.com) maintains lists, organized by industry, of professionals and the college they attended. Take some time to explore the site as a continuation of thinking like an admission dean at the top of the funnel. And in the spirit of seeing the larger landscape and learning more about your options, find out where some people you know (or know of) went to college.

1. The CEO of your favorite national/international brand

2. Your school's principal

3. Your town/city's mayor

4. Two or three of your neighbors' or parents' friends

5. Your favorite science or math teacher

6. Your favorite history, foreign language, or English teacher

7. Your favorite athlete

8. The owner of your favorite local business

9. Your favorite actor or musical artist

10. Your favorite national politician

11. A famous person from your state

CHAPTER 3

Wedges of College Admission

Let's stay together / Lovin' you whether
Times are good or bad, happy or sad.
"LET'S STAY TOGETHER" BY AL GREEN

If your family has ever sold a house, you know how all-consuming it can be. First, you have to prepare to sell by decluttering inside, touching up outside, and buying odd, decorative items for show, such as doilies and cookie-scented candles. Once your house is on the market, you are at the mercy of potential buyers. When your real estate agent alerts you to an upcoming showing, the news sets off a furious succession of wiping, cleaning, throwing a few random items into a box, and leaving the house to take refuge elsewhere until the potential buyers leave.

The buying side can be worse. After downloading multiple real estate apps—Zillow, Redfin, Trulia, Falsia, and one more for good measure—you set parameters for the desired number of bedrooms, bathrooms, location, price, and so on. Then the notifications start coming in—or they don't. Either way it is maddening. If your family is moving locally, every trip to the grocery store can lead to a detour "just to see if a new home has popped up on the market." It is easy to become manic about getting in to see houses before other potential buyers. Even the most normal people can find themselves cruising slowly through neighborhoods, while eight-year-olds on bikes give them curious and suspicious looks.

The conversation at every meal is about particular houses, pricing, or speculation about what you should do or should have done or what might happen next week. Everyone in the family (even those who do not live with you or even visit often) seems to have an opinion or a suggestion.

WE'RE MOVING!

There are a lot of parallels between home buying and college admission. You are constantly receiving glossy brochures advertising amazing "properties" that you simply must see! They tout all the amenities and provide testimonials that encourage you to dream about what life would be like living there. So you tour colleges and create pros-and-cons lists about size, price, location, and other factors. You inevitably find conflicting or incomplete information online, just like with real estate apps.

> The college admission experience can be exhausting, confusing, and filled with tension.

Everyone from coaches to aunts to baristas asks you questions and expresses their opinions about which place you should choose, which are overpriced, and which are undeservedly popular. It is an uncertain and protracted timeline. And let's face it: as humans we just hate the waiting.

Every year we see that the college admission experience for many students and families is as exhausting, confusing, and full of tension as the home-buying and home-selling process. The truth is that in recent years, as mis- and disinformation campaigns have increased and distrust of institutions and organizations has worsened, the consternation surrounding college admission has escalated for students and those supporting them. In this chapter, we identify the primary wedges that divide families and provide you with ways to stay on the same page.

WEDGE #1: TIME

If you are not intentional about when you have family conversations about searching for, applying to, and ultimately deciding on a college, the subject can bleed into almost any discussion. Parents' non sequiturs are the first sign of this problem: "Will you please put the ketchup back in the fridge, and be sure to ask Mrs. Thomas to write that recommendation for you." "Remember, it's your grandma's birthday, so let's call her later. And when is that deadline for UConn?"

Left unchecked, these queries and reminders seem to students like Zillow notifications pinging incessantly—after practice, on the way home from school, during breakfast, through the bathroom door, or while sitting on the porch trying to relax. Students begin to feel like every time they come downstairs for a meal, the "college talk" begins. Parents feel like their intelligent offspring have somehow lost the ability to string together consecutive words coherently or convey ideas using multisyllabic words. More importantly, these situations create unnecessary tension and division. Beware the creep of college conversations!

☑️ **QUICK QUIZ**

Parents: Are you bringing up college options, deadlines, or test dates at unnatural times with unchecked frequency throughout the week?

Students: Do you commonly answer your parents' many questions about college with "Good," "Okay," "No," or "Huh?" or find yourself pretending your phone is ringing whenever Mom asks, "Have you taken that practice SAT yet?"

If the answer to these questions is yes, we strongly encourage your family to establish a time each week when college talk is on the proverbial table. Specifically, we recommend that you agree on and schedule an hour a week beginning in the spring of a student's junior year. Occasionally, this weekly meeting may extend to two hours at points in senior year. Perhaps you set aside time on Sunday afternoons or Thursday nights. If you will create this regular time (and cancel it in weeks you don't need to meet), you will help bolster family unity and ensure that your relationship does not unnecessarily narrow to focus solely on college.

House Rules

Parents: You *get to bring* brochures you have noticed in the mail. This is *your time* to say, "Hey, look, honey, aren't the leaves pretty in the fall in Ohio." You *get to ask*, "Have you written your supplemental essays for SMU?" Or "Do you still want to take that trip to California to look at schools in November?" This is your time for "Did you get your ACT results back?" It's all fair game.

You *don't get to bring* outdated stereotypes of colleges and universities based on your experiences of 20 or 30 years ago. You *don't get to* fold your arms or have knee-jerk reactions. This is a family conversation. Resist the temptation to discuss other students or families and their college search or application experience (and please do not compare your student to their siblings or some other kid in their class or your neighborhood).

Students: You *get to bring* ideas about the colleges you are interested in and permission slips for your parents to sign for your school-sponsored college trip. This is *your time* to ask for another set of eyes on an essay or to tell your mom you plan to apply to her alma mater's biggest rival college. It is also your time to explain why you are losing interest in a specific major, location, school, or anything else.

You *don't get to bring* your cell phone or really crunchy snacks. You *don't get* to stare at your shoes more than three times or longer than six seconds before responding to a question. Come ready to engage fully in the conversation. Use intonation. Do not use sarcasm. Have some questions of your own ready. Show up the way you do for an athletic practice—prepared to put in the work and improve individually and as a team. One time a week, for an hour or two. That's 1 percent of your entire week. You got this!

The reason your parents are bringing up college, asking you questions, and expressing their opinions is partly because they are not convinced you are on top of things. If you answer their questions in detail, articulate a plan, and demonstrate that you are making progress on setting up campus visits or completing applications and paying attention to deadlines, you will dramatically diminish the seemingly incessant nagging. In truth, though, it is not really nagging at all. Instead, it is simply them doing what they have always done— loving you by trying to look out for you. Think about it: all of these questions are really just love in disguise. The time your parents make, the questions they ask, their desire to see things taken care of—these are absolutely grounded in deep affection. They know you are going off to college soon. There is some fear in that, as well as excitement. Every now and then they cannot believe you are taking Advanced Placement Biology or standing over six feet tall. Somehow training wheels and carpool lines do not seem to them like that long ago. Fear, excitement, love—these all warrant you being fully engaged, so meet their love halfway and err on the side of giving too much information. Answer their questions, look them in the eye, put down your phone, and for bonus points, start and end the time with a hug. Yes, we are serious.

> Let your application sit for a week and then come back to it with fresh eyes.

The good news is that, when you're a senior in high school, the two-hour max holds true for working on your applications too. You will find that if you devote that time consistently (not just hours before the deadline!) for six or seven weeks, you can absolutely do a great job on your applications. Your essays will be better by drafting them and then revisiting them in multiple sittings. Like many important things in life, there's a lot to be said for letting something sit for a week and coming back to it with fresh eyes and a new perspective. In fact, do yourself and your parents a favor, and start this all in the summer before senior year, when you are not as busy or distracted by homework and other school activities.

WEDGE #2: COMMUNICATION

One of the main issues with home buying and selling is how public it becomes—suddenly you are exposed. Everyone can see pictures, prices, and details on square footage and the number of bathrooms posted on flyers, apps, or websites. Neighbors chat in front yards and speculate about why someone is moving, when the house will sell, who might move in, and whether it is over- or underpriced.

Too often we see the same type of unnecessary, unhealthy, and unbridled noise occur in the admission experience because families share too much publicly. We strongly encourage both students and parents to limit what you broadcast in conversation and post on social media. Volunteering where you are applying to or talking about your first-choice college opens you up to questions from teachers, relatives, friends, and friends of friends about admission decisions and personal considerations about your ultimate college selection.

Keep It Private

Parents: You have the ability to reduce the speculation and consternation surrounding college admission in your community by refraining from sharing stories at athletic games, cocktail parties, or online about where your student is admitted, denied, or offered scholarships. The college admission experience can be a roller coaster ride because you love your kid. You want the best for them. You know they are going to leave home soon. You see the big tuition bills coming. You are going to experience a variety of emotions along the way, and it is understandable to want to share those worries, hopes, frustrations, or celebrations with friends and extended family. Being disciplined, however, in keeping these considerations and deliberations private has incredible potential to build trust and strengthen bonds in your family during a highly personal experience. We know this is not easy, but it will make the celebrations over admittance or scholarships sweeter when they come.

We would also challenge you not to ask other parents about their family's college admission search. Not only is it really none of your business, but also the information you hear could well be exaggerated, inaccurate, and biased. Typically, knowing it only makes you— and by extension your family—more anxious. When your kids were young, you looked to people who had hindsight and wisdom to share based on their prior experience. The same approach holds value here. Our strong recommendation is to talk to fewer parents of high school students and to more parents of current college students or recent college graduates about the college admission experience. They have tremendous perspective and encouragement to provide. (We also guarantee you that none of them will say they wish they'd made their college admission experience more public.)

Students: Consider holding your college admission experience close to your vest (or sweater or shirt for non–vest wearers) and letting only a small subset of trusted people know the details of your college search. Build a "College Support Team" around you. This might include your parents, a classmate or two, your school counselor, and a teacher. These are the people you will use as your sounding board. Ask them to listen to your answers to "Why am I going to college?" and to honestly critique or challenge your rationale. These are the opinions you can trust when building your college list. Talk to them after you visit colleges; consult with them about your essay topic; count on them to read and improve your writing with their suggestions; and request their help as you prepare for interviews.

Assembling and counting on this team is not just an opportunity to learn more about yourself through their feedback but also a chance to deepen these relationships as they invest in you, keep you accountable, and encourage you along the way. When you are deferred, denied, or wait-listed by a college, you'll have a group ready to console you, empathize, and also to provide the priceless perspective you will need. On the flipside, when you are accepted or awarded a great financial aid package, this group will be there to celebrate and validate all you have done to earn those opportunities.

Watch Your Pronouns

Setting aside consistent time to discuss college and keeping your discussions relatively private will help your family significantly. The other primary issue with communication is that parents, in their desire to help and support, often overreach by trying to drive the entire search and application experience. When this happens, students get frustrated and can shut down.

Parents: We have already established that you love your kids—but *you are not them*. Every year admission officers receive calls where parents say things like this: "*We* were deferred from your college" and "I know you've received *our* transcript because I made him give me his log-in information." "I see from your website that you don't consider additional letters of recommendation, but I'm going to have two of my business associates email you on my son's behalf anyway." When parents freely substitute *we* for *he* or *she*, students slide down in their chair during information sessions (or even get up and walk out).

When Dad launches into question number fourteen or Mom grills the tour guide about gluten-free options in the dining hall, students slowly fade to the back of the tour hoping not to be associated.

☑️ **PARENTAL PRONOUN TEST**

- *If* you've recently said, "We are taking the SAT next weekend," *then* you might be overly involved.
- *If* you said to a friend in the bleachers last week, "Our first choice is Columbia," *then* you might need to go for a walk.
- *If*, as your daughter was leaving for school the other day, you said, "Let's ace that calculus exam!" *then* you might need to take a deep breath and rethink your approach.

Our hope is that you will shift your stance from a *we* that can be overreaching and at times divisive to one that is helpful in maintaining unity, such as in the following statements:

We can discuss financing college at the outset.

We can limit talk about college to one day a week.

We can challenge each other to think beyond reputation, assumptions, or preconceived notions.

We can tour a range of colleges and each form different impressions.

We can be aware of expectations and talk openly about these as a family.

We can remain committed to controlling what we can control.

We can resist the temptation to make comparisons to siblings, relatives, or friends.

We can laugh, cry, celebrate, and be disappointed—sometimes simultaneously.

We can realize that change is inevitable and full of potential.

We can listen attentively to others and ourselves.

We can be authentic and not try to game the admission
    experience.

We can accept that a college does not define a person.

We can acknowledge that while we each have our own story,
    our stories are wonderfully and undeniably intertwined.

Matthew Hyde, dean of admissions and financial aid at Trinity
College, has thoughtfully shepherded thousands of families through
this journey and makes these observations about how "we" can all be
in this together while also allowing students to shine:

> The college search experience, when well-informed and good-
> intentioned, creates an awesome opportunity for young people to
> gain agency over their narrative. These college hopefuls can (and
> should) begin to get comfortable penning their own story and
> owning the opportunity (arguably obligation) to take charge of
> their narrative. If not yet co-authoring their own story, this rite of
> passage moment presents excellent footing for college applicants
> to begin to do so—honoring those who have raised and cared for
> them but confidently taking charge of outlining the chapters to
> come. Cutting out those who know them best is a bad idea on an
> applicant's part, but refusing to allow applicants to take charge is
> equally bad. The "royal we," when appropriately inserted, reflects
> a nicely balanced evolutionary moment and the passing of the
> narrative-writing "pen."

In his *Washington Post* article "The Compelling Case for Being an
'Intentionally Lazy' Parent," Scott Lutostanski (2018) discusses the
executive function of human cognition, which includes faculties such
as organizing tasks, managing time, and planning a course of action.
He asserts that parents need to be intentional and disciplined about
empowering their kids to develop these skills. Searching for, visiting,
applying to, being accepted by, being disappointed by, and ultimately
choosing a college are all opportunities for a student to hone these
skills.

Periodically checking your pronouns is an easy way for a parent to
avoid the communication wedge. It will also steer you toward asking
questions about your student's college essays and making helpful

edits or suggestions rather than attempting to rewrite the essay with words like *lugubrious* or *obsequious*. The communication wedge is real but avoidable. In a short year or two, your student will be on a college campus, and *they* will need to be able to navigate and advocate for themselves. Watching your pronouns allows you to step back without stepping away.

Students: Go find some pictures of your family from various points in your life. Maybe those are hanging on your wall or piled in a drawer or carefully assembled in an album or saved on a laptop or phone.

> The communication wedge is real but avoidable.

Look at the smiles and locations in those photos. Think back on all the time your parents dedicated to you, all the love they have shown you, and the sacrifices they've made for you—the number of carpool lines endured, the recitals and games watched, the lunches packed and dinners prepared.

Read the "Parental Pronoun Test" above. That was hard for them. This is *all* hard for them. They love you so deeply that their life (and sometimes their words) has become interwoven with yours. Take some time this week (and ideally at some point during each of your weekly meetings) to say two things to them: (1) Thank you. (2) I love you. Trust us—they need to hear it. If you can keep doing that at least once a week until you head off to college (and keep doing it once you're there), no wedge can drive you apart. (Don't worry; we will remind you to do this at the end of the book.)

I tell my students to take ownership over the college admission process. While that partly means taking responsibility for all moving parts of the process, it really means taking ownership over their own voice. Parents, friends, and family members usually have the best intentions about giving college admission and selection advice, but the student needs to take inventory about what drives them. Ultimately, compromise and agreement is the goal, but students need to know they've had an opportunity to be the driving force in *their* future plans. —Brandi Smith, college access advocate

WEDGE #3: MONEY

Recently, my (Rick's) family was on vacation at the beach. A house near the one we were renting was for sale, and our daughter, Elizabeth, suggested, "We should buy that!" I was intrigued. I was also optimistic—it was a cute home, great location, and not too much grass to cut. Pulling up Zillow, I found the property and saw the listing price: $2 million.

"Two million!" I said, spitting out the sip of water I had just taken. "Sorry, sweetheart. That's not happening."

"Why?" she asked innocently.

"Well . . ." I took a deep breath and refrained from accusing the owners of being insane for asking that price. "Even if we sell our house and cars and all of your stuffed animals, we just can't afford that."

"What if we win the lottery?" she countered.

"Maybe, babe. Talk to Mom about buying a ticket."

Just like I cut the conversation short at the beach, parents frequently do not share many details with their children about paying for college. This is unfortunate. In our experience, we have found too often that parents underestimate the importance of having comprehensive discussions about money early in the college search. In many cases, we hear loving parents say they've avoided honest conversations about money because they don't want to limit their kid's dreams. Or parents believe that bringing up paying for college too early will put an unnecessary burden on their kid. Ultimately, though, shielding students from candid talk about costs and the implications of very real financial responsibilities does them a disservice that can turn into a divisive wedge down the road.

The topic of money takes us back to our real estate metaphor. When you are looking to buy a house, price is often the first filter you apply to your search. *What can we afford? What are we willing to pay?* Location, size, number of bathrooms, and considerations like brick versus siding or attached versus detached garage all matter, but typically cost is your top narrowing factor. To determine what is affordable, you take a number of factors into consideration: down payment, current interest rates, monthly payments, and how those investments and obligations factor in with your other financial commitments and future goals.

A similarly holistic review of money, which accounts for the short- and long-term implications of paying for college, is critical to the college search. In chapter 4, we will do a deeper dive into college costs, discussing grants, scholarships, loans, and the process and timeline for determining net price. For now, though, our focus is on providing your family some practical language and a logical approach to having discussions about paying for college. What we don't want for your family is a conversation like Rick's at the beach, where the buck gets passed and hope depends on a winning lottery ticket.

Putting Off Money Talk

Any financial aid director can share countless painful stories about families coming to the aid office in tears sometime in April of the student's senior year. Having received a financial aid package, the family is grappling with the reality of paying for college, and in most of these cases, they have not had earnest conversations about cost along the way. Now, after the student has been offered admission, bought the college hoodie, and posted their intent to enroll on social media, financial lines are being drawn and emotions are running high on all sides.

The money wedge is real but avoidable. According to the Education Data Initiative, only "39% of parents have talked with their child about how cost may affect which college they can afford" (Hanson 2022 "College Savings Statistics"). Please don't belong to the other 61 percent. You have a real opportunity to build trust and work together in the college search and selection experience, so we encourage you to sit down as a family sometime in the student's junior year and have an initial discussion about your finances. You do not need to itemize all of your assets and income, but we do encourage you to provide perspective on your financial situation in how it relates to paying for college. Consider covering these topics:

- monthly or annual earnings

- taxes

- fixed/consistent costs (mortgage, insurance, car note, utilities, groceries, tuition if the student attends a private high school, organizational membership fees, donations)

- savings (for retirement, future purchases, health-related expenses, college costs)

- lifestyle (a second home, vacations, entertainment, eating out, trips to visit family and friends).

We understand that this topic may be uncomfortable to broach. However, talking through *how* you afford the life your student has known can have tremendously positive implications. While most students know something about finances and may even have taken a course in economics, a personal discussion about taxes and monthly expenses will help them appreciate money and costs in a completely new way. Often students have no idea how much an average mortgage payment is and have given no real thought to the way their college tuition will factor in other financial obligations.

"Opening the books" shifts the financing-college conversation toward a partnership and a collective investment. When making one of their first significant adult decisions, students should be privy to the expense and implications of their college choice. Talking openly about money shapes how you discuss and evaluate ways a student might offset college costs with a job, co-op, or internship; provides you with better questions to ask about return on investment and starting salaries; and informs how selecting a major is relevant to employment and life after college.

Talking Money

The Education Data Initiative's mission is to collect data and statistics about the US education system and about higher education in the United States and to organize them in an accessible, comprehensive fashion for students and educators. Its compilation of data is extremely helpful for framing grounded discussions about scholarships and paying for college. Here are a few stats to consider:

- Seven percent of college students will receive a scholarship (Hanson 2022 "Scholarship Statistics").

- The average scholarship is worth $7,400.

- Less than 2 percent of high school student athletes receive athletic scholarships.

"When parents initiate conversations about finances early, students deeply value that respect and are way more aware, responsible, and interested in making college choices that make financial sense," says Ron Diaz, director of student awards at Stanford University. Conversely, anxiety and frustration are born from a lack of knowledge, and the money wedge gets driven down when parents are unwilling to have a cards-on-the-table discussion about finances.

Our hope is that after walking openly and honestly through family finances, you will be on the same page as a family about how paying for a college education fits into your broader financial framework. You should have a ballpark idea of how much your family can pay annually, excluding any student loans. There is a fundamental difference, however, between the ability to pay and the willingness to pay. This is where the conversations can get emotional if you do not intentionally discuss limitations, conditions, expectations, and loan tolerance.

Limitations

What are you willing to pay for? Particularly in states with strong public university systems, we often hear parents say, "I am willing to pay for any of our state schools or the equivalent price if my daughter chooses to go out of state or to a private school." Parents should consider and honestly discuss what limitations they want to establish. We are not suggesting that these parameters keep you from visiting or applying to a school that will likely cost more than your determined ceiling, but setting these limitations during junior year will keep you from feeling "gut punched" in April of senior year when financial aid packages show up.

Conditions

"My parents will not pay for a school south of Washington, DC." Or "they have already told me I'm on my own if I look at schools in Canada." Or "we will pay $40,000 a year for College X, but we are simply not paying that for Y University." Or most alarming: "We will only pay for a college that is ranked in the top 50." (Don't be that parent.) What are your conditions? College is an investment. Your family's goal is to be comfortable with, and ideally excited about, the dollars you will spend on higher education because you believe in the experiences and opportunities your student will have. If you can talk about why you are putting conditions in place, they will not come across as irrational or arbitrary but rather as helpful, instructive, and ultimately rooted in concern and love.

Expectations

What role should students have in paying for their college education? Even if your family is fortunate enough to be able to cover all costs, is there an expectation that the student will contribute a certain amount each year? We have worked with families who determined a flat amount, some who set a percentage, and others who defined their ceiling and left any additional cost to the student to cover. Is there an expectation of sharing costs in your family? In most cases, paying for college requires sacrifices, and sacrifices (physical, time, or monetary) bring some discomfort. However, they also clarify your commitment and belief in the end result. Setting clear monetary expectations before applying lets students consider how they can work and save money during high school, as well as ask the colleges they consider about opportunities for on-campus jobs or the prospects for—and salaries associated with—internships or co-ops while in college. Setting expectations will serve to unify your family because "the problem" of paying for college becomes a joint effort, one to solve and resolve together. We recommend that even if families can afford to pay for everything out of pocket, the student be expected to invest something—even if just spending money or the cost of books—so that they have a vested interest in their own success.

> **The money wedge is driven deep when parents do not have an earnest discussion about finances with their student.**

Loans

In the next chapter we describe how loans factor in financial aid packages, but if you believe you'll have to incur some debt to pay for college, we hope you will take the time to discuss loan tolerance, debt philosophy, as well as short- and long-term goals, sacrifices, and opportunities.

Currently, the average student loan debt nationally is more than $37,000, and the average student at a public university borrows $32,880 to attain a bachelor's degree (Hanson 2023). Knowing that an average starting salary for four-year graduates is approximately $55,000, according to the National Association of Colleges and Employers (Gray 2022), families should be having conversations and asking questions about their comfort level with taking out annual loans during college and projecting the reality of repaying several hundred dollars per month after graduation.

Direct PLUS Loans (also known as Parent PLUS Loans) allow parents to borrow directly from the US Department of Education. There are no set borrowing limits for Direct PLUS Loans; the amount you are eligible to take out will be dictated by the cost of attendance (determined by the school) minus any financial aid received (Federal Student Aid 2022). Interest rates are determined annually, but in recent years, as reported by Nerd Wallet, the average PLUS Loan amount nationally has hovered just under $30,000, with an interest rate of 7.54 percent in 2022–2023 (Helhoski and Haverstock 2023). For parents, understanding these options and numbers gives you an important opportunity to articulate your philosophy on, experience with, or personal observations of the risks and benefits of incurring debt to achieve longer-term goals. We have both worked with families who are averse to taking on any debt yet are unable to write a check to cover all college costs. These families should have candid conversations about college options and financial aid requirements.

Start by asking these questions:

- As parents, are we willing to take out loans for our student's college education?

- If so, what is our annual and cumulative student loan tolerance?

- What will graduating college with debt mean for the family's lifestyle in the near and long term?

- Do we know families with a recent college graduate who might give us some perspective on loans and the reality of paying for college?

- Does our willingness to incur debt vary by college, major, or other factors?

All of these considerations underscore why it is critical to make time to sit down as a family to clarify your financial limitations, conditions, and expectations. As we said in chapter 1, parents love their kids. Another significant element of life that parents care about, and worry over regularly, is money, so it is understandable that these conversations can be emotional, uncomfortable, and difficult to conduct calmly, rationally, and openly. None of this talk will be easy, we know, but it is important and, ultimately, will have big implications for your family. Wedges are real and serious. You love your kids! You got this!

WEDGE #4: EGO

We know that telling you to put your ego in a box during the college admission experience is much easier said than done, but for the sake of your family's relationships, we urge you not to let pride or presumption drive family discussions.

What Surrendering Ego Looks Like for Students

When brochures or letters show up in your mailbox from schools you think are not "as good" as where you hope to attend, check your ego. Have the confidence to think for yourself. Be willing to consider places nobody in your family or high school has gone before. Come back to your *why* and let that, rather than the noise around you, guide your approach and opinion. If you are able to articulate this *why* confidently to your parents, they will trust, respect, and support you along the way.

When you are looking at the admission statistics for a college and see that your academic profile falls in the middle or lower end of its ranges, we implore you to listen to your school counselor and submit another application or two to "likely" schools. We're reminded of the cinematic "masterpiece" *Dumb and Dumber* in which Lloyd Christmas (Jim Carey) asks Mary Swanson (Lauren Holly) what are the odds they could end up together. He suggests "one in a hundred," to which she replies, "I'd say more like one in a million." Lloyd pauses, considers, and then replies exuberantly, "So, you're telling me there's a chance!" Translation: applying to more schools with extremely low admit rates does not improve your chances of getting in at any one of the schools. We have established that there are lots of great options out there. Do not let your ego keep you from exploring.

> For the sake of family relationships, parents and student must put their egos in a box during the admission experience.

When your parents want you to visit or apply to a school not on your list, keep an open mind about it. Listen. There is a lot of emotion tied up in this whole process for your folks. They are starting to imagine a life where they do not get to see you every morning, hear your laugh each day, or wait for your car to pull into the driveway at night. So, when they want you to check out their alma mater or swing by a school they wished they'd applied to, ask yourself why you are resistant. Is it because that particular college isn't aligned with your goals and interests? Fine. Look for a kind, tactful way to express that. But if instead it is pride or stubbornness, be cognizant of that too. The wedge of ego can divide a family when you are not humble enough to recognize it and find a compromise.

When mom or dad wants to "look over your essay one more time," remember that they're asking because they love you. This is their way of showing that. Yes, we know their requests sometimes come across like a lack of trust or a desire to control things. Old habits die hard. They sang you to sleep on nights you do not remember. They paid for a decade of practice and supplies in [insert your sport or art or hobby] and loved you enough to make you stick with it, even when you pushed back. They have always hoped your life would turn out better than theirs and have sacrificed time and money you simply can't tally in support of your interests. You are often the last thought on their mind before they fall asleep and sometimes the reason they wake up in the middle of the night. Through mountains of laundry, endless debates over bedtime, and countless parent-teacher conferences, they have loved you more than you could ever, ever possibly imagine. Just let them look over your essay and make suggestions (not rewrite it).

What Surrendering Ego Looks Like for Parents

"Well, you know. We live in [La Jolla, Georgetown, Cambridge, Kirkland, Bethesda, Manhattan—insert your neighborhood here] and we went to [Rice, UVA, Williams, Northwestern, Berkeley—insert your alma mater here]. So I know you are saying there are lots of good schools out there, but most of those are just not OK for our family." We hear some version of this all the time—after presentations, in emails, over the phone, in meetings with individual families. Because of where you live, your alma mater, or your perception of what constitutes a "good school," there is a preconceived hierarchy that excludes many schools as unreasonable to consider.

When you say this kind of thing, whether it be off-handedly over dinner or directly to a tour guide or admission counselor, your child internalizes that. They feel increased pressure to succeed academically and distinguish themselves outside the classroom. The truth is that, on some level, all kids naturally have that inclination (whether they express or convey it is a different story), so hearing your comments only compounds anxiety about meeting your expectations. We are not criticizing your desire to see them perform well, but the problem—the wedge—is that they associate your approval and your love with an outcome: admittance to specific, and typically well-known and selective, colleges.

This can be divisive because students do not control admission decisions, the competition in a given applicant pool, or the institutional priorities and factors those colleges are using in decision-making. You drive the wedge when they realize that what you expect of them, despite their best efforts, is ultimately out of their hands. Additionally, the school or schools you are focused on may be terrible fits based on what your child is really looking for in a college. Each year admission offices receive essays or short-answer responses from students that read, "Please do not admit me. I did not want to apply here, but my parents made me." (Yes, this really happens.) We have seen some pretty creative ways to work this plea into applications, including limericks, code, and parenthetical statements.

One that stands out to me (Rick) was from a student who applied to Georgia Tech a few years ago. Our speculation was that he could not work his lack of interest into his essay for fear that someone would proofread it and catch his self-sabotage, so instead he used the biographical section (and capitalization) to make his point: "Mother: Bachelor's Degree from College of Charleston (where I really want to go). Father: Bachelor's Degree from Georgia Tech (WHERE I DO NOT WANT TO GO!)" Left unchecked this lack of unity will continue after students enroll. College academic advisors frequently talk to students who want to change their major but are reluctant to do so because of the expectations of and pressure from their parents.

When recruitment materials arrive at your home or you are having a conversation about which schools to visit, and especially when your student adds unexpected colleges to their list, we again urge you to "look beyond what you see." Fundamentally, this is about trusting them to make good choices and being willing to engage in honest conversations about your fears, as well as your hopes and dreams for them. Simultaneously, it is also about listening to and considering theirs as well. We urge you to really listen to what your student is saying about why they want to go to college and be objective in considering the places that logically fit based on their goals.

When you hear them express interest in the University of X and you remember it as a backup school from your high school days; when University of X makes you think, "If you drove slowly down Main Street with your window open, they'd throw a diploma in"; when you remember that many students and alumni at University of X would start tailgating for Saturday's game on Tuesday, we ask that you reassess your assumptions about University of X and not cling to potentially dated perceptions.

> Parents should really listen to what their student is saying about why they want to go to college.

The landscape of higher education has been changing radically in recent years. The college town of the University of X may now be regularly praised in major magazines as a great place for food, family, culture; the university may have invested heavily in student support and programs; it may now have students winning international competitions for research and prestigious scholarships and fellowships. Resist making dismissive, knee-jerk comments like "party school" or "diploma mill." Change your filter. Do not dilute your kid's excitement with comments or facial expressions that indicate disapproval. *Your goal is to fall in love with every college they choose to apply to—all of them.*

When admission decisions are released, remember that the decisions are not a validation or a condemnation of your parenting. Does that sound like a ridiculous thing to say? Trust us. Every spring we get calls from parents of denied students who are struggling to understand "what more we could have done?" and are second-guessing their choices about their student's high school, their divorce, their move to another city, or their change of career. When your kid does not get into a college (spoiler alert: this is likely to happen), do not make it about you. Do not look back over the last 18 years of lost sleep and believe for a moment that a college's decision correlates with your love, sacrifice, or influence.

Conversely, each time they are admitted or receive a scholarship or honors college placement (even from your alma mater's biggest rival), celebrate it. Go out to dinner as a family. Reflect on the hard work, late nights, and collaborative effort that brought it about. Don't diminish it if it's not *your* first choice. Don't say or think, "Yeah, but it's only [insert school name here]." No! This is a big deal. A new world of opportunity has been opened and offered. That yes-letter is an invitation to a social network and a degree that many talented students will never access. Your student needs to know that for each school they are invited to attend, you would proudly wear that school's T-shirt and show up excited for Family Weekend every year. Selectively celebrating only some acceptances will show your hand and betray your bias to your child at a time when they are attempting to discern their own independent feelings.

When financial aid and scholarship packages arrive, remember that every school has a different cost of attendance, endowment, and enrollment strategy. Do not let your desire to brag about a scholarship at a cocktail party cloud your math. Each year we see families select one school over another based on the difference in the amount of financial aid awarded rather than on the difference in actual cost. Here is how that sounds:

Parent: Awesome University gave us—oops—I mean my son a
   $20,000-a-year merit scholarship. Congratulations College
   named him a Dean's Disciple valued at $65,000 over four years.
   And you . . . you gave us nothing!

University Representative: Well, sir, first, congratulations. I know you
   are extremely proud of him. However, we do not have an honors
   college or merit scholarships here. You will see that we have at-
   tempted to create a package that makes attending here as affordable as possible, and we hope he will.

Nobody who works in an admission office ends a call like this feeling great. It may be honest, but it is disheartening. Robert Barkley, former director of admission at Clemson University, used to say, "If you don't get in, you want in. If you get in, you want money. If you get money, you want more. And those who got in and got all of the money want it from somewhere else."

Part of the reason why the admission experience can be so stressful for parents is that it brings together two things you regularly worry about: money and your kids. Understandably, it is not easy to keep your emotions in check when analyzing costs of this magnitude. If the relative costs of two colleges are similar, and you have confidence in your financial investment in either college, we urge you to choose the better overall match rather than the bigger scholarship.

Parents: We suggest that, once a week during your student's senior year, you make a point of telling them, "I trust you and I'm proud of you." The truth is that all "kids"—whether 5, 15, or 50—long for their parents' approval. They may learn increasingly effective ways to mask that desire, but invariably it is there. Do not forget that the only reason you are reading this book is because your kid has worked hard to get to this point. They have achieved a lot both inside and outside the classroom. You are worried about admission decisions and financial aid packages because those things are on the horizon. What a great problem to have! You are the only one who can say it, and they need to hear it more than they will ever let on, so tell them frequently, "I trust you and I'm proud of you." Simple to say yet tremendously important to hear.

 Try This

Consider which wedge you are most concerned about and take some time at your next weekly college meeting to discuss why. Check in on these wedges regularly. The truth is that wedges divide families when "getting in" supplants "staying together" as the primary goal. Ultimately, *how* you go through the college experience is far more important than *where* it all ends up.

 Talk about This

1. How do you foresee these wedges (time, communication, money, and ego) being a challenge for your family and why?

2. How will you go about addressing a wedge when you identify it as a problem?

3. Are there other wedges not covered in this chapter that you fear may be a challenge to your family during the college admission experience?

👍 **CHECK IN.** After reading this chapter, are you still on the same page as a family? If you are not all-in together, what do you need to do, discuss, or learn to get there?

⭐ **Extra Credit**

For parents: In her now famous TED Talk "How to Raise Successful Kids," Julie Lythcott-Haims provides parents and supporting adults with perspective, humor, tips, and relatable anecdotes geared toward helping you focus on both the short and long term. Take some time to watch it and discuss what resonates with you.

For students: The first three chapters of this book have asked you to think hard about why you want to go to college and to explore who you are and what you want in college and beyond. Check out Laurence Lewars's TED Talk "Questions Every Teenager Needs to Be Asked," which reinforces the importance of this self-reflective mentality.

Follow the QR code in the upper corner to an "Inner Circles" exercise that asks you to identify the people on your college support team who will provide you with resources, perspective, feedback, and support as you search for, apply to, and make your final college selection.

PART II

CHAPTER 4

Paying for College

Everybody look to the left / Everybody look to the right
Can you feel that? (yeah!) / We're paying with love tonight.
"PRICE TAG" BY JESSIE J

As you approach senior year in high school, you'll increasingly hear terms like *fit* or *match* used to describe finding and choosing a college. In most cases, these discussions center on where you will thrive once on campus or the characteristics of a school such as its location, size, academic programs, social life, ethos and culture, and level of selectivity. Later in part II, we provide you with tips and insight about visiting campuses, asking good questions, and determining how colleges may align with your academic and outside interests. The varying costs of colleges and how much your family is able or willing to pay, however, are also critical parts of finding a good match, and they are the subject of this chapter. How to pay for college should be a big part of your family's conversations about admission from the beginning.

While topics like the cost of college, return on investment, and student loans are prevalent in the media and politics, most colleges and universities do not address finances in depth during their admission presentations or campus tours. Instead, in the midst of a 45-minute information session, you will see only a few slides about tuition cost, scholarship opportunities, and the timeline to apply for financial aid, as well as one slide titled "Success Stories" featuring a few smiling graduates next to company logos. This lack of substantive discussion about paying for college may come from admission officers' understanding that each family's circumstances vary, so they don't want to speculate much about individual cases. Or it may be that a high-priced consulting firm told them that "too much talk about cash makes people dash."

It is true that your family's financial picture is unique, so we cannot give you specifics for each college to which you might apply. Instead, our goal in this chapter is to help you understand the basics: college costs; the purpose of financial aid; types of aid available; the terms, forms, and applications you will encounter as you pursue paying for college; and most importantly, approaches to having clarifying, healthy conversations about money during your college search and selection. Again, as we emphasized in chapter 3, this all begins with setting aside time to meet weekly as family, beginning no later than spring of a student's junior year. One purpose of this time is to have transparent talks about financial *limitations*, *conditions*, and *expectations* that will impact your family's college search.

Regardless of how much money your family makes or has saved for college, or even how much you may believe in the value of education, we can all agree that college is expensive. Anyone reading this book who attended a four-year residential private college over 25 years ago probably paid annual costs between $20,000 and $30,000. If you went in-state to a public flagship university or other residential public university, the amount was perhaps half that. Today, though, the figures are more than double what they were then. And while the twentieth century occasionally makes a comeback—in fashion trends (think "mom jeans") or movie remakes (*Top Gun: Maverick*)—turning back the clock does not happen with the cost of college. When you start comparing price tags on a college education, you likely have some legitimate *whys* on your mind: *Why* does college cost so much? And *why* does college now cost so much more than it used to?

You might have read stories in the popular press that blame tuition hikes on "student amenities gone wild," like lazy rivers and luxurious dorms, but the reality is more complex than that. In an interview on *The Daily* podcast, Ron Lieber, a *New York Times* columnist and the author of *The Price You Pay for College*, outlined some of the primary reasons that tuition and other fees have escalated. He pointed to the drastic reduction in state budgetary support for public universities, particularly following the Great Recession of 2008–2010, which resulted in tuition increases, as well as many state universities recruiting nonresidents who pay at higher rates (Lieber 2022).

Other drivers of cost, resulting in large part from colleges competing for enrollment, have positive implications for the student experience. Lieber spotlighted the wide range of improvements that colleges have made to woo and win students, including beautifying their campus landscapes, modernizing residence halls, augmenting campus amenities, and designing state-of-the-art health and recreation centers. Additionally, he discussed the significant investments schools have made to create robust and comprehensive student support, as well as the expense of hiring a large cadre of professionals (many of whom have advanced degrees) dedicated to bolstering student academic success, mental health, and exercise. In many cases, institutions now staff specialized resource centers for increasingly diverse student populations, with spaces for veterans, women, LGBTQ+ students, first-generation students, transfer students, and others. When you attend open houses or tour campuses, you will find that many of these facilities, services, and staff are among schools' points of pride.

So, while college is certainly more expensive than it was 25 years ago, the good news is that holistic support for the student experience has also greatly increased. As a result, colleges can correlate some of their investments with improved student performance data (as measured by grade point average, retention rate, graduation rate, or job placement rate). Despite the escalating cost of paying for college, the ultimate monetary value of earning a bachelor's degree (often referred to as return on investment) is clear. According to the Association of Public and Land-grant Universities (n.d.), "bachelor's degree holders are half as likely to be unemployed as their peers who only have a high school degree, and they make $1.2 million in additional earnings on average over their lifetime." Think of college as a multifaceted investment because that is what it is: an investment of your time and effort, as well as your money.

Let's shift from examining some of the *whys* behind college costs and turn our attention to the *hows*: How can you pay for college; how is the financial information you provide considered; how do schools vary in the ways they create financial aid packages; and most importantly, how will your family approach conversations, planning, and choices related to paying for college?

HIGH SCHOOL DIPLOMA	$1,304,000
SOME COLLEGE	$1,547,000
ASSOCIATE'S DEGREE	$1,727,000
BACHELOR'S DEGREE	$2,268,000
ADVANCED DEGREE	$2,671,000

Return on investment: lifetime earnings based on level of education.
Adapted from Anthony P. Carnevale, Stephen J. Rose, and Ban Cheah, *The College Payoff: Education, Occupations, Lifetime Earnings* (Washington, DC: Georgetown University Center on Education and the Workforce, 2011), page 3, figure 1.

THE BUCKET CHALLENGE

In 2014, pro golfer Chris Kennedy posted a video on social media of people pouring a bucket of ice water on his head. He challenged friends and fellow players to do the same in order to raise awareness for ALS (amyotrophic lateral sclerosis, a progressive nervous system disease that affects nerve cells in the brain and spinal cord, causing loss of muscle control). Quickly, the video went viral, inspiring other athletes and celebrities and eventually people from around the country and the world to take the challenge. The bucket challenge raised more than $115 million for ALS research. If you look back at the videos and photos posted that summer, you will see a big variety of buckets—some were the size of industrial trash cans, while others were not much bigger than a souvenir cup you would buy at a high school football game. You will also see that some of the buckets were filled entirely with ice, some with just cold water, and most with a mixture of both.

Paying for college is like planning your own bucket challenge. Each school has a different size bucket, and your goal is to figure out if, how, and with what money you can fill it. Like in the original bucket challenge, you are not alone, because each year the federal government, individual states, and institutions pour in billions of dollars to make college more affordable for families. Let's take a look at how this works.

Cost of Attendance. While tuition is a topic often covered in the news, understanding the real cost of any particular school begins by determining its cost of attendance, or COA. This is the total published price including tuition, room, and board, as well as averages for fees, books, supplies, transportation, and personal expenses. COA should be the real starting point in your financial calculations.

Example. For the academic year 2022–2023, COA for the University of North Carolina–Chapel Hill (for in-state students) was $25,250 annually, whereas Duke University's published total cost was $84,500 annually. Separated by only a few miles and shades of blue, these two institutions both have incredible reputations for enrolling and graduating students who go on to achieve tremendous success. If COA were the entire story, only families able to write big checks each fall could send their student to Duke. But don't forget this: while every college has a different size bucket, colleges also have different financial aid strategies for helping families fill it.

College Costs	Duke University	UNC–Chapel Hill
Tuition/Fees	$62,941	$8,998
Housing and Meals	$18,166	$12,254
Books, Supplies, Estimated Personal Expenses	$3,410	$4,006
Estimated Cost of Attendance	$84,517	$25,258

Source of data: "Cost of Attendance [2022–2023]," Karsh Office of Undergraduate Financial Support, Duke University, https://financialaid.duke.edu/how-aid-calculated/cost-attendance/; "Costs [2022–2023]," Scholarships and Student Aid, University of North Carolina at Chapel Hill, https://studentaid.unc.edu/current/costs/.

FILLING YOUR BUCKET

At its heart, financial aid exists because higher education is a public good and a driver of social mobility, and providing federal, state, or institutional money allows students from all backgrounds to access a college degree. As we mentioned in describing the ice bucket challenge, some people filled their containers completely with ice, others with only cold water, but most used a combination. Similarly, the majority of students and their families use a combination of resources to pay for college. Here are the primary ways you can fill your bucket.

Need-Based Aid

Need-based aid is given to students because of their financial circumstances, and it does not need to be repaid. At the federal level, Pell Grants, Federal Supplemental Educational Opportunity Grants (FSEOG), and Teacher Education Assistance for College and Higher Education (TEACH) Grants are the most common and well known. In most cases, there are also state-sponsored need-based aid programs designed to help residents pay a portion of the cost at their state's public colleges and universities.

So how do you demonstrate your financial need? And how does government (both federal and state) and individual colleges assist families in taking up the bucket challenge? They start by asking you to complete two primary applications.

Free Application for Federal Student Aid

Created by the US Department of Education, the Free Application for Federal Student Aid, or FAFSA, determines financial aid eligibility for US citizens and permanent residents. The most well-known aid federally distributed is the Pell Grant, which helps support over one-third of undergraduates on an annual basis. Disbursed amounts do change, but in 2023–2024 the maximum Pell Grant award was $7,395, with students receiving various overall grant amounts. These funds are intended to serve families who would otherwise not have the financial means to afford a college education for their child. In fact, over half of Pell Grants go to students whose families earn less than $20,000 a year, while only 5 percent go to families earning over $60,000 (Hanson 2023). It is important to know that the FAFSA also qualifies students for federal loans and federal work-study programs, and many states and colleges use the FAFSA to determine eligibility for their need-based financial aid.

Driven almost exclusively by your family's tax return(s), the FAFSA becomes available online each year on October 1 and asks for the "prior-prior" year's tax information. In other words, if you are applying for the 2024–2025 academic year, you will be asked to submit tax documents from 2022. When you google "fun," you will not see images of people filling out government forms, but fortunately the Internal Revenue Service did implement a Data Retrieval Tool, which allows students and parents to access their tax return information online and prefill data pertaining to annual income. Additionally, with the FAFSA Simplification Act of 2020, Congress took steps to reduce duplication and the overall length of the application. This is helpful since college students receiving financial aid are required to resubmit the FAFSA each year they are in college.

Once you complete the FAFSA, you will receive a Student Aid Index (SAI), formerly known as an expected family contribution (EFC). This is the annual amount of money the federal government has determined that you and your family has the ability to access and use to pay for college. SAI is used to determine your level of eligibility for all federal aid (including grants, loans, and work-study opportunities), as well as some state and institution-specific aid. If you are a fan of acronyms, you will appreciate that your SAI is delivered via your SAR (Student Aid Report) after you complete the FAFSA.

Is the FAFSA Required?

Families often ask whether they should complete financial aid forms if they do not believe they are eligible for need-based aid. While that is a personal decision to make, it is important to know that some colleges require the FAFSA in order to issue institutional scholarships and other grant aid. In recent years, an increasing number of states are requiring that all graduating high school seniors complete the FAFSA prior to graduation. Moreover, if you believe you may want the option of taking out a federal loan, whether a student loan or a Parent PLUS Loan (which we will cover), it is necessary to submit the FAFSA. Lastly, having the FAFSA on file is helpful in case there are any significant changes in your earnings or overall financial situation in the future. Because the policies of institutions vary and completing the FAFSA gives you more options, we recommend you consider completing it.

You will likely hear some colleges described as being "need blind" or "need aware." These terms can mean different things at different institutions, but generally speaking, need-blind admission means that an applicant's ability to pay will not influence an admission decision. Many colleges, particularly public colleges and universities, could describe themselves as need-blind in that they do not consider your ability to pay in making their admission decision; however, they do not meet 100 percent of students' financial need. Currently, there are fewer than 100 colleges in the country that promise to meet full demonstrated need, and an even a smaller number than that do so without offering any loans as part of their financial aid package.

In contrast, colleges that say they are need-aware in the admission process are, on some level, taking an applicant's ability to pay into consideration when they evaluate applications and make offers. As a result, some families who believe they have the ability to pay for all or a sizable percentage of the full cost of attendance are reluctant to complete the FAFSA or other aid applications, believing it will diminish their chances of being admitted.

In our experience, that is an unwarranted fear driven by misinformation and gossip. The truth is that the majority of colleges in the country either do not have your financial aid information by the time they make admission decisions or they do not consider ability to pay in their admission decisions. Furthermore, if you are applying to the handful of colleges that meet 75–100 percent of demonstrated need, and you end up not showing need, that logically will not have an adverse impact on their admission decision. However, if any doubt remains in your mind about this, ask any questions directly to the schools you are considering.

Note: Our focus in this chapter is on undergraduate students who are claimed by their parents as dependents for tax purposes; these students will have their parents' financial information considered in their financial aid equation. If you are unsure of your tax status, we recommend speaking with your school counselor for assistance.

CSS Profile

Another major financial aid application you may be asked to submit is the CSS Profile, a product created by the College Board and used by several hundred undergraduate colleges and universities across the nation. The CSS Profile is far more detailed than the FAFSA, and schools requiring it are attempting to get a fuller picture or more accurate assessment of a family's financial situation than the FAFSA provides. In the majority of cases, this is because those schools have significant institutional funds set aside to meet the demonstrated financial need of the students they admit, and they want to dedicate their institutional resources to students they believe will advance their institutional mission. While the FAFSA focuses on tax information and earnings, the CSS Profile does a deeper dive into a family's assets, untaxed income and benefits, equity, and other "accessible" finances. In the case of divorced parents, it also delves into the finances of noncustodial or adoptive parents.

Scoir, a company dedicated to assisting students with simplifying their college search and helping them find the best academic and financial matches, highlights fundamental differences between the two applications, FAFSA and CSS Profile, in the table below.

Information Required	FAFSA	CSS Profile
Student Information		
Income Tax Return Data	✓	✓
Bank Accounts *(Checking, Savings, CDs)*	✓	✓
Educational Savings Accounts *(529 Plans, Coverdell Plans)*	✓	✓
Parent Information		
Income, Taxes, and Exemptions	✓ *(prior prior year)*	✓ *(past 2 years plus current year estimate)*
Bank Accounts *(Checking, Savings, CDs)*	✓	✓
Liquid Investments *(Stocks, Bonds, Money Market, Mutual Funds, ETFs)*	✓	✓
Investment Real Estate	✓	✓
Tax-Deferred Retirement Contributions *(IRAs, 401Ks, Pensions)*	✓	✓
Family Business/Farm	✓ *(only if more than 100 employees)*	✓
Equity in Family Home		✓
Trust Funds		✓
Medical Spending Accounts *(FSAs, HSAs, Dependent Care FSAs)*		✓
Siblings' Assets Held in Parent's Name *(e.g., 529 Plans)*		✓
Siblings' K–12 Private School Tuition		✓
Total Retirement Savings		✓
Non-retirement Annuities		✓
Other Valuables *(e.g., collectables)*		✓

Source of data: "FAFSA & CSS Profile—a Straightforward Guide to Understanding Financial Aid," Scoir, 2021, https://www.scoir.com/blog/fafsa-css-profile-a-straightforward-guide.

Note: CDs = certificates of deposit; ETFs = exchange-traded funds; FSAs = flexible spending accounts; HSAs = health savings accounts; IRAs = individual retirement accounts.

Scholarships

Institutional Scholarships

As we outlined at the beginning of the chapter, one of the reasons that college costs have increased over time is because schools have been spending money to improve their campus, the overall student experience, their perception among families, and their reputation or position within the higher education landscape. Colleges also spend a great deal of money to attract students who will help them advance their institutional priorities. In the case of scholarships, this means awarding money to students who are either academically excellent (often based on GPA, test scores, class rank, or some combination thereof) or who have other special talents, which could include musical, artistic, or athletic talent, or who possess another specific trait, interest, or background that aligns with the college's mission and priorities. While *scholarship* is the term most high school students are familiar with, you will find some colleges using other terms to describe this type of aid, including *gift aid* and *merit aid*. Regardless of the terms used, you should think of this as water in your bucket that does not need to be repaid.

Outside Scholarships

Not all gift aid comes from colleges. You will find scholarships provided by states (sometimes funded through lottery dollars), by private companies or individuals, as well as by nonprofit organizations, community-based organizations, or other religious, social, or professional sources. As you would assume, scholarship eligibility is determined by the organization awarding the money. In most cases these scholarships have their own application, deadline, and time frame for decision-making; they may have other unique requirements as well, so applying for outside scholarships takes time to research, effort to apply, and attention to detail. On the upside, in most cases the money awarded can be used to attend any college you choose. Finaid, Fastweb, Niche, and BigFuture provide free search platforms to help students and families identify and apply for scholarships. Like so much of the college search and application experience, researching outside scholarships requires that you be proactive and organized. We encourage you and your family to talk with your high school counselor and spend time on your own looking into these resources, particularly as you approach your senior year.

Renewability

As you research scholarship opportunities, you will find that some are provided as first-year-only money or are not guaranteed for your entire college career. We urge you to learn whether the scholarships you are applying for, or the ones that colleges or organizations encourage you to apply for, are renewable for the full time you're in college. If you find that a scholarship is not automatically renewable, it is critical to understand the conditions of renewal (such as a GPA benchmark, particular academic major, or athletic performance). In our experience, too many students and families focus on year-one affordability, rather than thinking about paying for all of college.

Loans

Whether from a bank, government, or other institution, loans are funds you will eventually have to pay back. Also known as *self-help aid*, loans have added interest, which increases the total amount you have to repay. While you may not have thought of loans as financial aid per se, they are often a necessary contribution toward filling your bucket.

The three primary types of loans that families take out are subsidized loans, unsubsidized loans, and Parent PLUS Loans. *Subsidized* loans are need-based, and the government pays the interest while you are earning your degree. Some colleges will include loans in the financial aid notification you receive after being admitted as an option for meeting the cost of attendance. *Unsubsidized* loans are available regardless of demonstrated need, and interest applies immediately upon receiving the loan. Some of these loans allow for deferring interest during your time in college, but if you decide to pursue an "unsub" loan, you'll need to understand the terms of the loan clearly and apply for any exemptions you qualify for.

Currently, there are limits on student borrowing, and the amount you are able to receive depends on a variety of factors, including your year in college, your college's cost of attendance, and your other financial aid awards. In the years ahead, some of the federal policies for loans may change, but for now, students claimed as dependents on their parents' taxes can borrow a maximum of $31,000, with no more than $23,000 of that total in subsidized loans, over the course of a four-year undergraduate career (Federal Student Aid n.d.). And while there has been a great deal of conversation around sweeping plans for loan forgiveness, you should approach borrowing money with an expectation of having to repay the full amount with interest accrued.

Parents are also able to take out a loan to assist in financing their student's college education through the Direct PLUS Loan (Parent PLUS Loan) program. According to LendingTree, "Students and parents borrowed an estimated $94.7 billion in the 2021–2022 academic year. According to CollegeBoard, 46% of this was federal unsubsidized loans, 16% was federal subsidized loans, 13% was Grad PLUS loans, 13% was private or other nonfederal loans and 11% was Parent PLUS loans" (Shepard and Filipovic 2023).

A Critical Conversation

At this point, you may be feeling a little uneasy about going through the financial aid process. In our experience, that is partly why so many families avoid or delay conversations about paying for college. The truth, though, is that discussing *limitations*, *conditions*, and *expectations*, as well as your position on borrowing money, is an incredible opportunity to help students build financial literacy and keep your family aligned.

From time to time, life presents us with the need to have these crucial but frequently clumsy conversations. But as you know from experience, the anticipation is usually worse than the reality, and we end up being glad we had the courage, honesty, and openness to address the issue. After working on the ground in admission at the high school and college levels for over two decades, we can assure you that students who have a sound understanding of their family's financial considerations, and of how their college choice will play into that equation, feel included and responsible, rather than restrained or sheltered.

Net Price versus Published Price

Because of federal and state financial aid, as well as individual colleges allocating institutional aid to advance their mission, a college's published price is often not the actual price you will pay. In effect, the size of the bucket is not necessarily the size of the bucket. Here's the math:

NET PRICE = cost of attendance − capacity to pay
− all forms of aid awarded (need-based aid,
scholarships, gift/grant aid, loans)

In other words, the *net price* is the amount you can expect to pay to attend a particular college *after* receiving financial aid. To have productive conversations about paying for college, you first need an approximation of how much the schools you are considering will cost you. Because each family's financial circumstances are different, this can be challenging to determine, but a good place to start is the Net Price Calculator that each college makes available on its website as required by the US Department of Education.

John Leach, assistant vice provost for enrollment and director of financial aid at Emory University, implores families to use these calculators or other online assessments *"as soon as you start thinking about college."* He explains that by entering basic information into these online tools, you can typically get a good sense of what families with savings, earnings, and assets and financial situations similar to yours have paid for their student to attend in recent years. "It is not perfect," he adds, "but if you will take the time to put in accurate and thorough data, you can get an excellent idea of overall costs within an hour."

Net Price Calculators ask for information required by the FAFSA or CSS Profile, including

- previous year's tax return data

- adjusted gross income

- family context (i.e., other children in college, custodial and noncustodial parent information)

- business owners' accurate income and assets

- divorced/separated/never-married parents (some schools will want information from both parents, regardless of marital status; in some cases, one parent is not and has not been a part of the student's life, so schools will need some details to waive the requirement)

- complex situations (health issues/medical expenses, natural disasters, deaths, etc.)

While a Google search will lead you to the Net Price Calculator of each college, there are also several companies that partner with institutions to make things more convenient. For instance, on the MyinTuition and BigFuture sites, you can learn more about projected costs, anticipated scholarships and aid, and estimates of net price for a number of private and public colleges and universities based on your financial information.

If you want to dive into financial data even further, search online for the Common Data Set (CDS) for the colleges you are considering. In Section H, each school lists the amount of need they meet on average; the number of students receiving need-based aid, non-need-based aid, or scholarships; and details about financial aid packages. Using the CDS, you can also learn the percentage of a class that took out loans and the average amount they borrowed.

As we said at the top of this chapter, finding colleges that are affordable is key in your search. Your objective is to end up at a school where you can succeed academically, thrive socially, and feel financially secure. This starts by doing your research, asking questions, and using resources to determine the real cost of the schools you are considering as early as possible.

Chris Briggs, dean of college counseling at Durham Academy, has this to say about researching financial aid resources: "I encourage families to contact financial aid offices with their questions the same way they would contact admissions offices before they apply. Remember that staff members are trying to build a new class every year. They are experts who know their institution and have seen it all. Reach out to them." Briggs, who formerly worked at Duke University, says that estimating costs without assistance is not always easy for families to do: "People have all kinds of different situations and circumstances that can be tricky to account for, and that is particularly true for business owners."

COMPARATIVE CASE STUDY

Let's take what we have covered in this chapter and see how an investigation into financing college may play out for a fictitious student,

Maya, and her family. Here's what you need to know about their situation.

1. Maya is a senior in high school who applied to six colleges.

2. She was wait-listed by one university and denied by two others. Fortunately, she was offered admission by three great colleges that she's excited about: Kudzu College, Seaside College, and Flagship University.

3. Seaside College is the school Maya is most excited about because its marine biology program is one of the top programs in the nation, and her best friend has already decided to go there.

Note: After colleges offer you admission, they will issue a financial aid letter or award package. Typically, this is delivered through your student portal. Your aid award states your COA, lists your demonstrated need, and then includes the need-based and gift aid you can expect to receive. Because a package's layout and terms vary among schools, and some colleges include loans in their package while others do not, we recommend that you create a spreadsheet (something like the table below) to facilitate a comparison of costs.

Financial Factors	Kudzu College	Seaside College	Flagship University
COA	$70,000	$54,000	$20,000
Ability to Pay (EFC/SAI)	$25,000	$25,000	$25,000
Financial Need	$45,000	$29,000	$0
Merit Scholarships	$0	$15,000	$0
Need-Based Grant	$42,500	$2,000	$0
Student Loan	$0	$3,500	$0
Work-Study	$2,500	$1,500	$0
Total Aid Provided	$45,000	$22,000	$0
Unmet Need	$0	$7,000	$0
Net Price	$25,000	$32,000	$20,000

Maya's Buckets

1. Of the three schools, Kudzu College has the biggest bucket to fill because it has the highest COA. Kudzu, however, also happens to have a multi-billion-dollar endowment, which allows it to offer students a great deal of institutional aid. Over time Kudzu has eliminated merit scholarships, and it does not include loans in its financial aid awards. In Maya's case, Kudzu is effectively filling her bucket to the top by offering her a financial package that meets all of her demonstrated financial need—leaving her with a net price equivalent to her ability to pay: $25,000.

2. Seaside College's published cost is lower than Kudzu's, but Seaside is unable to fill Maya's bucket with enough institutional aid to meet her full demonstrated need. Some colleges have more money to allocate in financial aid than others, but ultimately every school has limited resources. Seaside, like the majority of schools in the United States, does not meet 100 percent of demonstrated financial need for every student it admits.

3. Each year, Seaside is forced to make difficult decisions and direct its finite aid and merit money according to its institutional priorities. Notice that a portion of the aid Seaside has offered Maya is in the form of a loan. With Seaside's net price of $32,000, Maya will need to decide if she or her parents are willing to borrow additional money or can come up with another way to meet the remaining cost to attend.

4. Flagship University has the lowest published cost of Maya's three options, and it is the school that Maya's family would pay the least for her to attend. Note that even though her ability to pay exceeds Flagship's COA, her net price remains $20,000 annually. There were some students admitted to Flagship this year who received merit money in their aid package, further reducing the net price, but Maya did not have a talent, trait, or skill that Flagship was prioritizing in this admission cycle.

Ability to Pay versus Willingness to Pay

The more admission officers you talk to, the more you'll notice they tend to dodge absolutes in their answers. They can answer almost every question posed to them with "It depends."

> Is it better to take a dual enrollment class or an AP class?
> *It depends . . .*

> Should I start my essay with a quote from a dead person?
> *It depends . . .*

> Will my discipline situation from sophomore year hurt me
> in the admission process? *It depends . . .*

Similarly, because every family's financial circumstances differ, and regulations and policies can change from year to year, financial aid staff also are unlikely to use the words *never* or *always*. One thing they can all agree on, though, is that they've *never* offered someone a financial aid award package who said, "I think you must have made a mistake. This is way too generous, and I would like to give some of my awarded money back." On the contrary, most families think the amount of money they are expected to pay is too high and the amount of scholarships and other gift aid they are offered is too low.

Imagine dinner at Maya's house one evening in April of her senior year as she and her family are comparing her award packages from Kudzu, Seaside, and Flagship. In addition to the meal's aromas, a mix of emotions fill the room: excitement and pride about getting acceptances, understandable nervousness about making a choice, and pressure to select a school soon. If everyone in the room had agreed, before Maya ever applied, that $20,000 a year was the most her family was able to pay, the decision now is made. She's going to Flagship University. Go Ships!

Would Maya still rather go to Seaside College to study marine biology and share a room with her best friend? Absolutely. And while she plans to study science, she is also good at math, so she understands the limits of her family's ability to pay for college. A price tag of $32,000 a year is simply out of reach. Could dinner be a little somber because of this? Sure. But disappointing is a long way from disastrous. And that is what Maya and her family would be dealing with if this were the first time they had broached their financial limitations as a family. Students understand a financial ceiling. You just don't want the food to hit the ceiling out of frustration.

Parents: We have all had conversations with our children about our *willingness to pay*. Over the years you have probably seen this conversation go terribly wrong and surprisingly right. Maybe the desired item was a phone, a bike, a certain trip or show, or "that thing everyone else is getting." *Willingness* means you do have the money and are willing to spend it, but being unwilling means you may well have the money but fail to see the value or necessity of the expense. It is much easier to talk about willingness to pay in junior year or fall of senior year than in spring of senior year.

Imagine being Maya's parent in April of senior year if you could pay the net price for Seaside but don't want her to go there because it's a four-hour flight away. Meanwhile, she's sitting across from you wearing a Seaside sweatshirt. Again, we can't say it enough: talk about money—especially as it relates to conditions, limitations, and willingness—early and honestly. Willingness conversations are honest and respectful. The best ones start with "I love you" and focus more on what you can do and will do rather than what you can't do or won't do.

Students: We started this book by encouraging you to ask, "*Why* do I want to go to college?" At this point we hope you have followed our advice, given that question some serious thought, and have written down some of your answers, because it will inform how much you are willing to work, invest, or borrow. And equally important, it will help you articulate your position calmly and cogently to your family.

What If . . .

Amy, my (Rick's) wife, has many strengths and endearing qualities. If you are familiar with the Enneagram, she is a type nine, peacemaker. Perhaps because she wants everyone to be happy and for life to go on without conflict, she is extremely reflective. This means she often looks back on conversations and decisions to dissect them and to wonder whether she could have or should have done something differently: "Do you think she understood what I was saying? I wonder what would have happened if I'd . . ." I call this the what-if loop. As you read above about Maya's options, you likely have some what-ifs rattling around in your mind.

What if Maya's family appeals to or attempts to bargain with Seaside's financial aid office? It's true that her family could ask the financial aid office to reconsider her package. Perhaps she left out a major piece of financial information or something has changed in her family's financial situation since she completed the aid application. Each year colleges receive a significant number of appeals from families asking for additional aid. Some schools may ask to see your other financial aid letters and have the discretion to use professional judgment in their evaluation of the situation. For instance, Maya may be able to bring Kudzu's offer to Seaside's financial aid office and ask its staff to see if more aid is possible.

Perhaps Seaside would be motivated by Maya's desire to enroll and would therefore work to reduce the gap between its offer and Kudzu's. Or Seaside's staff may say in all sincerity that while they would love for Maya to attend, the office has exhausted all budgeted dollars for that year. As hard as financial aid staff work to help make college affordable, each school is operating with a limited amount of aid that it must distribute not only to new students but to returning students as well. Bottom line: yes, a family can attempt to bargain. Results will vary.

We both have had families express the concern to us that going back to a college to petition for more money might "hurt them" in some way. Absolutely not. Schools will not rescind a financial aid offer just because you asked whether more assistance is possible. If you choose to appeal your financial aid award, we encourage you to read the school's website for instructions about its process and timing for considering petitions, as well as what counts as a valid reason for another review.

Parents: We understand the emotions that come when you combine money, your kids, and a tight turnaround for committing to a college. If you choose to inquire about additional funding, frame your emails or conversations with respect and empathy. Financial aid teams work tirelessly each year to serve thousands of new and returning students, and they have to do this with a limited budget and set policies. While the success of any appeal cannot be guaranteed, your exchange with the office should start with a tone of appreciation versus one of demand or entitlement.

What if Maya's sister is also a college student? In the past, there was consideration for having multiple children in college at the same time, owing to the FAFSA's formula for calculating the ability to pay. With the passage of the FAFSA Simplification Act, however, that factor is no longer considered in determining need-based aid eligibility. Therefore, it is up to individual colleges to determine whether and how they will take that fact into account when adjusting financial packages.

What if Maya had been working in high school and saving for college? A student's own assets will be considered in determining financial aid packages by the FAFSA, as well as by individual colleges. In general, the expectation is that if Maya has savings, she will contribute 20 percent of that toward her college education. As an example, if Maya had inherited money from her grandparents and had worked at an ice cream shop through high school, and so had total savings of $40,000, then $8,000 would be factored in her ability to pay. Obviously, she could choose to use as much of her savings as she wanted beyond 20 percent to help fill her bucket.

What if Maya receives an outside scholarship in her senior year? This falls under the umbrella of "it depends." For financial aid offices putting together aid packages, an applicant's scholarships are not always additive, or "stacked" on top of all other grant aid in the package to the student's advantage. Each college has the discretion to decide if and how it will incorporate outside scholarships into your aid package. In some cases, a school will view them as strictly additive and not reduce what it offers in its package, while another school may reduce your institutional grant / gift aid by the amount awarded from the outside source.

The takeaway here is to know that if you are applying for, or receive, an outside scholarship from a company, nonprofit organization, or perhaps a parent's employer, you should research the details of how that scholarship can be used and inquire with the colleges you are considering to learn how they will integrate these funds in a financial aid offer.

What if Maya attended Flagship for a year or two and then transferred to Seaside? We understand that most high school students think about starting and graduating at the same institution. Increasingly, though, students are transferring sometime during their college career. In fact, according to a 2022 report from the National Student Clearinghouse (Causey et al. 2022), more than two million students transferred to another institution in 2020–2021. Transferring can be a viable strategy for reducing costs and making college more affordable. Many colleges have developed transfer articulation programs, which provide a clear path for students in terms of the courses they need to take and the grades they need to make prior to transferring. As you visit colleges or consider schools you believe would be good matches, we encourage you to learn the extent to which transfer opportunities exist.

What if Maya plans to work during college or take on an internship or a co-op? Working on campus, in the local community, or getting a formal internship or co-op are all ways for students to defray part of the cost of college. Your family should make this possibility a topic of conversations around *expectations*: that is, How much can the student make and in turn contribute to paying for college during their college career? Because your primary job as a college student is to succeed academically, we recommend that your family be realistic about how much you can earn over the school years and summers to pay for college. It would be extremely difficult for Maya to make the $7,000 a year of unmet need for Seaside while keeping her grades up and still having some free time. Again, this is why conversations about paying for college should happen during junior year or the summer before senior year. When offers of admission are on the table, emotions can run high. If dollars are limited, you'll be glad you have already hashed out *conditions*, *limitations*, and *expectations*.

What if marine biology is part of a tuition exchange program? In all regions of our country, there are states with reciprocity programs that allow residents to attend a college or university in another state without having to pay out-of-state tuition. (The National Association of Student Financial Aid Administrators has compiled information about some of these programs: https://www.nasfaa.org /State_Regional_Tuition_Exchanges). This is a great opportunity for students to expand their list of colleges and seek matches in terms of location, size, and financial viability. (Because these agreements exist only among public universities, our imaginary Seaside College, a private school, would not be included.) We encourage you to learn about your state's participation in reciprocity programs.

As you can imagine, entertaining the what-if loop about financial aid could generate even more questions or possible alternatives. Let's try some activities that will help to personalize your family's financial considerations.

Try This

Write down the list of schools you are currently interested in learning more about. Take time to plug your financial information into the Net Price Calculators for those schools. Then make yourself a spreadsheet listing COA, with tuition, room and board, fees, and other costs broken out separately, so that you can look at the schools' costs side by side.

- How do the schools compare with one another?

- Has your perspective on any of the schools changed based on your understanding of expected costs?

We also encourage you to check out the guide to financial aid for students prepared by the National Association for College Admission Counseling (NACAC) to learn more about applying for financial aid (available for download: https://www.nacacnet.org/financial-aid-basics -what-students-and-families-need-to-know/). Some families find it useful to consult a financial advisor or use resources available in state-sponsored financial assistance programs.

 Talk about This

1. What would you do if you were Maya?

2. Discuss loan tolerance as a family. Assume that your starting salary upon graduation is close to the national average of $50,000. What does your monthly budget look like after graduation when you start repaying your loan? What amount of monthly repayment is too much?

CHECK IN. After reading this chapter, are you still on the same page as a family? If you are not all-in together, what do you need to do, discuss, or learn to get there?

☆ Extra Credit

On the *New York Times* website, check out Ron Lieber's series of articles on student loans, college pricing, and the cost of college. His insight, sources, and questions will be helpful as you think critically about schools that may be a good financial fit.

On the podcast *Admissions Decoded*, Angel Perez, CEO of NACAC, hosts important conversations about the ticket price of higher education and offers advice for families making difficult decisions about what they can afford. For starters, listen to episode 9 from season 3: "Fit, Finance, and Equity: Two Economists Discuss College Affordability."

CHAPTER 5

Creating a College List

I really want to know (Who are you?)
Tell me, who are you?
"WHO ARE YOU" BY THE WHO

Keep an open mind that this is an opportunity to learn more
about your child's true interests and deeper desires. It's also
an opportunity for your child to declare those interests and
desires by making the college choice their own choice.
A PARENT'S ADVICE ON THE COLLEGE SEARCH

Imagine that your name is drawn in a local lottery. You have the option
to choose a round-trip plane ticket or a helicopter tour. If you choose
the plane trip, your focus will naturally be all about where you are
going. Destination is king. In the airport and on the plane, you will be
surrounded by people singularly focused on getting somewhere specific. They are headed to a wedding or funeral, going to a graduation,
traveling to make a speech or presentation, visiting family or friends,
or interviewing for a new job. Everyone has a precise end point in
mind. As a result, delays are annoying, lack of coffee or spotty inter-
net service is irritating, and turbulence is scary. What you remember
about plane trips typically are the inconveniences—the length of time
it takes to get there, the uncomfortable seats, poor snack selection,
and annoying passengers constantly bumping you as they head to
the bathroom or remove something from the overhead compartment.

What do you remember later if the flight was smooth and arrived on time at its intended location? Nothing. Taxi, accelerate, take off, and land. That is all.

If you choose the helicopter tour, you will lift straight up off the ground with little effort or fanfare. Blades spin, seat belts buckle, doors close, and headphones go on. You are quickly airborne. Your focus is not where you are headed, because you know it will end in the exact spot it began. The point of the ride is not to get somewhere. Instead, it is to see, learn, explore, appreciate, and gain a new perspective.

The same is true of college admission. It is not intended to be a direct flight. Too many people expect the college search experience to be a plane ride. They have one specific destination in mind, so they strap in and hope not to be frustrated, delayed, or rerouted along the way. Our hope is that you begin to view it as a helicopter tour. Your goal is to look beyond what you see, to rise up rather than barrel down the runway, and to spend your time excited and learning rather than anxious and trying to control all the details or stay on an exact route. If the coronavirus pandemic taught us anything, it was to expect the unexpected: that life doesn't always go in a straight line, that we often learn and grow through reroutes and turbulence. This is a good lesson to take on board as you approach your college search experience.

This chapter encourages you to enjoy and appreciate the ride; gives you good questions to ask along the way; helps you look down over the landscape, observe your choices, and see things from a different perspective; and most importantly allows you and your family to "fly" together.

FIRST THINGS FIRST

The stress and anxiety people describe when they discuss college admission centers on the piece of the experience that you do not control—where and when you will be admitted and how much money that school will give you to attend. So it is easy to forget that you do control three-fourths of your college admission experience: *where* you visit and apply, *which* school you select to attend, and ultimately *how* you show up at the place you chose.

In part III, we will cover how you can put your best foot forward with your application. First, though, it is time to add another important building block to your cornerstone—matching your *why* with *where* to create a solid list of colleges to visit and apply to. If you remember the metaphor of the helicopter tour and keep an open mind as you explore different options, your list of colleges will continue to shift and change. Do not be disconcerted. That is precisely what you want.

FRESHMAN AND SOPHOMORE YEAR

We are often asked, "What should I (or my student) be doing in ninth and tenth grades for college?" The short answer is "Not much."

At this point, your job is simply to be a good high school student. Take classes that interest, challenge, and prepare you. Be a good member of your school and community—not because you think it is going to help "get you in" but because being involved is what makes a rich, rewarding, and memorable high school experience. Yes, colleges are going to look at your involvement, impact, and influence outside the classroom, but you should be volunteering your time, working, participating in clubs, or playing a sport because you are in exposure mode at this point. (Note that we are not suggesting you have to do all of these things.) Do what you enjoy. Try new things. If you hate tennis, do not join the team just because you think it will help you get into college. First, it will not. Second, there is no second.

Parents, please encourage your student (and frequently remind yourselves) to enjoy these all too brief and precious high school years. Resist the temptation to turn each event and grade into a discussion about the college résumé.

Keep it simple: Ask yourself some basic but invaluable questions: What do I choose to do when I have free time? What genuinely interests and excites me? What do I like to read on my own? What do I have the most fun doing? What am I good at? What would I research and explore even if it were not required in school? What kind of people do I enjoy being around? What parts of my state or country would I want to visit or live in? What jobs or professions appeal to me and why?

What did I miss during lockdown in the pandemic, and what was I glad I didn't have to do? Admission officers frequently ask applicants what they are "passionate" about during interviews. At age 17 (or 47 for that matter) that can be tough to have a good answer for. But in essence you are passionate about something (people, places, activities, or ideas) when you would miss if it were taken away. What are those for you?

Keep asking these questions and making notes as the answers change. Tara Nelan, formerly a college counselor in Florida and now the regional director of admission for Muhlenberg College, puts it perfectly: "Being authentic and honest with yourself in answering these questions, especially during the 12–20 months leading up to you actually submitting an application, can help your journey through high school to college be one of growth instead of a task to be done."

Look and listen: As a ninth and tenth grader, you are in a great position to be a casual observer. Don't miss out on this chance. Watch the juniors and seniors in your life, at your school, on your teams, in your clubs, at your job, or around your community. Listen to their conversations and deliberations. Explore some of the colleges the kids you admire are visiting and applying to.

What about some of the adults in your life? Relatives, coaches, friends' parents, leaders in your community, neighbors—what do they do for a living? What about their life interests you or seems appealing? Where did they go to college? As you get older, you will be hearing the incessant question "Where do you want to go to college?" Get out in front of it. Ask them now where they went and why. What would they do differently knowing what they do now? They will be thrilled to give you advice and insight, if you will initiate the conversation.

Go and see: Early in high school, we recommend that you make an effort to get on a few college campuses either close to home or while traveling on a family trip. Try to see the campus of a big state university, of a small liberal arts college, or of a technical or art institute if you are interested in those fields. Walk around, watch the students, subtly eavesdrop on conversations, catch a game, wander through buildings, eat in the dining hall or food court or at a popular restaurant on the edge of campus. Get a feel for the size of different colleges and how they connect with the surrounding community. Again, ask yourself basic questions: What stands out? What do I like here? What would I not enjoy if I went here? Your answers are hugely important because they point you toward the qualities of colleges you will be looking for in the future.

Explore online: One of the positive outcomes of the pandemic was that college admission offices leaned heavily into their online resources and programs. Register for online information sessions for schools that interest you and take the time to learn about different types of colleges. This will help you appreciate what to look for when your search ramps up later in high school.

JUNIOR YEAR

This whole college thing is probably seeming a lot more real. Breathe.

Separate needs and wants: In his book *Start with Why*, Simon Sinek introduces the "Celery Test." Sinek asks you to imagine that you're attending a dinner party where a number of people come up to tell you what food they think you should eat: M&Ms, Oreo cookies, and celery, to name a few. These recommendations come from highly accomplished, successful friends. When you later go to the supermarket, you spend a lot of money buying all of these foods, some of which will have little or no value to you. Sinek explains that if you know your *why* before you go into the store, you will make better decisions. If your *why* is to be as healthy as possible, you will leave the store only with celery (and have saved a lot of money).

> Identify your *needs* for a college as distinctive from your *wants*.

Identifying your *needs* in a college versus your *wants* is critical. Is being able to double major a *need*, or would a minor in one of those areas be OK? Would it be *nice* to have easy off-campus access to professional sports or Broadway productions or world-class restaurants, or is having those experiences *imperative* for you? Maybe you hope your college will have a rugby team or a marching band. Ask yourself if those are enhancing aspects or absolute deal breakers for you. Becoming confident in separating your needs and wants will help you tremendously in the admission experience.

BEGIN WITH THE BASICS

Location: When admission readers open your application, some of their first questions will be "Where does this student go to school?" and "What community are they coming from?" They ask this because context and place matter. Your goal is to find colleges where you are excited and confident about becoming part of the campus community. This starts with figuring out the type of setting (rural, suburban, small town, urban area), culture, and part of your state or the country you are drawn to. Weather is a big deal. Snow looks great in brochures and on social media, but walking around in subfreezing weather for months on end is a different experience. How early does it get dark in the winter? Do the number of rainy or cloudy days a year impact your mood or ability to focus, learn, and thrive? Will you be able to get outside as regularly as you're used to? What opportunities or limitations will the climate affect? If you are from Miami, visit Vermont in February, not June. Conversely, if you have never experienced extreme humidity, go to New Orleans in August.

Consider some helpful questions like these: Do you need or want to be able to drive home often and quickly, or are the costs and limitations of flying home OK? Did the impact of the pandemic change your feelings about location? What types of restaurants, activities, or cultural events do you want to have access to on a regular basis?

Size: Are you more comfortable with a smaller college of fewer than 2,000 students, or would knowing everyone in your class by graduation seem confining? If your high school's graduating class has 50–100 students, your perception of what a large college is will likely be different from someone whose high school has close to 3,000 students. On many college campuses, you will need to take a bus or shuttle between classes. Are you comfortable with that, or do you want a more intimate, compact, walkable campus? How important is the size, layout, and architecture of the campus?

Not all colleges of a similar size feel the same when you are on campus. For instance, if you are in the most popular major, your class sizes will likely be larger than the college's published faculty-to-student ratio, and that has implications for access to professors, research opportunities, classroom dialogue, and more. Many large universities in recent years have invested heavily in honors colleges or living-learning communities that create smaller, more intimate cohorts. Look beyond the overall enrollment number, talk to current students, and check out the student newspaper or online students forums to gauge what your experience would be like based on your major and interests.

Majors/programs: One of the many reasons that college rankings are—at best—misleading is that the strength and breadth of program offerings at schools vary greatly. The most selective college in the country might be amazing if you want to study biochemistry, but if it offers only one elective in your intended major, its rank and level of selectivity are irrelevant. If you are undecided on your major (like most applicants), you may want to explore colleges that allow or require you to take classes across academic disciplines in a general curriculum. About 80 percent of students in college end up changing their major at least once, according to the National Center for Education Statistics (2017). On average, college students change their major at least three times before graduating, so you should find out what a college's policy is on switching majors. Policies vary. Some schools allow students to change academic disciplines without any limitations. Others require that you apply to a specific major after a year or two of being on campus. Some colleges have GPA requirements or other internal transfer processes for their current students who want to change from one major to another. This is critical information with significant implications that too few students think to dig into before arriving on campus.

People: What kind of people do you want to be surrounded by for the next four or more years? Remember that a big part of going to college is creating a network of friends and colleagues. Your college career may last only four years, but some of the connections you make there will last a lifetime. Where do alumni from colleges you are considering tend to live and work? Alumni magazines, school newspapers, and social media accounts of student groups are good resources for getting a sense of the campus ethos.

Where students are from and the backgrounds they have will influence the conversations you have over pizza at 3:00 a.m. and the discussions you have at 3:00 p.m. in the classroom. Who are your people? What types of individuals bring out your best? These answers are hugely important to finding your best college matches. Is attending college with students from a variety of socioeconomic backgrounds important to you? Take time to learn what percentage of students receive some type of financial aid.

Do you want a school known for student activism, conservatism, or community engagement? Is it important to you that most students live on campus? Is evident school spirit and bonding with classmates at sporting events part of your vision for college? College brochures may all look the same, but the actual student experience varies widely among campuses.

Outside the classroom: When people say *college*, you probably think about life beyond academics. This makes sense because most students are in class or lab somewhere between 15 and 20 hours tops each week. Even after subtracting the additional hours spent studying and writing papers, you are still left with a lot of time to do other things on campus and in the surrounding area. What do you want your college experience to look like in the times and spaces beyond the classroom? Are you planning to study abroad in a certain country or region of the world? Would you like to have an internship or co-op in a specific industry or with a particular company? If so, how accessible are these opportunities for students? Intramural sports, clubs, ROTC (Reserve Officers' Training Corps), research, and service opportunities all vary from school to school. Are you a hiker, rock climber, biker, or caver? How active are the outdoor clubs at the schools you are considering? If you want to pursue an engineering degree and study in another country, make sure this is possible. If you want to play a varsity sport, are walk-ons eligible to try out for the team? If you are a recruited athlete, are there any limitations on the offerings of the college experience that you're allowed to access? Some colleges discourage athletes from studying abroad, while others encourage it. You can find information about all of this online or on social media. You should also make an effort to ask current students these questions when you visit campus or attend a virtual session.

Cost: As we discussed in the last chapter, a college's published cost should not keep you from visiting or applying. Learn as much as you can about the amount of financial aid you will need to make that place affordable enough to attend. Because money can be a wedge for families, now is the time to take our advice and have open discussions about earnings, expenses, savings, and how college costs factor into your family's lifestyle and goals.

Selectivity: We intentionally left this piece until last, and we hope you will as well. If you honestly ask and answer the questions we have posed, you will find many colleges (with widely varying selectivity) that match your criteria. This is great news because you want to have a few colleges on your list where your grades and test scores (if required) put you above their average accepted student profile. There is nothing wrong with applying to schools with single-digit admit rates. However, if those colleges constitute your entire list, you are setting yourself up for disappointment. Remember: your chances of getting into a school that admits 10 percent of applicants does not increase with the number of those colleges you apply to. That's just not how math works. A *good* list of colleges is not determined by where they rank or the percentage of applicants they reject each year. Instead, your job is to find colleges where you will be excited to attend if you are admitted. With thousands of options to choose from, we are confident you will be able to build a balanced list from a selectivity standpoint.

Research: College Scorecard, BigFuture, Princeton Review, Unigo, and other companies provide free online interactive tools that let you search for schools by key attributes (size, location, cost, academic and nonacademic programs) to discover and compare colleges. Your high school may also have access to a college search and application management platform such as Cialfo, Xello, Scoir, or Naviance. If you are staying open in your approach, we expect you will easily identify 15–20 schools that align with your criteria.

RANK THE RANKINGS

Given the rising cost of tuition and increasing debt for many college graduates, it is understandable why families might think of themselves as consumers of a college education. Schools traditionally avoided language describing tuition as a transaction or the cost of a degree as a purchase, but in recent years the concept of return on investment (ROI) has become prevalent. In response, colleges are focusing their marketing, presentations, and communications on "outcomes" for their students as much as they are on the student experience while in school. In other words, they are attempting to articulate the short-term value of attending and also the long-term dividends that a degree provides. This is a good thing. ROI should absolutely be part of your equation in making a college choice. As you research schools, we hope you'll seek out figures related to outcomes: the job placement rate at graduation, the average number of job offers students have upon graduating, and graduates' average starting salaries and mid-career earnings. These figures will vary by major, so be specific in your analysis and questions.

The downside to viewing college education as a consumer is the temptation to quantify, order, and draw lines. This is understandable, because in our culture we are surrounded by ratings and lists. We add a top-50 playlist to our online music account in a heartbeat. Reviews and metrics of products are everywhere. You cannot turn on the TV or radio without hearing ads touting how a new truck was rated number one for towing power or overall customer satisfaction. If we are car shopping, we pull up comparisons online about average miles to the gallon, safety ratings, and resale value. These can be informative, but in the end, would you buy a car ranked highest in fuel economy if you have a family of six and the car has only two doors? Are you swayed by a top ranking in power steering in a SUV that won't fit in your garage? No.

> Rankings can limit a constructive and comprehensive college search.

When it comes to considering colleges, families do fall into these traps. They take rankings and ratings at face value. They boil the college experience down to one number and assign it disproportionate value and then draw arbitrary, draconian lines in the sand. Each year students tell us they were counseled to apply only to schools ranked in *U.S. News and World Report*'s top 25; they were pressured only to visit schools ranked in the top 10 in their chosen field; and ultimately they were made to feel guilty or misguided if they did not choose the highest-ranked school to which they were admitted.

We believe this mentality inhibits a healthy and comprehensive college search. Fixation on rankings was criticized by author Malcolm Gladwell (2021) in a scathing two-part episode of his *Revisionist History* podcast; he took issue with the gameability of the *U.S. News and World Report*'s rankings, which he characterized as having incited a "horse race among colleges, to see who can rank the highest." In his exposé of commercial college rankings, he interviewed researchers at Reed College who had unpacked the data to reveal how colleges improve their standing by implementing strategic policies and practices. In his book *Who Gets In and Why*, Jeff Selingo (2020) also drives home just how absurd and irrelevant rankings are to your thoughtful and personal college search.

There are many sources of rankings, but here is the methodology of *U.S. News and World Report* as one example (Morse and Brooks 2022):

40 percent—Outcomes (including social mobility, graduation, and retention rates): How good of a job is the school doing at retaining, supporting, and graduating students?

20 percent—Faculty resources: How do faculty salaries and the number of students in the classroom compare with other universities nationally?

20 percent—Expert opinion and peer assessment: What do academic professionals from other colleges (presidents, provosts, deans, etc.) and counselors on the high school level think about that school? (Often these individuals are not familiar with the schools they are rating, or they delegate completion of the questionnaires to support staff.)

10 percent—Financial resources: What is the average per-student spending on instruction, research, student services, and so on?

7 percent—Student excellence: What is the school's admit rate, test score averages, and number of students coming from the top 10 percent of their high school?

3 percent—Alumni giving: At what rate are alumni giving back to their alma mater?

Maybe you skimmed over that list too quickly, so let's back up. Notice that one-fifth, or 20 percent, of the rankings are not based on numbers at all but rather on opinions. Let that fact sink in by imagining a scenario.

You walk into American history class on the first day of your senior year in high school, and Mrs. Bertha Ormse passes out the course syllabus. She announces in a gravelly voice, "On pages one to two, you can see what we will be learning this fall in US History, 1800 to 1910."

Scanning the syllabus, you pick up the highlights: War of 1812, Monroe Doctrine, western expansion, Missouri Compromise, rise of railroads, Trail of Tears, Civil War, Reconstruction. Nodding in agreement, you think, "Makes sense. I've heard of most of this."

Interrupting your ruminations, she continues matter-of-factly: "Page three breaks down how you will be graded." You flip to page three: quizzes, homework, tests, and projects count for 80 percent of the grade. "OK, Ormse. I see you. Personally, I would have weighted quizzes a little less, but . . ." And then you come to the next line: "No. Certainly not. Wait . . . the last 20 percent of my grade is decided by the opinions of the other students. Twenty percent?!"

That's right. Your fellow students, who have a vested interest in their own grade and position in the graduating class, will decide one-fifth of your final grade. You start looking around anxiously and suddenly your mind shifts into overdrive.

Who is that kid in the second row? I've never seen him in my life.

Oh, no. Zach. He has always hated me ever since that thing with the guy at the place back in third grade.

Crap. Sarah. Everyone loves her. She's . . . she's . . . she's . . . all the things I'm not. But does that make her better at history? Does that make her better than me in general?

Well . . . when the opinion of others accounts for 20 percent of the grade—probably. And that's how it goes for colleges with the rankings. Twenty percent is based on the opinions of others. Others in the same game. Others in the same class. Others with vested interests in their own results and position.

Raise your hand if you'd like 20 percent of your admission decision to be based on the other applicants' opinions of you. (You can put your hand back down now.) Oh, and to be clear, in most cases they have never met you, seen you, or have anything concrete to go on except where you are from and a vague recollection that a few years ago someone they met said you were "OK."

Our hope is when you consider the value of rankings in your college search or selection process, you will ask these questions:

- Do I care if a president (or their assistant) from one college looks favorably upon another (especially accounting for what we know about college competition)?

- Is a school's ability to pay a faculty member $2,000 more annually ($244/month or $8/day) of any consequence to my college search and decision?

- Do I really think there is a difference in prestige/quality/experience between two colleges because of the three-spot difference that places one inside and the other outside the top 25? The top 50? The top 75?

- If a college is in an ideal location, has a dynamic student body, is a good academic match, but ranks 10 spots below another, should that number (based on the factors above) matter?

- If the school is outside the top 100 but is offering me a scholarship and has graduates thriving in the field I want to pursue, should I turn it down for a higher-ranked but less-affordable option?

When you apply to college, you trust that admission officers are going to take much more into account than just your test score and grade point average. You do not want them to rule you out by drawing a line you happen to fall just below, despite your good grades, tough classes, and extracurricular impact. Similarly, we would encourage you to visit and apply to schools not because of a subjective rank but rather because they match your interests. Be holistic in your approach.

Opt in: In chapter 2, we explained the way colleges and universities search for students. Search is a two-way street. If you are not receiving information from a college that matches your criteria, opt in. Go onto university websites and complete their electronic form for prospective students. Typically you'll be asked for basic contact information along with questions about your academic and extracurricular interests. This is an excellent way to receive information from schools. It also puts you into their database so they can invite you to special recruitment events on campus and notify you of when they're coming to your city or school to conduct a prospective student session.

Visit campuses: During your junior year, you should be taking the opportunity to hit the road. We will expand on the importance of, and best practices for, visiting colleges in the next chapter. Ideally you will visit every college you plan to apply to, and often students need to visit twice as many colleges as they ultimately apply to. This might mean traveling to 15 or 20 colleges, so start early. We understand that traveling is a big investment of both time and money. If you are unable to get to some of the places that interest you, check out the virtual tours that schools provide on their websites. YouVisit and CampusReel are two companies that partner with colleges to show pictures, videos, student testimonials, and online campus tour information. One silver lining to the COVID-19 pandemic is that colleges were forced to invest in robust online visit options after their campuses were shut down and students were unable to experience the school in person. We encourage you to do your initial tour of schools online and narrow the list of those you will visit in person.

Show up: Admission representatives for colleges travel extensively in the fall, and increasingly in the spring, to meet students and build excitement for their college. Keep an eye out for college fairs in your area. These can draw reps from several hundred schools, who gather to speak with prospective students and their families. Regardless of the event's location, you will find admission officers

> **College fairs are a great way to gather information, network, and learn about schools.**

standing behind folding tables and displays with their school banner, glossy brochures, and often some free swag. College fairs are a great way to gather information, network, and learn about schools you have not yet considered. Do not waste this opportunity. It will be crowded, and your time with each college will be limited. Be prepared with two or three questions you could not easily find answers to on the school's website. The reps will be able to collect your contact information or point you to a webpage where you can share it. Do this. It is an excellent way to receive follow-up information about majors, application tips, or campus visit programs. In some instances, this interaction will be noted as a demonstration of your interest in that particular school. There are many online college fair options as well, and the platforms offering these get more engaging and interactive every year. Don't discount these opportunities. You will find fairs focusing on specific types of schools, like arts schools or colleges specializing in the STEM fields (science, technology, engineering, and mathematics). Search online or ask your school counselor about these events.

Similarly, when colleges come to your high school, either in person or virtually, make every effort to attend. Do not just passively absorb information. Use that time to connect with the admission officer (often the same person who will be reading your application). Do not let them go through their canned speech. Be sure to get answers to your specific questions about your needs and wants. Having presented to hundreds of high school groups, we can attest that admission officers appreciate students who ask thoughtful questions. If you join a virtual event, be prepared to present yourself well and be in a space where you can interact comfortably.

Whether you are reading a college guide, looking online, or taking advice from a sibling or teammate, remember that this is *your* search, *your* list, and nobody else's. No one person's opinion is the absolute truth about a school—no alumnus, current student, admission director, or college president. Your job is to solicit as many opinions as possible and to look for themes and commonalities while staying mindful of *your* needs. What is the story the college is telling, and does it match the story you are building for yourself?

Change the question: One Sunday after lunch, I (Rick) was watching college football highlights of a back-and-forth battle in Happy Valley between the University of Illinois and Penn State. At the time, my 10-year-old daughter was stretched out on the living room floor next to me. With her head touching the ground next to her foot, she asked, "Penn State? Is that a good school?" Without hesitating, I said yes. Now standing with her foot pulled behind her, toward her shoulder, she asked, "How about the University of Illinois?" "Absolutely," I answered. Over the next 15 minutes, we saw another eight games recapped. Private colleges, land-grant public schools, and military academies whose teams covered every geographic region of the country. Elizabeth, after a few questions about mascots or comments on helmets, would ask the same question: "Is that a good school?" And each time (including once when my wife scrunched her nose), I'd respond definitively. Ole Miss? Brown? University of New Mexico? Gonzaga? Yes to all.

Yes is a satisfactory answer for a double-jointed 10-year-old who is more concerned with touching her foot to the back of her head, but it is not a satisfactory answer for you. Your job is to dig deeper. Your job is to stay focused on your *why* and to think for yourself. Your job is to ask lots of questions. And that starts by being honest with yourself and changing the question from "Is that a good school?" to "Is that a good school for me?" Trust us. Adding these two words changes everything. Are we good? Good!

LATE SUMMER AND EARLY FALL OF SENIOR YEAR

Trust your gut: Are you excited about schools you had not heard of a year ago? Have some colleges dropped off your list even though you bought their T-shirt when you visited campus? You are on the right track. Has the order of your list changed? You are doing this right! Do you remember Sinek's "Celery Test" from early in the chapter? Look at your "shopping list." Confirm again that all of the colleges you are still considering align with your interests, values, and priorities—your *why*. Did you really not like the campus, or did you just have a bad tour guide? Did you lose interest in a school after hearing an offhand remark from a peer? Remember: it is *your* list, *your* choice, *your* college experience.

Finalize your list: Our advice is to arrive at a final list of five to nine colleges where you believe you would thrive and where you would be truly excited to attend. If a college does not check those boxes for you, do not waste your money or time or the college's effort to review your application. Too many students feel pressured to increase the number of schools they apply to for arbitrary reasons.

Here is a framework of categories you can use to put together a balanced list of colleges:

- Two to three *reach* schools—colleges where your grades and test scores put you below their average admitted-student profile or where it seems impossible to predict an admission decision based on their admit rate and high volume of talented applicants. If you do not love any schools that fall into this category, please feel no compulsion to include one on your list.

- Three to four *target* schools—colleges where your academic profile matches their average admitted student. Ideally, you will find colleges in this category with admit rates closer to 50 percent than to 20 percent.

- One to two *likely* schools—colleges where you are above the average admitted-student profile. (While you may hear the term *safety* school, there really is no such thing.) Again, the national admit rate average is over 60 percent. We are confident you can find at least one or two colleges at or above that admit rate where you would have a phenomenal college experience.

In the end, the driving question is this: Would you be excited to attend every school on your list? Barbara Tragakis Conner, director of college counseling at Foxcroft School in Virginia, advises students to apply to *five first-choice* colleges. Her point is that each school on your list should be a great match where you believe you would be happy and successful; that way you will not be disappointed if you are not accepted at any one institution.

Unlike the traditional college fair, at Kentucky Country Day School's Finding Your Fit Fair, college representatives leave the recruitment literature behind, along with their name tags and school banners. In lieu of that, each representative is asked to submit a list of five distinct characteristics or programs at their institution, which are printed on sheets of paper. Students then wander from table to table, not knowing the institutions' names but focusing instead on the programs or experiences they offer. Next, students and representatives gather for a debriefing, at which time the representatives reveal the names of their schools. The group discusses what the students—and the representatives—learned, what surprised them, and how their preconceived notions were challenged. Finally, the representatives get to return to their tables (with brochures and banners) and meet with students again. This format encourages engagement and discernment rather than reflex and judgment. It is the ideal approach to building a college list—one that focuses on values, programs, and the experience. Consider ways you can conduct your search in a similar manner—focusing less on name and more on how the schools match your criteria.

> The ideal approach to building a college list is to focus on values, programs, and the experience.

☼ *Try This*

In the table opposite, list the top-five needs (things you must have) and the top-five wants (things nice to have) that are important for your college experience. Are there certain majors that must be available or other desired programs, opportunities, or features that will inform the college list you build?

Compare your current list of colleges with that of a family member you have asked to write down a list of schools for you. Explain why each school was included on your two lists. Ideally, there will be some overlap but also some different colleges on the lists. What are the commonalities? Differences? What can you learn about each other's expectations, hopes, goals, and priorities based on these lists?

Needs	Wants

Talk about This

1. What outside influences are going to affect the college list you build? Rankings? Family connections? Finances? Friends? Parents and student should both make lists of influences and then share your responses.

2. What is one thing you need to communicate to your parent/student about the schools being considered?

3. What resources are you going to rely on for information about colleges? Are they objective or subjective? In what way?

CHECK IN. After reading this chapter, are you still on the same page as a family? If you are not all-in together, what do you need to do, discuss, or learn to get there?

☆ **Extra Credit**

Listen to Malcolm Gladwell's podcast episode "Lord of the Rankings" from season 6 of *Revisionist History*. He takes a deep dive into university rankings, including their history, methodology, and how universities make strategic adjustments to improve their position from year to year.

We think you are smarter than the makers of commercial rankings. And we know you can tailor your criteria and weight your priorities in an individualized way that can help you build a list of schools that match your needs, wants, and goals. So take some time to do your own ranking of the colleges on your list. Follow the QR code in the upper corner and use our Real Rankings worksheet, which will guide you in creating your own rating scale based on what is important to you.

CHAPTER 6

The College Visit

I hope you never fear those mountains in the distance
Never settle for the path of least resistance
Livin' might mean takin' chances, but they're worth takin'.
"I HOPE YOU DANCE" BY LEE ANN WOMACK

As we pushed the faded motel sofa in front of the paper-thin door, I (Brennan) knew this was one of those father-son moments I would never forget. We were in a questionably safe motor lodge in upstate New York that looked as though it was right out of a 1970s police drama. At the time I expected an escaped convict to kick in the door at any second, so a sofa barricade seemed like a reasonable precaution. This is now one of many great memories I have of my weeklong college tour with my father. Similar memories abound from the trip that my mother and I took months before. On that adventure, my brother and I had spent the week desperately trying to convince her that she didn't need to ask the tour guides if girls were allowed in the boys' dorms.

Despite the inevitable missed flight or meal or highway exit, we want these trips to be memorable for your family too, the source of stories you'll retell 3, 5, or 15 years later. Our hope is you look at these trips as an adventure—a time to explore, connect, and enjoy the experience.

WHY VISIT

Visiting a variety of schools—large, small, urban, rural, private, public, near and far from home—is the best way to separate your needs from your wants, as we discussed in chapter 5. Just as you would not buy a car sight unseen, it makes little sense to choose a college without first comparing it against a checklist of desired features and experiencing it firsthand: to kick a tire and take a test drive. You need to try before you buy.

The disruption of the global pandemic greatly enhanced opportunities for virtual visits, interviews, and admission programming. Most schools now have robust offerings for students and families who cannot step foot on campus. While websites, videos, social media, and virtual tours can be helpful, there is simply no substitute for visiting a campus to get a sense of the school, its programs, and its community. Visiting is also an important way to demonstrate to an admission office that you are sincerely interested. Increasingly, institutions are using "demonstrated interest" as one criterion in their review of candidates. Admission professionals want to know that applicants have done their research and are applying because they are informed; these applicants are more likely to enroll if offered admission. Visiting campus virtually and in person is one of the best ways to demonstrate your interest.

> There is no substitute for visiting a campus to get a sense of the school, its programs, and its community.

WHEN TO VISIT

Students frequently ask, "When should I start going on college tours?" The answer is simple: "When you are ready." You may want to begin exploring campuses early in high school, or you may have to be prodded by parents or other adults in your life as senior year approaches. The most important thing is that you are open to experiencing a campus and are intentional about the visit. The time to start is different for everyone. There are no rules that dictate when you should or should not visit a college, but there are best practices that the in-formed "consumer" should keep in mind.

The ideal time of year to visit colleges is when school is in session and students are on campus. A weekday tour and information session and/or interview will provide the best feel for the campus, culture, and community. Since summers and high school holidays are among the busiest times for college visits, planning ahead will make it more likely that you can schedule tours and interviews while they are still available.

If a college offers on-campus interviews, take advantage of this opportunity when you visit as a junior or senior. Some families do an initial tour of schools to see which ones interest the student, and then they return later to interview. Do not postpone the opportunity for interviewing; it is a waste of time and resources to have to return to each campus. Interviews are a great way to get to know a school, and even if you wind up not applying there, at least you had practice at a valuable life skill. We provide some helpful tips for interviewing in chapter 10.

HOW TO VISIT

Most colleges have a "visit" link on their website providing options for in-person and virtual opportunities to get to know their institution. You will be able to book visits online or with a phone call. If a school allows you to sit in on a class, we highly recommend doing so; the more exposure you have to what life will be like there, the better. One mistake families often make is trying to pack too many visits into a day or a week. Be conscious of travel time, and give yourself space to process your impressions and enjoy being in these campus communi-ties. We advise you not to schedule more than two visits in a day, and any more than five or six visits in a week will likely leave your head spinning. To facilitate comparisons across schools, try choosing a common theme for each visit. One of my (Brennan's) students and his father made it their mission to find the best burger restaurant nearest to every college they visited. Imagining yourself as a student on that campus and in that area takes time. Do not rush it.

CRITICAL QUESTIONS

Traveling to colleges is a big investment. By now you have likely seen how similar college marketing emails and brochures can be. Campus visits can also seem predictable after you've sat through hours of PowerPoint presentations and watched enough tour guides walk backward and talk about the same topics: the opportunity to play intramural sports, the chance to conduct research, the option of studying abroad. If you do not ask questions that matter to you, these visits will blur together until every admission officer and tour guide sounds like the schoolteacher in Charlie Brown cartoons: "Wah wah, wah wah wah." Mary Wagner, executive director of strategic higher education enrollment leadership at the College Board, advises families to ask themselves, "What is the campus culture like? What do students think is important, and do I agree with much of what they get worked up about? Which place makes me feel most welcome? Can I see myself fitting into many of the activities and academic pursuits that current students enjoy?"

Asking the right questions, and being persistent in asking them, is the trait of a good high school student, a good college applicant, a good college student, and a lifelong learner. As you go through the college admission experience, staying curious is absolutely vital. Our hope is that when you visit college campuses, you will commit to being a relentless inquirer. Consider the following ways to reframe your questions for greater depth of understanding.

Student-to-Faculty Ratio

You ask: "What is your student-to-faculty ratio?" This may include faculty who are primarily doing research, those who teach only one undergraduate class, and even those who are on sabbatical. Take a look at an online college guide like BigFuture or Unigo. You will find that many schools are listed with ratios under 19:1 of students to faculty. Does that mean you and 18 classmates will be sitting around a table in Introductory Calculus your first year? In most cases, the answer is no. These statistics include courses at all levels (those with 2 students and those with 200), so while not entirely unhelpful, these ratios do not tell the whole story.

You *should* ask: "What is your typical introductory class size?" This question focuses on the classes you'll probably be taking in your first and second years. Schools rarely publish average SATs or GPAs of admitted students; rather they publish bands or ranges. Likewise, you want to look at ranges and variations in class size. At Georgia Tech, for example, the most common class size is 26–33 students, and around 7 percent of courses have over 100 students in them. The student-to-faculty ratio, on average, is 19:1. When you visit a campus, ask questions about class-size percentages and ranges. For instance, you might ask what percentage of classes have 30 students or fewer. That information will be more helpful to you in setting expectations for what kind of experience you would likely have there. Ask current students what their typical class size is, who teaches them (tenured professors, adjuncts, graduate students), and how accessible instructors are outside class.

> When you visit college campuses, commit to being a relentless inquirer.

And *then* ask: "How does that vary from first year to senior year? Is the range higher or lower for the major(s) that I am considering?" You will find schools often have introductory classes in chemistry or economics with rosters four or five times larger than their averages. It is helpful for you to understand the variance, because it may also be the case that upper-level chemistry and economics classes are half or a quarter of the average size.

Your job is to probe. Your job is to understand what your experience could look like.

Graduation Rate

You ask: "What's your graduation rate?" Colleges will have a variety of answers to this question, and with national averages below 50 percent, you need to dig deeper. Some will give you their four-year graduation rate; some will provide a five- or six-year rate. The variance is not an attempt to mislead you; college representatives have been trained to respond with an answer that is reflective of their students' experience. Most private liberal-arts schools will not talk much about their five- or six-year graduation rate because there is no significant difference by years and their goal is to graduate students in four years. That is how they structure their curriculum and campus culture. Alternatively, some colleges have a high percentage of their students interning, working a co-op job, or studying abroad for multiple semesters. As a result, many students there take more than four years to graduate but pay tuition only for eight semesters. Digging in with good questions helps you understand the numbers and the culture and may lead you to ask follow-up questions.

You *should* ask: "What are your four-year and six-year graduation rates? For both groups of graduates, what percentage has either a job offer or an admission to graduate school upon graduation?" This will help you understand the school's outcomes. You will find that some colleges have a high graduation rate but low job placement or percentage of graduate school admission.

And *then* ask: "How does the graduation rate vary by major? What percentage of students who double major, study abroad, conduct research, and/or have an internship finish in four or six years?" You should try to learn whether graduates are finishing school with a social network and opportunities rather than whether they are finishing in four years after someone hit start on a stopwatch. Often the reason graduates take more than four years to graduate is because they have used their time to gain work experience, contacts, or international exposure that translates into lower loan debt and higher earning potential. If that is the case, who cares about the clock? You might even ask, "How many students finish in less than four years by taking advantage of a summer term or other special programs that allow them to save money or time?"

Test Score Policy

You ask: "How do you consider test scores in your admission review process?" Expect responses that you could just have easily found online. *We are test-optional. We are test-free. We require tests.* Honest, yes. Accurate, yes. But not necessarily helpful. A college can be test-optional and still prefer to receive test scores. Or a college may give you the flexibility of not submitting scores but still recommend that you send in something additional if you take that option. Alternatively, a school may require test scores and use them in a formulaic manner to make decisions for scholarships but not for admission. Or a school may require tests because of a policy of the state or the board of regents, but the school leans more on grades and other elements of your application to make its decision. While the pandemic pushed many schools to adopt various approaches to standardized tests, their use of those tests is anything but standard. Dig deeper.

You *should* **ask**: If a college is test-optional, we encourage you to ask, "What percentage of your admitted students sent in test scores with their application last year?" And then probe further to learn the average scores for that group of students versus those who sent scores after being admitted. Your aim will be to put your best foot forward in your application, and knowing this information about actual practices by applicants is an important place to start.

And *then* **ask**: "What about for students like me?" Again, *standardized* testing does not mean *standardized* review. Ask whether submitting or not submitting scores is expected or more common for Early Decision applicants versus Regular Decision applicants. Ask whether applying with your major or residency status or other demographic should impact your decision to send or not to send scores. These questions are not off-limits. Your questions are valid. Ask them!

Retention Rate

You ask: "What is your first-year retention rate?" This is a great and important question. The national average for students returning to their college for their second year is typically around 65 percent in four-year colleges. Therefore, when a school reports that its first-year retention rate is 85 percent, it sounds impressive.

You *should* **ask**: "Why are those other 15 percent leaving the school?" Is it financial? Is it because the football team lost too many games? Are the students who leave disproportionately in certain majors or from out of state? Is it because the school is too remote or too urban or too big? Your job is to dig deeper. Ask the school to explain who is leaving. The school should know the reasons. Some colleges have retention rates below the national average, but they are losing students who succeed in transferring to state flagship institutions or into specialized programs in the area. These answers provide context beyond the bottom-line number.

And *then* **ask**: "What resources are there on campus for academic student support?" Many colleges have invested significant human and financial resources to ensure a positive campus experience. Is there an office dedicated to retention, intervention, and enrichment?

Campus Diversity

You ask: "What is diversity like on campus?" In response, get ready for a litany of statistics and websites, reference to an annual symposium, and mention of a vice president or office dedicated to this work. All of that has value, of course, but it won't give you a sense of what your experience of diversity might be like there as a student.

You *should* ask: "Have you seen campus become more diverse and inclusive in your time here, and if so, how?" The answer to this question will likely be anecdotal, although you still might get a website or two thrown into the response. Ask not only for numbers but also stories. You'll want to determine if the websites and programs the school has created are actually benefiting diversity in students' experience and in the campus community.

And *then* ask: "Can you connect me with a first-year student and an upper-class student (possibly even someone in your major)?" Ultimately, you want to hear firsthand perceptions and experiences. Getting a range of perspectives is critical, so also attempt to speak with faculty, staff, and recent graduates, in addition to looking online—particularly at the social media accounts of campus clubs and organizations. Reddit threads and online student newspapers often provide insight into the real conversations, criticisms, and varying views about diversity and inclusivity on campus. Beyond the surface numbers, you'll want to know how engaged the campus is in this dialogue.

Outcomes

You ask: "What percentage of your graduates have jobs when they graduate?" Given the amount of money, time, and effort you are going to invest in earning a degree, this is a critical question and one you should absolutely dig into. In most cases, admission officers will provide you with a number. But what does 87 percent really mean? Is 91 percent good? In most cases, schools stop with the statistic and do not offer much context, leaving you with more questions than answers.

You *should* ask: Lots of follow-ups. How many students in *my major* have jobs upon graduation? How about within six months or a year of finishing? Are they hired into jobs they are excited about? How many other offers did they have? What percentage go on immediately to graduate school? What does that look like for my major? What are some of the companies regularly hiring on campus? Can you tell me the average starting salary of your graduates? These questions will provide you with details, expectations, and, yes, more questions.

And *then* ask: "What support does your career services office provide and when?" Now that you know something about placement rates and salaries, you'll want to understand how the college is getting these results. How many students are participating in internships that lead to jobs? At what point does the institution begin coaching students with résumé review, interview preparation, and workshops or seminars to help them understand how to use their degree in the workplace? Return on investment is a measure you will see ranked and referred to. Your questions, however, are a more holistic way of learning how a college develops its students and prepares them for work after graduation.

A VARIETY OF VOICES

When you visit schools, your goal is to gather answers from a range of sources so that you'll get a balanced perspective. No alumnus, tour guide, faculty member, or current student has a corner on the market of a school's story. Colleges and universities are big. Experiences vary. Ask the *same* questions to as many people as you can. The answers may align and create a consistent picture, or they may differ dramatically. One result is not necessarily better than the other, but asking a variety of people will help you form opinions and determine how you feel about the school.

What makes this college different from other schools? This question is essential. If a student, tour guide, admission counselor, or faculty member cannot answer that question, *run!* One of the most challenging parts about the college admission experience is discerning how one school stands out from the thousands of others in the country. If you find some common themes in the answers you hear, despite varied experiences, you have likely found the school's real identity and can consider whether it resonates with you. In contrast, if you find people there unable to identify a distinctive culture, it should give you pause.

What is the most exciting thing happening on campus? Perhaps the answers you'll hear are all about sports when you are not much of a fan, or they may focus on a major that doesn't interest you, or they center around political activism, the new vegan dining options, and the 12-screen movie theater nearby, but you are an apolitical carnivore who dislikes popcorn and surround sound. All of this is helpful to hear. This is what *match* is about: campus culture and ethos. Maybe the answers you hear instead are about the entrepreneurial spirit on campus and students' interest in start-ups, and this emphasis resonates with you. Congratulations! You have broken through the noise and found a real match.

What question has not been asked today that should be asked? We suggest asking this at the end of a tour, information session, or interview. It gives the presenter an opportunity to hit on something that really matters to them. The good news is their response will not be scripted, so you can count on it being authentic, honest, and reflective of their priorities.

What do you wish you had known before coming to this college? Ask this to students, tour guides, and even to professors or admission staff who may not be alumni. Are their responses generally positive? (Like excitement about the number of hiking trails or good restaurants in the area.) Or are they predominantly negative? (Like shock over the expense of living in the area or the lack of direct flights to most places.) These responses will give you great information to consider as you make your decision to apply or attend.

How has this college set you up for success and fulfillment in the future? We suggest you ask this question to first-year students as well as to seniors while you are on campus and then, later, to recent graduates and to alumni who are well into their careers. This is a pertinent question for faculty and upper-level administrators as well. Are you hearing answers like "the incredible network" or "amazing reputation" or "ability to think critically and work collaboratively toward solutions"? Do the answers resonate with your goals?

Bonus questions: What has disappointed you about the college? What do you wish were different? What is the most frustrating thing you have experienced? Where would you like to see this school in five years or ten years? What is the most important thing for a prospective student to know about this school?

Understanding context and gathering a more complete story is your goal for college visits. Do not spend money and time traveling and missing school just to accept the answers that colleges give you in their presentations or tours. Ask your questions! Be resourceful and use your network to find individuals who will share their experiences. Maybe friends' parents or your parents' friends or your school counselor can connect you with alumni of the college who formerly attended your high school. Online resources such as LinkedIn can also be helpful in building connections. Social networking apps have made connecting easier to do. As a student, this is *your* job. It is not your mom's job, and it is not your counselor's job. *Do your job!*

> **Understanding context and gathering a more complete story is your goal for college visits.**

Here are some other ways you can use your time to maximize your visit:

1. Develop a list of questions that you want answered at each school about academic programs, as well as life outside the classroom. These might relate to internships, career counseling, first-year retention, social life, safety, study abroad, mental health counseling, or tutoring services. (But don't ask, "How is your biology department?" because you will just get "It's great!")

2. Try to connect with the admission representative who is responsible for your high school or the area where you live. If that individual is not available, get their contact information.

3. Allow time to wander the campus after you finish the tour and leave the admission office.

4. Ask at the admission office if you can have lunch in the dining hall or where you can grab a coffee on campus.

5. Try to find a random student (not a tour guide) and ask their thoughts on the accessibility of professors, school spirit, support services (tutoring, writing center, career resources), and what it is like to live in the area.

6. Stop by the academic department you are most interested in to talk with a professor and/or a student. Better yet, contact the department before you go to see if you can schedule a meeting

with a professor. Ask about their research or the department's offerings. Even if you cannot meet with someone, walk around the department's building to see examples of student projects on display.

7. Contact coaches, music directors, or others beforehand to set up meetings while you are on campus. Better yet, attend a game or concert or production or exhibit. This will give you a snapshot of school spirit and student engagement.

8. Pick up the student newspaper; it generally offers an uncensored take on the issues facing students and the college as a whole.

9. At the end of your visit, ask yourself what story the college was trying to tell through its tour and information session. Is this consistent with what you value and the experience you're hoping for in college? What differentiates the college from others? Make some notes for yourself, as your visits will run together in your memory if you don't take time to record your impressions when they're fresh.

BEEN THERE, DONE THAT: VETERAN ADVICE

Wisdom comes from experience, and we suggest heeding the sage advice of students and parents who have visited some campuses and lived to tell about it. Here is what they had to say.

Students to Students

"Pay attention to small things . . . posters on the wall, how harried or at ease the students appear. Imagine the campus in the dead of winter (cold, dreary, miserable days, and would you want to be there); look for what social activities go on, look at the range of clubs and class sizes. Take advantage of any 'stay the day' or 'stay overnight' experiences."

"Get off the propaganda path. Eat at the cafe, read the student newspaper, wander around campus without the group, go to a class, talk to students you meet, etc. Visit as many colleges as you can in small bursts."

"Stay close to the tour guide so you get all the info during the tour. Don't be nervous about asking questions. Ask them why they chose that school—it usually says a lot about that place."

"Stay away from your parents during the tour! Make your own opinions about the school and do not let their impressions rub off on you. Same goes if you happen to be touring with friends. You can debrief on the way home or on the way to lunch."

"Keep an open mind that there is something to be gained from each visit, even ones you found least appealing, because you learn what you like and what you don't like along the way. Make notes immediately after the visit, what was liked and what wasn't. When deciding which college to 'accept,' you might not remember details."

"Don't judge only by the tour guide. Don't be scared to talk to students that aren't tour guides."

"Take a virtual tour of the campus before visiting, so it feels familiar from a physical point of view, and you can spend your actual time there focusing on how it feels—the atmosphere, the people, etc.—rather than on amenities."

"Find a student that you have a connection with: a graduate from your high school, someone who went to your summer camp, your cousin's friend from high school, your club sport teammate's older sibling. Go to eat in the student center with that person, ask them all your questions about the school. You will get much better answers than from your tour guide, and you will have a better idea of the background and perspective of the person answering the questions."

"Enjoy the journey!"

Parents to Parents

"Let your child be in charge; stay in the background."

"Start early (if the child is ready) as time is a premium as the student approaches senior year. Be realistic. Don't waste all of your time visiting schools that are a reach for everyone. Make sure you visit a mix of selectivity so that your child has more likely options he/she can get excited about. Have fun! Chill out and enjoy the time with your child."

"Ask your kid what they think of the school before you give your input so that they can develop their own opinion about the place before you sway their answer."

"If your child says they don't like the school, don't push them to stay and keep looking. Listen to your student. They are the ones who will have to live there."

"Visit colleges early in the process and use it as an opportunity to further build relationships with your child. Embrace the process."

Other Helpful Tips

"Asking offbeat questions at information sessions and tours. It throws off the propaganda agenda and you start to see truths."

"Having a tour guide who told a lot of stories about their experiences at the school was the most helpful way that I learned what life was like on that campus. It helped a lot to ask them for moments or stories about their favorite class or experience."

"Don't try to convince yourself you like a school because it is a 'good school.' If you don't like it, you don't like it. Don't let the name cloud your judgment."

"When I first began my search, I knew nothing about what I was looking for in a college. The least helpful for me was going into a college tour without knowing what abbreviations like 'LLC' or 'RA' meant, how a college class schedule typically worked, what a meal plan was, or what college dorms typically looked like. Basically, not doing enough background research beforehand was really the least helpful."

"Research smaller, lesser known schools when visiting an area; you never know when you might find a hidden gem."

"More than two visits a day is too much, and all the schools end up blending together."

"You will never know everything about a college in a day, so have a goal to learn about your interests and where they sit within the college."

"When visiting, don't just visit the school and leave town directly after. Is there a town life? Is there something beyond the campus gates? This will help you decide if the area is right for you. For example, going to the Dr. Pepper Museum with my mom after visiting Baylor showed us how interesting the town was, but it also gave us a memory together and took away a lot of the stress I get when I visit a college."

"Students and parents, have fun with each other while it lasts and try to make college visits educational about the institution but also a fun time together. This is a great tradition to have while touring!"

"Thank-you notes. Beyond this being a good practice and a lost art today, it can't hurt a student's file."

·ϕ· *Try This*

Scavenger hunt. Who doesn't like a good game or challenge? A little creativity will turn your college visits into more adventurous and memorable experiences. Is your brain going to explode if one more time you hear how many books are held in a college's library or you endure another explanation of the blue safety light system common on most campuses? Why not create a scavenger hunt that will keep you alert, while allowing you to dig deeper into a college community and providing an innovative way to contrast schools.

The items or challenges on your scavenger hunt will be uniquely yours depending on your interests, areas of study, or other priorities you may have, but here are a few suggestions to get you started.

(continued)

- Collect a student newspaper on campus.
- Find out the name and location of the favorite late-night student hangout.
- Get a picture of yourself standing in front of the most important landmark or statue on campus. (Many schools have traditions related to these attractions.)
- Collect a pen, postcard, or other item from the college.
- Take a photo of or with the school's mascot or its likeness. (Some schools make this easy, like the University of Richmond, which has a cutout of its human-sized spider mascot in the university's admission center.)
- Visit an academic department with a major you are interested in and talk to at least one professor there. You might come with a list of questions you want answered about access to courses, intriguing internships, or graduate school placement.
- Come up with your own addition to this list and share it with friends.

The options are endless for what you can put on your scavenger hunt list, but the more challenging you make it, the better, as this will push you to gain greater familiarity with each institution.

 Try This (Bonus)

Get lost. This tip comes from Joe Greenberg, a former professor and retired regional dean of admission for George Washington University. He said one of the best ways to get a read on the culture of a campus is to identify a busy hub of campus life (a quad, dining facility, or student center). Position yourself in the center of activity, and do your best impression of a lost visitor. Wait and see how long it takes for someone to stop and ask if you need help finding something. Does everyone just navigate around you with earbuds in or eyes fixed on their phone? Do you get strange looks? Are you tackled to the ground by campus security? The reactions of those around you and your observations of what students are engaged in will provide a window on the vibe of the campus.

Talk about This

1. What role will each family member play in arranging college visits and trip planning?

2. What environmental factors might affect your visit in unexpected ways? For example, a rainy day, a really hot day, a tired or overly enthusiastic tour guide? How will you ensure that you still get a good grasp on the story of the school?

3. What types of follow-up discussions will you have after each visit? Students, do you want your parents' impressions, or would you prefer they withhold comment? What will you use to make notes or take pictures on your visits?

👍 **CHECK IN.** After reading this chapter, are you still on the same page as a family? If you are not all-in together, what do you need to do, discuss, or learn to get there?

 **Extra Credit**

The College Tour is a TV series that tells the stories of colleges and universities from around the world. In the spirit of helping you come up with campus tour questions, keep an open mind, and explore broadly, we invite you to check out a few episodes.

As you seek out a variety of perspectives on campus, follow the QR code in the upper corner to a helpful worksheet for recording the answers you get to those questions about college life that are most important to you.

PART III

CHAPTER 7

Admission Plans, Deadlines, and Application Review

No one really knows how the game is played / The art of the trade
How the sausage gets made / We just assume that it happens.
"THE ROOM WHERE IT HAPPENS" BY LIN-MANUEL MIRANDA

We do not have time to write this chapter in rhyme, although our intuition is "The Room Where It Happens" would be a great title for a musical about college admission. Now that you have formed a list of colleges, visited campuses, and refined your criteria, we are going to build on your *why*, *what*, and *where* by turning your attention in part III to *how*. *How* do you apply to college? *How* do schools set their deadlines? And *how* do they review the information you submit and make their admission decisions? Or, to hat-tip Lin-Manuel Miranda's *Hamilton* again, we will walk you through *how* the parties get to yes. Let's enter the room where it happens.

There are several ways to submit a college application: an institution-specific application, the Common Application, Common Black College Application, and the Coalition on Scoir.

Some colleges and universities require that students use their institution-specific application. This also exists at the state level. Two prominent examples are the University of California System and the California State University System. Each has a uniform application that students complete in order to apply to any of the schools in the system. This format is simple for students and allows system schools to easily access and distribute applicant information to the appropriate campus for review. Like California, some other states have university systems where one application lets students apply to multiple campuses if they wish.

The Common Application, established by 15 private colleges in 1975, has grown to become an association with more than 1,000 member colleges and universities, both public and private, in the United States and around the world; these schools have agreed to provide one universal undergraduate application for admission (Common Application n.d.). Students can fill out the application online and send it (typically for a fee) to as many schools as they wish. In many cases, member schools also have supplemental questions or essay prompts that they require as part of the Common Application. Member schools that also offer their own institutional application as an alternative must agree to give equal consideration to all applicants regardless of how they choose to apply.

> **Pay attention to any requirements beyond the standard application that are specific to a college.**

The Coalition for College was established in 2015, and over 100 public and private member institutions use this platform. Coalition member schools are united by their mission to help students have an accessible, affordable, and transformative college experience (Coalition for College n.d.). In 2022 Coalition partnered with Scoir (a company committed to helping students navigate their search and application process) to create a more seamless application experience for students. Coalition is an alternative to the Common Application; however, many schools allow students to apply with either application.

What does this all mean for you? If a school offers more than one application option, that school does *not have a preference for which application you use.* The school is simply interested in obtaining accurate and complete information about you. If all of your chosen colleges accept a particular application, we recommend that you save time and energy and use that one. You will need to pay close attention to any institutional requirements beyond the standard application, such as additional essays or other materials specific to each school. Some colleges and universities will ask you to submit these additional requirements through their admission portal after you have submitted the standard application.

If having multiple applications does not sufficiently confound you, perhaps facing an array of deadlines will. You'll discover that many schools have multiple admission plans to choose from. Here is a primer on the options you are likely to come across.

Rolling Admission. Under this plan, students may apply at any time once the application period opens (usually in late summer or early fall). Many colleges that offer rolling admission try to review applications and make decisions in a set time frame (such as three weeks after submission). These colleges make admission offers on a rolling basis until all spots in a class are filled, at which time most schools will still accept applications for their waiting list.

Early Decision (ED). This plan is a binding agreement by which a student can apply only to one school where they will commit to enrolling if admitted. A growing number of institutions are now offering two rounds of ED, with the first deadline usually in early November and the second in early January. Most ED I applicants are notified of a decision in mid-December, and ED II applicants are notified in late February or March along with the rest of the applicant pool. There are even a few colleges that allow applicants to apply ED on a rolling basis, meaning that at any time during the admission cycle, an applicant can enter into a binding agreement. Because admitted students promise to enroll if admitted, the acceptance rate for ED applicants is often significantly higher than it is for other application plans. Increasingly, many selective schools are enrolling more than half of their class under this plan.

Early Action (EA). Like Early Decision, under an Early Action admission plan, students typically submit an application in October or November and receive a decision in December or January. The primary difference between EA and ED is that students are not bound to attend if accepted under an EA plan, and they can submit EA applications to multiple schools. The benefit of applying EA is that you'll get a decision sooner. As with ED, more and more colleges are admitting larger percentages of their classes through EA.

Restrictive Early Action (REA)/Single Choice Early Action (SCEA). This plan is like Early Action but with a condition. These schools let students apply and receive a decision early under a nonbinding application, but in doing so the students agree not to apply to another college under a binding ED plan at the same time. In some cases, these plans prohibit students from applying EA to another school, although they may make exceptions for public university applications.

Regular Decision (RD). Yes, this option still exists and remains a common way for students to apply to college. Most RD deadlines are in January or February, with notifications going out to applicants in mid- to late March.

Priority Application. This can mean different things at different schools. At some colleges and universities, a priority application has an early deadline (often November 30 or December 1) by which a student will be considered in the school's first round of review. This plan is often offered by large state systems. Priority applications are also sometimes called "VIP applications," "snap apps," or "fast apps," which all refer to streamlined application plans that encourage students to apply early (and boost a college's application numbers). Application fees are often waived, and essays are not required.

What do all these plans mean for you? As we said, schools are agnostic when it comes to *what* application you use. However, you should talk to your school counselor and closely review historical data in order to determine which application plan makes the most sense for you. Colleges have different admission plans with different deadlines for three primary reasons.

1. **Institutional Priorities**. We will do a deeper dive into institutional priorities in chapter 11, but for now all we'll say is that admission offices have specific goals for the size, shape, and profile (academically and financially) of their incoming class. The admission plans they offer are designed to achieve those goals and fulfill their mission.

   Example: The University of California System has an application filing window between October 1 and November 30. Was that window (which is academically intense for seniors in high school and includes the Thanksgiving Break) chosen because it works well for applicants? Nope. The application plan exists because it works for the schools of the University of California System and their collective admission process and enrollment goals.

2. **Competition**. Higher education may not be a perfect example
of Newton's third law of motion: for every action there is an
equal and opposite reaction. But higher education does function like an ecosystem where the decisions of one institution
have impact on others. This is particularly true when it comes
to admission and enrollment models. Schools are constantly
comparing their class size, academic and geographic profile,
admit rate, and yield rate with those of other institutions.
Boards of trustees and college administrators, and state leaders
keep a watchful eye on the policies, practices, and programs of
peer and aspirational institutions. The trend to adopt, maintain, or reverse test-optional admission policies in recent years
is a great example of how this plays out. The bottom line is that
colleges create their admission plans and set deadlines after
considering what is done at schools they are competing with
or aspiring to be more like in the future. If you are a sports fan
of any kind, none of these actions or thought processes will
surprise you.

   Example: If a school gives students the opportunity to apply
in the summer before their senior year in high school (which
is well before the October or November deadlines that are
common), you can be assured that the school has been losing
students to other colleges and thus pulled back its application
timeline to gain a competitive edge.

3. **Financial Aid**. You may not realize that admission deadlines are
related to financial aid and the cost to a college of enrolling its
class, but the two are inextricably linked. The timing of application plans (and their corresponding schedule for releasing decisions) affects how schools dole out financial aid, as well as the
amount of money they have available to offer admitted students
at different times in the admission cycle.

   Example: If a school has multiple early deadlines (ED I and
II, plus EA), it is generally attempting to get early commitments from students whose families have the financial ability
to pay, even if it means forgoing later applicants with a better
academic profile.

HOW DO COLLEGES REVIEW APPLICATIONS?

Depending on the college's enrollment goals, the number of applications it receives, and its institutional priorities, the admission office will take one of two approaches when reviewing your application.

Formulaic Admission Review

Formulaic review is typically used at public universities that have decided that academic factors alone are sufficient to determine which applicants will likely succeed at their institution. Formulaic admission review is based on just that—formulas, which factor in the courses you took and the grades you earned in high school, possibly along with your standardized test scores, in order to assign your admission "score." These formulas are simple to understand because they are transparent. Think of formulaic review like running the hurdles in a track meet, where you have to clear the bars at the height they're set. A college's goal is to ensure that the students it admits will succeed in the classroom. To do this, it evaluates the performance of current students (by college GPA, retention rate, graduation rate) and then uses that information to set admission standards. You can look on a school's website or admission publication to find the high school courses, GPA thresholds, and standardized test scores (in some cases) you will need to be admitted.

> With formulaic review, a university's primary goal is to admit students who will succeed in the classroom.

A good example of formulaic review is found in Iowa, where students can apply to the University of Iowa, Iowa State University, and the University of Northern Iowa with one application. Each school sets its academic requirements using what is known as the Regent Admission Index (Board of Regents, State of Iowa 2022).

Prior to applying, students can enter their GPA and test scores into the online calculator provided to find out whether they will be admitted to each of the three universities. In Georgia, most of the state's public universities use the Freshman Index (the equivalent of Iowa's Regent Admission Index). Here again applicants know the height of the hurdle in advance. This is purely about numbers, rather than being a humanly judged event. Anyone who can clear the bar will be

> ⊞ **How to Calculate Your Regent Admission Index, or RAI**
>
> Primary RAI Formula
>
> (3 × ACT composite score)
>
> +
>
> (30 × Cumulative GPA)
>
> +
>
> (5 × Number of years of RAI-approved high school courses completed in the core subject areas)
>
> = RAI Score

Source of data: "RAI Calculator," Board of Regents, State of Iowa, https://www.iowaregents.edu /institutions/higher-education-links/regent-admission-index/rai-calculator.

admitted. Arizona State University, Penn State University, and many other large public institutions, including a number of state flagship schools, employ formulaic review to admit and enroll tens of thousands of students a year.

Inside One Admission Office

I (Rick) am extremely familiar with formulaic review because in 2003, when I arrived at Georgia Tech, this was the way we made the vast majority of admission decisions. That year we received around 8,500 applications for first-year admission. Our admit rate was about 62 percent, or roughly two of every three applicants (Georgia Tech, Institute Research and Planning 2003). I loved traveling to high schools and college fairs at that time because my answers were quick and clear. "What are your GPA and SAT score?" If an applicant scored 1250 or higher on the SAT and had a 3.7 or higher GPA, I could say confidently they were going to be admitted because we were utilizing a formulaic, "plug and chug" admission review model. We had room enough in our incoming class to accommodate students who met those academic thresholds, and we knew based on our student data that they would probably do well once enrolled. So we ran the Microsoft Excel formulas, plugged admission decision codes into our student information system, and voila! Change the toner, print the letters, grab a coffee, lick some stamps, and call it a class. That process worked for us at the time based on the quality and size of our applicant pool and the enrollment goals we were attempting to achieve. It was easy, clear, and stress-free. The beauty of having formulaic review was that it allowed me to have more direct and productive conversations with prospective students. I didn't have to hedge about a student's chances of being admitted, so we could move on to discuss whether the student *should* apply based on the kind of college experience they were seeking.

A decade later, in 2013, after the recession, and with return on investment at the forefront of the nation's consciousness, families were asking pointed questions about graduation outcomes (employ-ability, average starting salary, etc.). Simultaneously, the tide of STEM fields was pulling more students into majors that Tech offered. In that year, we received more than 17,600 applications (or more than 100 percent growth compared with 2003). Because we were not signifi-cantly increasing the size of our first-year class or undergraduate pop-ulation, our admit rate dropped by one-third, to 41 percent (Georgia Tech, Institute Research and Planning 2013). This trend has continued in recent years: for the class of 2026, Georgia Tech received 50,600 applications with an admit rate of 17 percent. Given the sharp rise in both application quantity and applicant quality, cutoff numbers alone are no longer sufficient for making admission decisions. When the supply of talented applicants far surpasses demand, an institution moves away from formulaic review and adopts a holistic approach to admission decisions.

What is the takeaway from this change in admission practices at Georgia Tech? I am still in touch with many of the students who entered Tech when our admit rate was above 60 percent and we were not considered "highly selective." They went on to run companies, earn PhDs, or travel the world after selling their patented products. They are smart, successful, incredible people who are influencers in their communities all over the world. Remember this when you are evaluating colleges. Unfortunately, far too many students correlate a college's quality with the number of applications it receives or its selectivity (admit rate). Students begin to believe (perhaps after being repeatedly told) that their success potential is tied to these numbers. Do not make that mistake. Willard Dix (2016), an independent college counselor in Chicago, remarked on this mistaken tendency in a piece he wrote for *Forbes* called "Rethinking the Meaning of Colleges' Low Acceptance Rates" in which he states, "Although colleges love to crow about these numbers, they conceal a fact that few outsiders realize: A low acceptance rate, along with high scores, grades and other characteristics, indicates inputs, not outputs. It says nothing about what, how or whether students learn once they're there."

There are a number of websites that help you compare the admit rates, retention rates, and graduation rates of colleges you are considering. Check out the following table with data taken from College Raptor, a company committed to helping students and families "make smarter decisions about college." This is just a small sample illustrating how admit rates do not correlate with retention rates.

Institution	Freshman Retention Rate (%)	6-Year Graduation Rate (%)	Admit Rate (%)
Penn State University	93	86	50
University of Wisconsin	95	85	54
University of Michigan	97	90	27
Franklin & Marshall College	92	87	34
Villanova University	95	90	36
Gonzaga University	94	83	65
Wichita State University	73	43	94
Florida Atlantic University	79	49	60
Montana State University	76	52	83

Source of data: Lynell Engelmyer, "2 Key Statistics For College Cost Comparison: Graduation Rate and Retention Rate Explained," College Raptor, updated November 5, 2021, https://www.collegeraptor.com/find-colleges/articles/college-comparisons/2-key-statistics-for-comparing-colleges-graduation-rate-and-retention-rate-explained/.

Holistic Admission Review

If formulaic admission is like running the hurdles, holistic admission is like competing in the all-around competition in gymnastics: you are asked to demonstrate more abilities, and your demonstration of them is judged subjectively. John Barnhill, the assistant vice president for academic affairs at Florida State University, often jokes that holistic admission means colleges "can do whatever they want and not have to tell you why." In holistic review, schools do not simply set an academic bar and accept everyone who clears it. These colleges receive too many applications from students who could do well academically once enrolled. Holistic review admission has been characterized as a blend of science (objective quantitative evidence) and art (subjective considerations such as character and talents). Schools with holistic review have developed additional criteria for comparing applicants in order to shape the class they want to enroll.

> Holistic review is a blend of science and art.

At universities that practice formulaic review, admission staff are primarily recruiters. They travel to college fairs, visit high schools, and deliver campus presentations, but their admission decisions are based on numbers. The opposite is true in holistic review. While the staff of these admission offices also recruit, much of their work each year is devoted to reading applications, reviewing student files in committee, and making admission decisions based on context.

The Room Where It Happens

After you submit your application, the admission team checks that your file is complete by assembling your transcript, letters of recommendation, test scores (if submitted), and any other supporting documents. Some offices will send complete files immediately to an admission officer's queue to be read. Other schools read geographically, reviewing all applicants from a high school, city, county, or state at one time. Often the first person to read your application is the individual who recruits at your school and local area. Their job is to get to know your high school and community environment both inside and outside the classroom. They read your application and make a recommendation to admit, defer, deny, or wait-list. They then pass it along to a second reader, who also reads your file in its entirety. Often the second reader is more seasoned, and if that reader agrees with the initial recommendation, they have the authority to make a final decision. In some cases, though, an application will be passed on to a committee to review, discuss, and decide.

Each school reading holistically determines its own model for review based on application volume, staff size, and institutional priorities. At some universities, faculty are involved in reading undergraduate applications, while at others faculty appreciate never being included in the admission review process. Some colleges move a file immediately following its "first read" into committee. Others use what is called "committee based," "team based," or "partner based" review, in which multiple readers simultaneously review each application so that they can discuss it in real time and make their admission recommendation. The COVID pandemic provided schools an opportunity to evaluate, alter, and improve their review process in a number of ways. It also accelerated the prevalence of synchronous online review by pairs or larger groups of reviewers.

As you visit colleges and speak with admission representatives, you will usually find them to be very clear about their approach to making admission decisions. (If not, be sure to ask). In the next few chapters, we will help you understand *what* admission officers are looking for, *what* questions they are asking one another as they review applications, and *what* types of conversations they are having in committee review sessions.

 Try This

Find a university system in your state or a neighboring state that uses formulaic admission review. Plug in the information used in the formula (your grades, test scores, etc.). What was the result? Did you clear the hurdle? Do your numbers qualify you for consideration at some of the system's campuses but not at others? Are there things you wish were considered that are not part of the formula?

 Talk about This

1. Is there a reason why Early Decision or Early Action admission plans would be positive or negative in your circumstances?

2. How do you think your application will read in holistic and in formulaic review? Which type of review is used by the schools you are interested in?

3. Having read about the two types of admission review, what encourages you? What concerns you?

👍 **CHECK IN.** After reading this chapter, are you still on the same page as a family? If you are not all-in together, what do you need to do, discuss, or learn to get there?

☆ **Extra Credit**

The AXS Companion is a free online resource designed by admission professionals and consultants to be used side by side with the Common Application as you work your way through it. Each section of the application has corresponding explanatory videos, tips, a glossary of application terms, and links to resources mentioned in the videos. We encourage you to take advantage of this phenomenally helpful resource if you decide to apply to schools by using the Common Application.

CHAPTER 8

Classes, Grades, and Testing

Gonna cruise out of this city / Head down to the sea
Gonna shout out at the ocean / Hey it's me
And I feel like a number.
"FEEL LIKE A NUMBER" BY BOB SEGER

In chapter 7 we set the stage for the ways in which you can apply to college and the two approaches that schools take to review applications. In this chapter we explore what admission officers want to know about your academic opportunities, achievement, and potential.

RIGOR OF CURRICULUM

The first question that an admission officer asks when they open your application is "Where does this student go to school?" They want to understand what curriculum choices you have. Does your school offer Advanced Placement (AP) and/or International Baccalaureate (IB) classes? What are the levels of rigor in the curriculum at your school? Gifted, magnet, honors, advanced? An application reader wants to understand the classifications your school uses to categorize its courses. To see what courses you had access to, they refer to the *school profile* that your high school counselor provides along with your transcript. If you have not seen this document, we encourage you to take a look at it on your school's website. For admission officers, this is a gold mine of context and insight.

An admission officer's aim is to understand *what classes you could have taken versus what classes you chose to take* in high school. When you hear admission representatives speak about the rigor of curriculum, you'll catch them saying they want to see that "you challenged yourself" with your choice of classes. Often, however, they do not explain why this is important.

Admission readers want to see rigorous courses on your high school transcript because it demonstrates your willingness to push yourself. In a sense, they see your choices as a character trait. Your academic preparation in high school is also critical because college courses are challenging, and professors want to know you can keep up with the pace and depth at which they cover material.

To evaluate the extent to which you've challenged yourself, some schools will count the number of "rigorous" courses you took (AP, IB, dual enrollment) from the offerings listed on your school's profile. Other schools have their own rubric for categorizing classes that allows their admission readers to rate the strength of your curricular choices. As you can see in the example below, the scale is not used to rate the quality of an applicant's high school in a comparative fashion; rather, the scale is used to evaluate an applicant's choices within the school's curriculum.

5—Extremely challenging course selection in all classes

4—Strongly challenging course selection in all classes

3—Moderately challenging course selection in some or all classes

2—Less challenging course selection in some or all classes

1—Not academically challenging classes

Here are some other questions admission readers will ask as they review your school profile:

- What percentage of graduates from this high school go to college (four-year and two-year institutions)? This is one way colleges assess the strength of a high school.

- Are there any limits to the number of courses that students can take per year? At some schools, for instance, students are not permitted to take more than two or three AP classes a year.

- What is the highest level of each academic subject offered, and what courses are required for graduation? Answering these two questions gives a reader insight into what they can reasonably expect from your choice of classes, given your school's curriculum and what, if any, required courses impacted your choices.

- Are all classes "open enrollment," or do students need a recommendation to take any of them? At some schools, you cannot simply register for any class. Instead, a teacher may need to recommend you for certain courses, and a cap may limit how many students may enroll.

- Have students from this high school attended our college in the past, and how have they done? Increasingly, colleges are tracking student performance by individual high school and using this information in their evaluation.

- Did the student switch schools during high school, or did the grading scale or curricular offerings change? When students switch schools, admission readers ask why that change occurred and what impact (if any) it had on course choice and performance.

Note: Admission readers know that most high school students do not get to pick which high school they attend. If you go to a public school, your address influences where you go to high school. If you attend a private school, you may have had some say in that choice, although your parents' preferences, as well as factors such as proximity, cost, opportunities, and culture, were likely also determinants. Before reading your essay or looking at your test score, admission readers focus on understanding *your* school context, *your* school's curriculum, and *your* choice of classes.

GRADES

The proliferation of different grading scales in our nation's high schools has been both maddening and comical to college admission offices. There was a time when the 4.0 ceiling for GPA, numeric grading scale of 0–100, or alphabetic grading scale of A–F was the norm, but the permutations today are astounding. Admission readers may review the academic records of students who were graded on numeric scales that run to 80 or to 120. Some schools use the traditional 100-point scale but start at 50. Admission readers still see a 4.0 maximum for many GPAs (though some of these GPAs are weighted, with additional points given to rigorous courses), but ceilings of 5.0, 6.0, 13, or 15 points are becoming more common.

Not to be outdone, the alphabetic grading scale has its modifications as well. Some schools still use the conventional A–F grading system but assign + or – to grades to make finer distinctions. In some cases, schools no longer issue the grade of D, so the scale jumps from C straight to F. In the years ahead, we wouldn't be terribly surprised to see a G–K scale pop up, because, clearly, A–F is tired and antiquated. Alas, some institutions, particularly independent schools, now write narratives, instead of assigning grades, in assessing a student's achievement. Narrative "grading" is also popular in homeschooling situations, and a growing number of schools use mastery-based assessments that are not based on numbers or letters. Emojis and GIFs may be the next frontier of grading!

As you can imagine, for colleges using holistic admission, it is challenging to publish GPA ranges and averages and speak with precision about their expectations for applicants' grades. (Imagine a student in an information session who has an 11.3 GPA on a 15-point scale hearing that the average GPA of admits is a mere 3.7). Mike Sexton, former vice president for enrollment management at Santa Clara University, explains how admission readers make sense of all the variations they see: "We ask, 'What have the students done with what's available to them at their particular school?' We get applications from over 3,000 schools around the world and have seen every conceivable combination of curriculum, grading, and weighting. It's not the GPA that matters. It's what's behind the GPA that is important."

Regardless of your school's grading scale, here is what colleges look for to assess course performance:

- Grade distribution and number of students in the class: this provides admission readers with a percentage of the students in a class who received various grades, and it helps them understand how compressed or distributed students are relative to one another on the grading scale. This information is increasingly helpful due to the trend toward grade inflation.

> **Admission reviewers want to know whether an applicant has taken challenging classes and done well in them.**

- Number of students taking (or scoring above a certain threshold on) AP or IB exams: understanding performance on standardized tests in particular subject areas provides admission readers with a concept of academic achievement apart from grades. Does the school issue high grades even though its students do not score well on these exams? Or is the opposite true? Comparing grades to test scores can be extremely helpful.

- Highest GPA in the class: sometimes found on the school profile, this datum is something students may be asked to supply on college applications. Again, it provides perspective to admission readers by giving them a ceiling on student performance in an applicant's graduating class in high school.

Note: To enable better comparisons across their applicant pool, some colleges will recalculate applicants' GPAs according to their institutionally determined scale. You can usually find this information on their admission website. If not, feel free to ask whether a school does this when you visit campus.

Regardless of grading scales, recalculations, and weighted or unweighted GPAs, when it comes to assessing applicants' academic performance, admission readers ask the same question: "Has this student taken challenging classes and done well in them?"

Another consideration for admission readers is whether an applicant's grades changed over time in high school. This is known as a grade *trend*. Did a student earn higher grades in more difficult courses as they progressed through high school (showing an upward trend), or did they start out strong and then struggle academically? Admission readers also take note of anomalies in your academic record, such as a low grade in one class, a dip in grades for one semester, or something else that doesn't fit the pattern. You will have an opportunity to explain all of this in a section of the application called "Special Circumstances" or "Additional Information," which we discuss in the next chapter. Again, context is critical for admission readers, so you'll want to provide that when given the opportunity to do so.

Takeaway: Colleges practicing holistic review will not simply enter your GPA in a spreadsheet with those of all other applicants and sort the column from highest to lowest to make their admission decisions. Admission readers are making notes and focusing on your course choices and progression over time in the context of your high school. Their assessment of your academic career in high school is nuanced, not black-and-white.

What Does This Mean for You?

Each spring, when the line forms outside my (Brennan's) high school counseling office and I have a backlog of messages in my email inbox, I know it is course-selection time—quite possibly my least favorite week of the year. Students at all grade levels and their parents seek out their school counselor with the hope that we will bless their course selection and assure them it will lead to the college acceptance of their dreams. Instead, we share the "truth as we know it" from years of working in the admission profession; undoubtedly some leave our offices frustrated because we did not make their decisions for them or could not give them the answer they were wanting. Here are some of the questions we hear that you might be wondering about yourself:

> "Is it better for me to take the regular class and get an A or choose the advanced class and risk a B?"

> "I want to drop my foreign language class, but I also want to be admitted to a highly selective school. Will they care?"

> "Should my son take three or four AP courses to be competitive for admission?"

> "Can I double up in English and history and drop math and science senior year?"

"My daughter is a recruited athlete, so she doesn't need to take advanced classes, right?"

"The college's admission website says only two years of high school history or social studies are required, so can I stop after taking US History junior year?"

As with so much in college admission, the answer to these questions is "It depends." If you will be applying to engineering programs and your course selection lacks rigorous math and physics classes, that will raise a red flag in admission review. If you are considering a technical institute and you decide to double up in math or science at the expense of a fourth year of foreign language, that will not raise as much concern as it would were you applying instead to a liberal arts college. There are, however, some generalizations about what colleges are looking for that we (and some experts below) can share with you.

You have just learned that admission committees are paying close attention to context. They do not expect you to take every AP, honors, or advanced class that is offered at your high school. What they are looking for is intentional challenge in your course selection.

Expert Advice

We want to see students continue to take challenging courses— math, science, English, social science, and a language. Some students also manage to schedule that sixth or seventh subject—an extra language, science, or math. Avoid the tendency to coast through senior year by avoiding the subjects you are less enthused by. —Beverly Morse, former Associate Dean of Admissions, Kenyon College

It's not just the level or rigor of classes you take that matters but also the selections you make in given subject areas. Though there can be some exceptions, we are usually looking for four years of all the core subject areas. Things like taking Calculus after Precalculus or taking Spanish 4 after Spanish 3 (what we call the progression of a curriculum) really do matter. —Owen Bligh, Senior Associate Dean of Admission, Providence College

Selective colleges put a lot of weight (a *lot*) on applicants' curricular choices, so not taking a class each year from what I call "the big 5" can be a deal breaker: English, math, science, foreign language, and social sciences. —Jonathan Webster, Senior Associate Dean of Admission, Washington and Lee University

It's good to bend, but not break. In other words, it is wise to stretch yourself but not so much that one overdoes it and becomes overwhelmed. A father whose daughter was not admitted recently asked me about her challenging high school experience. "What was it all for?" asked this father, who saw his daughter's high school experience through the narrow lens of the college admission process, rather than through the broader lens of preparation for college and life. She is someone who is incredibly bright, accomplished, and promising. She will do great things in college and beyond. She is very well prepared for what lies ahead. Her father had lost sight of the value of her high school experience, outside of a desired college admission outcome. The point of course rigor is to prepare for a smooth transition to college and to prepare for more advanced coursework in college—not to use one's course selections as a means of being admitted to the most selective college possible. I think stretching is good preparation for a productive college experience. —Paul Sunde, Director of Admission, Dartmouth College

The theme running through this expert advice is clear: selective colleges expect your high school preparation to be broad, sustained, and appropriately rigorous.

Practical Tips for Completing Applications

You will be asked on applications to list senior-year courses. Be sure to do this accurately, especially if your high school does not include senior classes on the initial fall transcript it sends to colleges. An increasing number of colleges are asking applicants to complete the Self-Reported Academic Record (SRAR), for which you enter every class you took in high school and the grade you earned. Ask your school counselor for a copy of your transcript so that you can be as accurate as possible. Later, after you are admitted and choose to enroll at a college, the college will ask you for an official final transcript so that it can verify what you reported.

In the academic section, you also have an opportunity to report any honors you earned. If you make your school's honor roll or a similar distinction, you can state that. This is also a place to list National Honor Society, Phi Beta Kappa, or other academic affiliations or awards from high school. (Please don't list every honor you have received since elementary school, even though you are understandably still proud of your fourth-grade writing prize.)

STANDARDIZED TESTING—
THE NOISE IN THE NUMBERS

Many books, documentaries, and op-eds have criticized, defended, or otherwise unpacked standardized testing. Research (and research about the research), advice, and analysis on standardized testing are rampant, and large test-prep companies continually insert themselves into any conversation about these tests. Unfortunately, while there is a lot of information available in this space, there is a lot of misinformation too. The cost of taking these tests, combined with their length and the often ungodly hour at which they are administered, compounds the anxiety many feel over standardized tests.

Parents, you may already be a little queasy as you recall sharpened pencils, a roomful of bleary-eyed teenagers, and a test proctor who was either displeased about being there or, worse, was taking pleasure in watching you endure this rite of passage. We get it. Standardized testing may be a long-standing feature on the admission landscape, but it does frequently change. Since the first edition of this book came out in 2019, the SAT Subject Tests and writing section were eliminated. Tests are now primarily digital, so don't rush out and buy a sharpener for those number-two pencils. Then again, if you read 1840s French literature (Jean-Baptiste Alphonse Karr) or listen to 1980s rock (Jon Bon Jovi), you may know the saying *plus ça change, plus c'est la même chose,* or "the more things change, the more they stay the same." This is certainly true with standardized testing. Despite the many changes, tests continue to be a part of the admission equation that families must understand and consider strategically. Here is what you need to know.

ACT versus SAT

Originally, the ACT and SAT were far more distinct in format and style, and their regional footholds in the country (mostly SAT on the coasts and ACT in between) further distinguished the two tests. In 2012, due in large part to extensive lobbying for state contracts, more Americans took the ACT than the SAT for the first time in our nation's history. The gap widened in 2013, and in 2014, the College Board, maker of the SAT, revised its test to look remarkably similar to the ACT. We often hear students speculate that colleges prefer one test over the other or want to see scores from both exams. Colleges, by and large, are test agnostic and give no priority to one of them, nor do admission committees speculate about why you took one over the other.

For schools that do require or consider standardized testing, like all factors in a holistic review process, your scores will be viewed, well, holistically. Think about it this way: testing probably matters *a little more* than most admission directors or deans typically admit but *much less* than most students or parents imagine. Colleges do not simply take your GPA at face value without considering course choice, school context, and grade trend. The same is true of testing—they will ask some questions to help them understand your scores.

How Do Colleges Consider Test Scores?

What are this student's highest combined test scores? "Superscoring" is what colleges do when they combine your highest scores on the different subsections of the SAT or ACT across multiple test administrations.

	Reading Score	Math Score	English Score	Science Score	Composite
June ACT	30	28	29	30	29
September ACT	28	30	30	29	29
Superscored ACT	30	30	30	30	30

In the example in the table, the composite scores are the same, even though the subsection scores varied from the June to the September administrations. Superscoring allows an admission committee to take your best combined performance into consideration. Colleges superscore because, like in most parts of college admission, they are looking to give you the benefit of the doubt rather than penalize you for a lower score. They understand that sometimes the school bus breaks down on your way home from a band trip on the Friday night before the SAT administration. After waking up the next morning on the couch with barely enough energy to get dressed and eat a few crackers, you may score lower on the math section than you did previously. Superscoring is their way of saying, "We get that."

Is this student competitive in our applicant pool? When an admission reader opens your transcript, they have an expectation: that you will have done well and appropriately challenged yourself. The same is true when they review your test scores. Additionally, they are comparing your scores to those of other applicants. If a college's middle-50-percent test-score band for admitted students is 1370–1460, its admission readers will *not* take note if you are within that range. Testing would, in this instance, be deemed neutral (essentially a nonfactor). If your scores are well above a college's average, it is certainly to your advantage. Conversely, if you are in the bottom 25 percent, an admission reader will then expect more from the rest of your application.

In formulaic admission, and certainly when awarding merit-based scholarships purely by test scores, colleges use *cut scores* (prescribed thresholds, such as >28 on the ACT). In selective holistic review, though, that is generally not the practice. Admission committees will read every application. If, however, your GPA and test scores are both below their normal class profile, do not count on your school counselor writing what we call a "Lazarus recommendation."

How many times did this student test? The majority of colleges are only going to be interested in your highest combined totals. Students worry about whether this is true, but in many cases admission offices use an online system programmed to pull only the highest relevant scores from a database. With that said, there is a small minority of schools that will require you to send your entire testing history. They are asking questions concerning your timeline, trend, and access. Did you take the test four times across your junior and senior years, or was October of your senior year the only time you took the test? Just like questioning "how you got your GPA," they ask the same for testing. Testing, at these colleges, is taken as a body of work.

Is this student's test score in line with those of other applicants from their high school? Just as admission committees will consider the courses you chose from your high school's curricular offerings, they may also consider how your test scores compare with those of other applicants from your high school or region. Many colleges also maintain historical data so that they can compare current applicants to past applicants from your high school who enrolled.

Schools may ask for or allow you to submit your AP, TOEFL, or other test scores. Some schools require specific tests or permit you to send a combination of SAT, ACT, and specific subject-area exams. In these cases, an admission committee has determined that those test results have value in predicting your academic potential on their campus, so you can be sure they will evaluate your performance relative to other applicants and current students. For schools that recommend you submit scores on these content-based tests or say they will review submitted scores, they are looking to see whether your test results correlate with your grades and course choices. There is no firm expectation that you will send these test scores, but it is an opportunity for you to demonstrate your knowledge in a content area, as well as your interest in that college.

Takeaway: While the majority of colleges superscore and are truly interested in your highest combined subscores, you should explore a school's website so that you have a clear understanding of how testing is used in its review process. You will find that schools typically do an excellent job of explaining (sometimes in tedious detail) their practice. This could also be a good question to ask when you talk to an admission representative who comes to your high school or when you visit a campus.

Test-Optional: There is good news for those who are standardized-test-averse: not all colleges require them. Bowdoin College was the first school to make testing optional in 1969, and over the half century since then, the number of schools with a test-optional policy has steadily grown. In 2018 the University of Chicago, Colby College, and the University of New England (among others) went test-optional, joining around 1,000 other schools that had determined they did not need to see test results in order to enroll students.

After the University of Chicago made its announcement, Jim Nondorf, vice president for enrollment and student advancement, reported that three-fourths of the school's applicants were scoring above 1480 on the SAT (32 on the ACT). With so many students bunched into a tight range of scores, standardized tests no longer served to differentiate applicants.

Then came COVID-19. For much of 2020 and 2021, access to testing sites was severely restricted across the United States and practically nonexistent in other parts of the world. In response, the vast majority of colleges were forced to adopt a test-optional or flexible policy for a year or more. This gave boards of trustees, college presidents, and state leaders an opportunity to see how removing testing requirements affected an applicant pool and an enrolling class. In many cases, after reviewing the data on student performance and retention, as well as the policies adopted by their peers regionally and nationally, colleges decided to remain test-optional or abandoned a test requirement altogether. In fact, in 2023 more than 1,700 accredited four-year colleges and universities were test-optional and more than 80 were test-free. To find out what institutions are test-optional, check out the list kept by the National Center for Fair and Open Testing on its FairTest website at www.fairtest.org.

Does Optional Really Mean Optional?

Growing up, my (Brennan's) mom hung a sign in the kitchen that read, "You have two options for dinner: take it or leave it." The message was clear: we had a choice, but not really. The truth is that test-optional policies, unfortunately, are not that clear cut. There is nuance to the choice of whether to send scores, which can create anxiety for students and their families. If a college has a test-optional policy, it means the ball is truly in your court. You must decide what value your test scores have for you at each school. Our friend Akil Bello, senior director of advocacy and advancement at FairTest, has years of working in the test-prep industry. He tells students, "If your test score makes you look good, then you should send it. It's like sending your résumé, cello recital, or pastel drawing to colleges. The more positive info you give a college, the more likely you are to get admitted."

The reality is that some colleges have higher admit rates for students who submit test scores than for those who do not. There are many factors that might contribute to this, and none of them can you control. What you do control is how your scores enhance or detract from your application to the school. Bello says, "If you have evidence the test score will help you, then send the score. Helpful could mean you've identified scholarships based on scores that you can access (some colleges have merit aid for scores as low as 1000 on the SAT or 21 or the ACT). Helpful might also mean it offsets something in your admissions profile that isn't great. If your academic rigor or GPA is slightly below the average for a school you're interested in, an SAT above average might offset that."

What Does This Mean for You?

Your head is probably spinning by now: subscore, superscore, test-optional, test-free, middle-50-percent. Just unpacking the lingo of standardized testing and how it applies to you seems like its own exam. Here is the reality: the pandemic disrupted standardized testing for US universities, but it didn't make it any simpler for students to understand or navigate standardized testing. For some colleges and universities (especially many of the most selective), standardized tests are a necessary evil in college admission. Yes, there are an increased number of schools that no longer require submission of test scores with an application, but if you have your heart set on a college that still does, standardized testing is going to affect your candidacy. If your scores are well below a school's testing profile for admits, and if you lack a significant extracurricular "hook" or don't fulfill an institutional priority, your odds for admission are likely not good.

Rather than feel confined or limited by standardized tests, there are ways to take back control. For some, this could mean buying a test-prep book and taking multiple practice tests. For others, it might mean taking an online test-prep course or subscribing to a daily email listserv that delivers a test question of the day to your in-box. The options for test preparation are plentiful, from peer or professional tutors to group classes to Khan Academy. Some students see significant gains of more than 100 points per section, while others' scores remain the same. The point is that you may have to "play the game" if you are applying to an institution that values test scores.

When you confront standardized testing, you should also be ready to accept when you have done all you can to raise your scores and thus have to live with what you've got. When your scores do not increase across administrations despite the hours you've devoted to studying, it eventually becomes a self-imposed exercise in frustration. Determine the cost-to-benefit ratio of the time and resources you are spending on preparing yourself for this one exam, and return to your cornerstone of *why*. You might need to revisit your college list to make sure your scores meet the thresholds of the colleges you aspire to attend. Perhaps you will need to focus on applying to test-optional colleges. Also, be aware that some test-optional schools require or recommend an additional essay or other submission to accompany your application. Remember: your job is to put your best foot forward, so if you are not submitting test scores to a test-optional school, the admission office will weigh the other parts of your application more significantly as a result. Look at the whole picture of what you are presenting with your application and at what story it tells about your past performance and future potential.

> **For some colleges and universities, standardized tests are a necessary evil in admission.**

Practical Tips for Completing Your Application

The Common Application asks you if you wish to "self-report" your test scores. If you are applying without submitting test scores to any of the schools on your list, answer no to self-reporting scores. You can then send official test scores from the College Board or ACT directly to the colleges that require them. If all of your colleges require standardized test scores, it doesn't hurt to self-report your test scores on the Common Application. In fact, institutions are increasingly allowing students to report unofficial test scores with the understanding that if you are admitted and enroll, you will need to provide official scores. This saves you money and gives you more discretion over which scores colleges receive.

Be sure to understand what each college on your list requires for test score submission, and plan accordingly. It is your responsibility as an applicant to know the requirements of the colleges to which you are applying and to be timely in registering for testing dates to meet these requirements. If you have questions at any point, reach out to the schools you are considering. You are not alone. Admission staff is there to help, so be proactive and ask your questions.

Try This

Create a spreadsheet with the colleges and universities that you are considering. List the test score ranges, average GPA, and other academic criteria for admission at each school. Based on these numbers and your current profile, identify whether each school is a *reach*, *target*, or *likely* one for you. Discuss your classification of schools as a family and with your high school counselor to determine whether they agree with you.

💬 Talk about This

1. What have you learned that surprises you about the way admission committees review your grades and test scores?

2. How much time are you willing to commit to improving your test scores if needed? Consider what else you could be doing with that time if you choose not to do test prep.

3. What picture do your classes, grades, and test scores paint about you as a student?

 CHECK IN. After reading this chapter, are you still on the same page as a family? If you are not all-in together, what do you need to do, discuss, or learn to get there?

☆ Extra Credit

College Guidance Network is an organization committed to helping students, families, and the educators who support them "confidently navigate the college admissions process to make good, financially responsible decisions." Explore the Network's treasure trove of online recordings of experts discussing a variety of topics, including standardized testing and the academic component of admission file review.

Channel your inner admission officer and review your own transcript for rigor. Follow the QR code in the upper corner to try this exercise on your own or with a friend.

CHAPTER 9

Essays and Short Answers

I'm gonna write you a letter / I'm gonna write you a book
I wanna see your reaction / I wanna see how it looks
"AMSTERDAM" BY GUSTER

You can read entire books on writing essays for college applications. With titles along the lines of *Writing a Winning Essay* or *Confident, Clear, Concise: College Essays That Worked*, these books promise that, by following their advice, your words will jump off the page and convince any admission reader to make you part of their next class. Online you will find plenty of TikTokers and YouTubers claiming to have the right formula or magic tips for writing the perfect essay for Duke or Brown. They don't.

We understand why, though, there's a demand for such advice. In presentations and individual meetings, we often ask students which part of the application makes them the most nervous. Invariably, they cite the essay and short-answer section. Perhaps this is because it feels like the last piece of the application that you still control or because it can feel uncomfortable to write about yourself or because you do not have a sense of what colleges are looking for. Good news: we can tell you. Better news: we can cover the basics in one chapter rather than a whole book. And best of all: you can save your screen time on TikTok, YouTube, or elsewhere for cat videos, dance moves, or ironic parodies, rather than tips about writing.

APPLICATION ESSAY / PERSONAL STATEMENT

We want you to take a minute to think about your classmates in high school. Think about those who have classes and grades similar to yours—that is, a similar rigor of curriculum and around the same GPA. We are guessing you have a decent number of peers in mind at this point. Now, just think about those who likely also have standardized test scores comparable to yours. Great. Next, consider classmates who also have about the same amount of involvement and impact outside the classroom as you. Not all the same clubs, sports, jobs, and volunteer or paid employment, but people who, like you, have contributed to your community outside the classroom. With each filter you added, the number of people you were imagining probably shrank; inevitably, you still have a few classmates in mind. If you can imagine several people you know who "look" similar to you on paper, think about an applicant pool of 8,000 or 21,000 or 47,000. *That* is why schools require an essay or personal statement in their application. They want—and need—you to distinguish yourself. Writing is important because it helps admission committees *hear* you in a unique way that is not evident in other parts of your application. You could say that the *test* of the essay is your ability to concisely articulate your point.

Here are some of the questions that admission readers commonly ask themselves when they rate your essay or comment on your writing:

- Did I gain new insight into the student's life, motivations, values, character, or intentions?

- Do I see evidence of growth, maturity, or self-awareness?

- Is this piece compelling, unique, reflective?

- Would this voice add value to our campus culture?

How are admission readers arriving at their answers to these questions? Bear in mind that they *are* reading quickly. At schools receiving thousands or tens of thousands of applications, reviewing 30–50 applications a day is a common expectation for an admission reader. This means that your first line and first paragraph need to grab the reader's attention. Many will read the first line of each paragraph or the first and last paragraph of your essay to get a sense of your style and subject. In some cases that is enough for them to rate the quality of your writing and determine whether the topic you selected provides them new insight.

They *are* wanting to learn something new and deeper than what they already discovered about you as a student, a family member, and a community member from reading the rest of your application. Your essay fills in color and adds texture to that picture. They want to know what inspires and excites you. A wasted essay is one that simply reiterates what they already know. Readers do not want a résumé in paragraph form. Your writing, unlike other sections of your application, supplies the *why*, not the *what*. When reading it, committees make notes about your character, your motivations, and your mindset more so than your accomplishments.

What Does This Mean for You?

The glow from the laptop reflects off his forehead as he stares at the screen with a pained look of paralysis. The application essay prompt is copied into the open blank document. His mind races from topic to topic, each of which he dismisses immediately. The championship soccer game . . . too cliché. His meaningful relationship with his deceased grandfather . . . overdone. Reading the prompt for what seems like the hundredth time, he searches in vain for an event, challenge, accomplishment, obstacle, interest, or talent. And so he sits with the cursor flashing.

Do you worry that this will be you? Writing the application essay is about getting out of your head and opening your heart. It is an exercise in exploring self—about conveying what makes you who you are, not who everyone thinks you should be. Who are you outside the constraints placed on you by school, parents, friends, and society? How do you demonstrate character in your own unique ways? Simple, right?

Here are a few tips for writing an authentic, effective college essay.

Ignore the prompts. If an application provides multiple essay questions (as the Common Application does), don't read them first; read yourself. Many students stifle their unique voice by attempting to respond to a specific prompt that the application provides. What results is often a generic statement that lacks energy or personality. Write the story that you want to express, and then choose the prompt with which it best aligns. If the directions ask you to respond to only one question or prompt, then by all means do so—and do not exceed the maximum word count.

Don't repeat the question. Which of these sentences makes you eager to read more?

1. "There are a lot of events and realizations that have sparked personal growth for me."

2. "Before I started this job, the only time I had been to a bowling alley was to bowl."

You want to grab the reader's attention from the start. Do not write your way into the essay by simply restating the prompt or question like sentence 1 does. Instead, put the reader in the moment by painting a picture, and then elaborate on why it is important.

No Jedi mind tricks. The application essay is not a test to see if you can read the minds of admission officers and know what they want to hear. Plain and simple, they want to know about you, how well you write, and how self-aware you are. Write the essay for you, not them.

It's not us, it's you. Regardless of the topic you choose, be sure the resulting essay reveals more about you than about the other characters or places in the essay. When Erik DeAngelis, upper school dean at Harvard-Westlake School in Los Angeles, worked at Brown University, he advised, "Don't fall into the trap of telling us why you're a great fit for our school by telling us all about our school. We know our school. Tell us how you'd take advantage of the resources and experiences available. Don't spend precious word space impressing us with your knowledge of the school; rather present your argument for how you envision yourself participating in academic and social life."

Happily never after. The moral to the application essay is that there need not be a moral. You are writing a personal narrative, not a parable, so don't feel compelled to conclude with a lesson learned or a happy ending.

Always ask why. When you have finished a draft of your essay, read it over and ask yourself why you wrote it. If you cannot answer this question, you might not be going deep enough or painting a vivid enough picture of who you are and what is important to you.

Did your essay hit its mark? Have you effectively communicated who you are and what you value? The best way to tell is to have your parents or a friend give your essay to someone who doesn't know you and ask that person to read the essay and then respond with three adjectives that describe you and a sentence that captures what they learned. Does that person's impression reflect the message you hoped to convey? If not, go back to the drawing board.

Print it out. Let's be honest. We've all sent a text or an email with a missing word or two put words in the wrong order (see what we did there?). Sometimes you look at a computer screen for so long that your writing sounds good in your head, but it could be clearer. After writing your first draft, and again before you submit your application, print out and read your essays and responses to short-answer

> **For your application essay, you are writing a personal narrative, not a parable, so don't feel compelled to conclude it with a lesson learned.**

questions. By changing your perspective, you will see ways to improve the wording, catch mistakes, and feel more confident as a result. Trust us: print it out.

Drop test. Imagine taking your printed essay without your name on it and dropping it in the hallway or a classroom at school. Could a classmate pick it up, read it, know it was yours, and learn something new about how you think or see things? If not, then start over.

Read it out loud. Once you have a full first draft, print out your essay and grab your phone. Go to the voice notes app and hit record. Now read your essay aloud and then listen to the recording once or twice. We are guessing you won't make it past 18 words without pausing to revise. That's a good thing. Continue to record yourself reading revised drafts aloud and listen to the recordings until you're satisfied with what you have. This is your best simulation of how an admission reader will hear your voice in your writing. Does this sound a little awkward? Sorry. Sometimes feeling awkward is a step on the path toward improvement. So read it out loud.

Managing editor. Colleges are not looking for grammatical perfection or a certain number of multisyllabic words. Yes, you should run spell check. Yes, you should have someone else edit your writing and provide feedback to you. There is a fine line, however, between an editor and a coauthor. Parents, do not steal your student's voice by overediting or replacing *related* with *consanguine* or *a lot* with *plethora*. Compelling, memorable essays are what distinguish an applicant. Fancy word choices and an absence of comma splices won't achieve this; rather, it comes down to your distinctive voice. A colleague used to equate admission readers to bank tellers who handle money constantly. They know when it is fake. If you are funny, that's great. By the time an admission reader gets to application number 36 of the day, they appreciate some humor. If you are not funny, though, don't try to be in your essay. There is truly nothing worse than the unfunny funny essay.

Waste not, want not. Are you being redundant? If your essay simply reiterates information that appears elsewhere in your application, then you are squandering an opportunity to elaborate on your story. Don't make your essay a résumé of your activities or the awards you have won. Ask yourself if you are telling readers something new. If the answer is no, start over.

Am I done yet? Every student asks this question, so you are not alone. We know that writing an essay can bring on angst because it is one of the last things you control when applying. Your classes and grades are not going to change. You either did or did not join that club or play that sport in your junior year. But the essay . . . *that* you still hold, can continue to massage, and will perhaps be what tips the scales in your favor. Trust us: if you have followed our advice to this point, your essay is in great shape. So, yes, you are done. Let it go.

Todd Rinehart, vice chancellor for enrollment at the University of Denver, puts the application essay into perspective:

> Students should know that while essays are important, they are rarely the reason a student gets admitted or denied. Students shouldn't feel the pressure of having to write a Pulitzer-winning essay to gain admission to their college of choice. With that said, they also need to know that an award-winning piece won't supersede poor academic performance. Most admission committees are looking for capable and competitive students academically— once academic ability is vetted, an essay plays an important role in helping committees build their class with interesting classmates and roommates. Committees aren't looking for the perfect essay, topic, or set of activities and achievements—we simply want an interesting, authentic, and well-written glimpse into a student's life.

ADDITIONAL INFORMATION

On applications you will find an open-response section that allows you to add more information. This section may be called "Additional Information" or "Extra Information" or "Special Circumstances." What are schools looking for in this section, and how do they incorporate what you put there into their review of your application?

Significant life events. You had mono as a junior and missed the first two months of school. Or your parents' divorce was finalized in the summer before senior year, and the end of eleventh grade was filled with turmoil. Or you moved three times during high school due to a parent's job transfer, promotion, or loss. These are examples of things we see mentioned in this section. Admission readers appreciate the perspective you can provide, and they will make notes or highlight pertinent pieces of your application that they believe are relevant to their admission decision, especially as it relates to overcoming adversity, persevering, and demonstrating grit.

Academic context. Readers want to know if your choice of courses was limited somehow in high school. Was there a schedule conflict that prevented you from taking a class? Was a course that you'd hoped to take canceled because too few students were planning to take it that year? Did your school change its grading scale or not offer a certain class in your junior year? If you moved multiple times during high school, readers will see that on your transcript, but in this section you have an opportunity to tell them about the academic impact it had. Maybe your move made you unable to take a desired course or to pursue a particular curricular track. This is where you can explain that.

Additional activities. If you are unable to convey the extent to which you contributed through your activities because the activity section of the application is too limited, you can expound on your involvement here. You might detail a business you started, a fundraiser you organized, or additional levels of achievement in one of your activities. That said, you should put your strongest, most compelling information in the activity section itself, and do not feel obligated to use this additional section unless it is necessary to convey the degree of your work or time spent.

In general, the Additional Information section is your chance to explain pertinent *whys* or *what elses* that affected you during high school.

This is not the space for another essay. This is not a place to make excuses or try to draw sympathy. Readers evaluate this section by looking for pieces of information that provide valuable context (inside or outside the classroom), which you could not include elsewhere in the application. If you believe you have something noteworthy to add, use this section. However, for most students it will not be necessary.

Community disruption. The Common Application also provides a space (of 250 words) for students to share information about any "*Community disruptions such as COVID-19 and natural disasters.*" Colleges realize that events such as these can have a significant impact on students. Not only can classes and learning be disrupted, but family health, finances, and safety can be as well. This section was added in 2020 during the pandemic. In that year only a third of applicants used it. The following year that number was cut in half, and it will likely continue to decrease. If you need an opportunity to inform an admission committee of such extenuating circumstances, this space is designed for you. If not, count yourself fortunate and move on to the next section.

What Does This Mean for You?

The Additional Information section is not your opportunity to wax poetic. Use this space (if necessary), but be succinct. If an admission reader is wondering why you filled it in, you didn't need to. The old saying from the paper-file days of college admission applies here: "the thicker the file, the thicker the student." If you find yourself justifying choices or making excuses, then reconsider.

You could use this section to insert a URL link to some creative work you have posted online, without which it would be hard for an application reviewer to truly know you. Two words of warning, though: Be discerning. Don't tell them what they are not asking for.

SHORT ANSWERS / SUPPLEMENTAL ESSAYS

In addition to the main essay or personal statement, you will find that many colleges ask you to respond to short-answer questions or write supplemental essays in the school-specific portion of their application. You might have a choice of several prompts, but some colleges will dictate exactly what they want you to answer. Here are a few past examples:

> "Describe the world you come from (for example, your family, school, community, city, or town). How has that world shaped your dreams and aspirations?" —Massachusetts Institute of Technology

> "What is the hardest part of being a teenager now? What's the best part? What advice would you give a younger sibling or friend (assuming they would listen to you)?" —Rutgers University

> "Write a brief thank-you note to someone you have not yet thanked and would like to acknowledge." —University of Pennsylvania

> "Tell a story from your life, describing an experience that either demonstrates your character or helped to shape it." —University of Washington

Have fun with these and approach them as another opportunity to shine a light on your personality, circumstances, or experiences. Often colleges ask a version of "Why us?" as a short-answer question. Keep in mind that admission readers do not want to read what you could (or did) write for another school. They want specifics. They want you to have done your homework about their school. Why do you want to study at Colgate or Colorado or Colby (or some other C-o-l school)? Do not write the same answer for each. You should be spending time digging through those brochures or websites or notes you took in an information session to give details on *why*. Your answer should be related to specific professors, opportunities, or campus culture. Do your homework because admission readers will expect it of you when they are reviewing and discussing your responses. A supplement essay answering "Why us?" is a love letter. Be specific. Saying "you're pretty" is not going to cut it.

What Does This Mean for You?

It means you have more work to do, especially if you are applying to multiple schools with short-answer questions on their application. Nobody said this would be easy, but it can be a way to highlight how you are a good match. Too often students belabor the main essay, writing draft after draft and getting extensive feedback, but then crank out something quickly in response to short-answer questions. Colleges include these because they help differentiate applicants, so answer them thoroughly, specifically, and thoughtfully.

 Try This

Get out your computer or a pen and paper. Set a timer for 20 minutes. Choose one of the prompts below (or better yet, work your way through each one on different days) and just start writing. Do not try to write a college essay and do not overthink what you are writing. Try not to stop writing before the 20 minutes have elapsed, even if you begin a new idea or change direction in what you are putting down.

Prompt 1. "Dinner at our house . . ."
Prompt 2. "The things I carry . . ."
Prompt 3. "Sunday mornings . . ."
Prompt 4. "The hardest thing . . ."

 Talk about This

1. What is a story that only you can tell?

2. How might your short-answer responses differ for the various colleges you plan to apply to?

3. Who is going to read your essay drafts, and what kind of feedback do you want?

👍 **CHECK IN.** After reading this chapter, are you still on the same page as a family? If you are not all-in together, what do you need to do, discuss, or learn to get there?

☆ Extra Credit

The emergence of artificial intelligence (AI) tools such as ChatGPT and others is dramatically influencing the way we brainstorm topics, edit writing, and formulate ideas.

Should you use one of these platforms to assist you with your essays or short-answer responses? If you do use AI, how can you ensure your voice and style are authentic, personalized, and memorable? And what important factors should you consider in employing these platforms to enhance your writing for college applications?

Follow the QR code in the upper corner for answers, insight, additional resources, and tools to help guide you through the rapidly shifting space of AI.

CHAPTER 10

Activities, Interviews, and Recommendations

It's a little bit of everything / It's the matador and the bull
It's the suggested daily dosage / It's the red moon when it's full
All these psychics and these doctors
They're all right and they're all wrong
It's like trying to make out every word
When they should simply hum along
It's not some message written in the dark
Or some truth that no one's seen
It's a little bit of everything.
"A LITTLE BIT OF EVERYTHING" BY DAWES

To enroll students who will help fulfill its mission, a college may rely heavily on nonacademic or qualitative factors to make admission decisions. Chapter 8 made the point that even grades and test scores are not always black-and-white, and this chapter focuses completely on the gray, which can be disconcerting to families at times.

The good news is that investigative researchers recently discovered the perfect formula for being admitted to all colleges, even if you are not competitive academically. Get out your pen or phone because we are only going to go through this once. To get into any college in the country, you need to follow these steps exactly. *Note: You must complete each task in the listed order, and failing to include one negates the guarantee.*

1. Take AP Physics.

2. Volunteer as a translator at your local hospital.

3. Use either *bucolic* or *grandiose* in the opening line of your application essay (ideally both).

4. Score at least 70 points higher than your current score on the SAT.

Wait. Stop writing. As you already know, there is no script or blueprint here, so we cannot provide you with that. And despite their confidence, dance moves, and graphics, nor can the admission "sages" on TikTok, YouTube, or Reddit give you one. What we can do is give you an idea of what colleges value and how to use that knowledge when you apply.

EXTRACURRICULAR INVOLVEMENT

Admission committees spend a great deal of time trying to understand not only what you have been involved in outside class but also the contributions you've made to your community during high school. They want to know what your commitments have been beyond coursework. The reason they care is that they're building a campus community to advance the mission of the institution and enrich the experience of students on campus. In order to do that, these are the key questions admission readers ask about an applicant's activities.

What Is This Student *Involved* with outside the Classroom?

In our culture, time is a precious commodity. As a high school student taking a full load of classes that come with homework, papers, and exams, this is particularly true. When colleges are reviewing your extracurricular activities, they look at them as reflective of both your interests and your values. They are far more concerned with understanding *how* you have used your time when not in class or studying than in judging your choices. In other words, they are not splitting hairs between your becoming an Eagle Scout or working 30 hours a week at a grocery store.

What Is This Student *Invested* in during High School?

Students often feel they need to have "done it all" so that they'll come across as "well rounded" to colleges. This is a big misconception. Do not forget: admission committees are made up of human beings. Humans who have families, go on vacations, and have an Instagram account and walk dogs. In fact, one silver lining of the pandemic is that it humanized admission officers. It reminded families that these admission representatives are not judges or robots. They don't hibernate all summer only to emerge and read applications each winter. All of a sudden in 2020, instead of giving information sessions on campus, they found themselves presenting on Zoom with their kids, cats, and plants behind them. And these kid-raising, cat-petting, plant-watering folks know that no matter what you do outside the hours spent in school, there are increasing demands on your time. Coaches, bosses, and club advisors all want more hours from you in the week and more of your weeks through the year.

> Pursue what you love to do in and out of high school, and make that clear on your application.

If you are a musician in your high school band, you likely have multiple-hour practices, competitions on weekends, camps in the summer, a mandatory class during school, and optional (but not really optional) practices for your own instrument section. The same is true if you play soccer, tennis, or another sport: club teams, school teams, traveling teams, indoor, outdoor, tournaments, summer camps, winter camps, and the list goes on. Trust us—admission officers *do* get it. They *do not* expect you to have played three sports, worked two jobs, walked old ladies across the street every day before school, and cured a disease on the side. While they do admit well-rounded students, "pointy" students who are committed to one or two activities with a deep level of achievement and experience are also great candidates for admission. Pursue what you love to do in and out of high school, and make that clear on your application. If you dislike tennis and see no benefit in participating, stop. One more season is not going to make or break your application. Admission readers also realize that logistical, family, health, or financial circumstances may have limited your ability to be as invested in activities as you might have wanted.

What *Impact* Has This Student Made?

Two students could list identical activities on their application and be read totally differently. One simply showed up—a "joiner." He signed the roster, went to some meetings, and smiled in the group shot for the yearbook. He was on the Homecoming Committee one year, ate a baguette in French Club, and played on the tennis team one spring. He was involved but did not make an impact. Meanwhile, another student started working on the Homecoming Committee as a freshman and was in charge of publicity as a junior and senior. He had no official title but can describe the successes of his work. He helped the French Club connect online with a class in Metz, France, and began an exchange program between the two schools. He played tennis year-round and also taught younger players in the community. His impact is clear, and this is a big part of what committees pay attention to in their review.

Notice in these examples that what stands out to admission committees is not necessarily the positions a student held. Colleges have broadened their definition of leadership beyond focusing just on titles to looking into a student's contributions. You can demonstrate impact through taking on added responsibilities at a job, helping to raise three younger siblings at home, or serving as a translator for your parents. Impact is not photobombing pictures for the yearbook or sporadic and minimal involvement. Instead, impact is exhibited by longevity and depth. Admission committees are essentially asking, "Will this student be missed when they are no longer part of that community?" Your goal is to use your activities to answer that question.

How Has This Student *Influenced* Others?

Admission readers consider how you have used your time outside the classroom because they know that being committed in high school will translate into being influential in your college career and beyond. They are looking to admit a class of students who will complement one another in their skills, interests, and talents. Their hope is that in residence halls and classrooms and on practice fields and in laboratories, and even over pizza at 2:00 a.m., the students they admit will stretch, push, challenge, and enhance the experience of others on campus.

Colleges generally use a rubric to rate your longevity and commitment in activities, as well as your impact and influence. Here is an example:

Extraordinary (1): Major impact within school, community, or subject matter; influencer, intentional movement, with depth either as a leader or independently. Sustained activity and influence over four years in three or more major activities.

Strong (2): Strong involvement with some influence. Extreme depth in one or two areas or moderate depth in multiple areas. Sustained activity over three to four years.

Solid (3): Involved but lacking influence. Busy but hasn't demonstrated growth in involvement. Involvement that isn't necessarily sustained but rather pieced together over multiple years.

Average (4): Sustained activity over two to three years. Has some gaps in involvement.

Lacking (5): Minimal involvement. No sustained activity or evidence of influence.

What Does This Mean for You?

Involvement, impact, investment, and influence—no problem, right? Now you know what colleges are looking for, but you are staring at your computer screen, and the application is asking you to distill your high school years down to ten activity slots. You are likely either thinking, "How can I possibly fit all my extracurricular involvement into this restrictive form?" or panicking because you can fill only four slots and are sure that every other "competitive" applicant has ten activities to brag about. Instead of fearing that you will not measure up or will not impress the person reading your application, consider what story you want to tell about what you have chosen to do and—you know this is coming—*why*.

The college application is your megaphone, so make sure your message is clear in your broadcast. Before you start filling in dropdown menus on the application, step back and make a list of what you do when you are not in class, how much you do it, and then write down for yourself the reasons for your involvement. Start with the activities that are most important to you (even if they are not the most consuming ones), and work down to your less critical involvement. It might look like this:

Model UN: 3 hours/week since ninth grade, because I love the interaction with students from all over and am into global issues and debate.

Swim team: 10 hours/week in eleventh and twelfth grades, because I enjoy being part of a team and my friends convinced me to join.

Grocery cashier: 20 hours/week tenth to twelfth grades, because I have to save up for college and also earn my spending money.

You get the point. Writing these out ahead of time will help you articulate the choices that you have made. This will not only help you complete the application but will also be useful if you interview at a college. If you have more activities to list than the application has room for, look at the entries at the bottom of your list and determine if they say anything significant about your involvement, impact, investment, and influence. If not, omit them. If they do seem important to the story you want to tell, make the application work for you. Some schools allow you to upload a résumé. If you choose to do this, aim to keep it to one page.

> **Consider what story you want to tell about the activities you have chosen to do while in high school.**

Practical Tips for Completing Your Application

Don't add fluff. If you are struggling to find things to add, it means you probably shouldn't add them. Listing "waste management officer" because you take out the trash at home once a week is stretching it!

Don't assume. Many high school clubs have fun acronyms. That is great for a club's members, but the admission office won't know your abbreviations.

Leadership. Yes, the application will ask for your position/title, but that doesn't mean it has to be filled in or that an untitled role you may have had is any less important. When possible, use numbers or other facts to emphasize your involvement (for example, "one of four members who . . .").

Time commitment. Give your best estimate of the number of hours per week you participated and the duration of your participation. Admission readers are not going to conduct an audit and find that you're off by a week. Again, readers want a sense of your investment and how you spend your time.

Remember: quality over quantity. You do not have to fill in all the boxes.

INTERVIEWS

One way to showcase your involvement, impact, investment, and influence—as well as your academic journey and community context—is through an interview. Not all colleges conduct interviews as part of their admission process, and those that do vary in how they conduct them. Some schools offer in-person interviews on campus with an admission officer. Others have interviews at a local coffee shop or at your high school. Increasingly, virtual interviews, for reasons of efficiency, access, and convenience, are gaining popularity. Interviews conducted by alumni, current students, or faculty are also common. Regardless of interview format, colleges that have interviews in admission are committing valuable time to meet you, listen to you, and learn more about you. Here is what they will be looking for, noting, and discussing later in committee.

They expect you to be prepared. Interviewers want to know that you have researched their school and can articulate why you want to be part of their community. They want you to provide specifics about how your background and interests align with their campus culture. Hint: this is not where you discuss how big a fan you are of their sports teams or the fact that lots of your friends or family members have gone there. Interviewers appreciate when students have researched particular academic programs or enrichment opportunities outside the classroom and can authentically discuss why these are interesting, exciting, and a logical match. They want you to convince them that this college is one of your top choices and not simply another school on your list.

Interviewers do not want a laundry list of your activities and accomplishments. They want to discuss your motivations and goals. *Why* did you decide to start tutoring seventh graders in math after school? *Why* did you choose to operate stage lighting for the drama club? Interviewers do not want you to get into the weeds about the amount of time you practiced. Instead, they want to hear about lessons learned. *What's next*, now that you have discovered or experienced X?

> **Interviewers want to know that you have researched their school and can articulate why you want to be part of their campus community.**

This is your chance to provide context for your life in high school, to explain what you are curious about, and to give the interviewer a sense of your intentions and hopes for the future. Remember, they want to understand who you are and what you will bring to their campus.

They do not want to ask all of the questions. Whether you are sitting down with a current student or someone who graduated 20 years ago, remember that this is someone who is not just affiliated with the school but also deeply committed to it. They are hoping to see how you will contribute on campus as a student as well as how you will later represent the school as a graduate. Your responses matter, but so too does your demeanor, tone, facial expressions, and body language. They do not expect every response you give to be a TED Talk. In fact, they want a give-and-take. They want to see your personality shine through. They appreciate seeing how you respond, build on prior answers, demonstrate curiosity, and generally interact in a conversation. Interviewers make notes and later make comments in committee about students' confidence, eye contact, and engagement in the dialogue.

They want you to do well. Perhaps the biggest misconception students have—and one of the reasons they are often uneasy about interviewing—is they think their interviewer is a judge who is looking to find fault and to document any shortcomings. This could not be further from the truth. Interviewers do understand that at age 17 or 18, this interview is the first or one of a few you've had in life. They are genuinely looking for sincerity and excitement about what you discuss. They enjoy when you "light up" or "nerd out" about your interests or opportunities on their campus.

We cannot tell you whether you'll be admitted to your first-choice school. We cannot tell you what to write about in your essay or if you should take a certain science class in your junior year. What we can tell you about an admission interview is that, at some point, the interviewer is going to pause, look at you, and say, "What questions do you have for me?" Be ready for this. That question is coming. What are they looking for in asking it? They want to see that you've done your homework—they almost appreciate being stumped by what you ask. This is not the time to ask, "What is your mascot?" or "How many students are on campus?" When you reference a professor by name or a campus group and talk about wanting to take part in research or to check out the group, they make note. You can also mention an article you read in the student newspaper or alumni magazine and ask how the campus reacted to its news or point of view.

InitialView is a company that interviews thousands of students a year for some of the most well-known colleges and universities around the world. Terry Crawford, its CEO and founder, gives this advice: "The interview is all about being able to strike the right balance: be yourself, but really that means be the mature version of yourself. Talk about and promote yourself, but don't come across as arrogant. Be humble and sound smart but don't be a know-it-all. If all that sounds both ambiguous and challenging, well, it is." He adds,

> My advice is to do what almost no one does: practice. And by practice, I mean really practice your interview skills, which should involve doing a mock interview with a stranger (perhaps a colleague of a parent or a teacher who's willing to play the role). Record the interview with your smartphone and review it along with a teacher or counselor or other adult who can give you good advice. Yes, it's awkward to see yourself on camera, but the good news is that with relatively little effort you can do something that might significantly improve your chances. The ability to connect with a stranger and get them to like you is a critical life skill—perhaps the one most critical to your future success.

What Does This Mean for You?

If a college you're applying to offers applicants an interview, we strongly encourage you to take advantage of this opportunity. In fact, if the school's admission materials say, "interview recommended," you should treat it as though it's required, especially if you live within the distance of an easy drive, the school offers virtual interviewing options, or it conducts regional interviews in your area. Chances are the colleges that make interviewing applicants part of admission (at a significant cost of staff time and resources) value "demonstrated interest" by applicants. If nothing else, interviewing is a useful life skill to practice, one you will use in college and afterward, so start practicing now. If you are nervous, try a mock interview with your school counselor, a friend of your parents, or just record yourself on your phone answering questions to get a sense of how you come across. Does that sound a bit awkward? Sure. But it is absolutely worthwhile and a great way to get comfortable before your real interview. Here are some more tips and some sample questions:

Tips for Your Interview

- Things to take with you: A copy of your high school transcript to share with the interviewer (and don't hesitate to talk about your course selection with them); an athletic or extracurricular résumé if you have one; a portfolio of creative work if applicable; and a notebook with some questions to ask during the interview and to record your impressions after the interview.

- Before you go: Talk with your parents or whoever will accompany you to agree on what their role will be. You, not a parent, should check in upon arrival, if the interview setting is the admission office. When the admission officer comes out to greet you, be sure to introduce your family member.

- How to dress: Dress appropriately for the institution. Be yourself, but put your best foot forward. Avoid wearing T-shirts with slogans or the names of other colleges. Don't wear clothes that are dirty or have holes. Leave your hat in the car. (We've seen all of these ill-advised choices and more.)

- How to carry yourself: Don't flirt, slouch, put your feet on the furniture, or chew gum. Do make eye contact and give a firm handshake before and after the interview.

- How to communicate: Be yourself, but be the sophisticated side of you. Avoid slang, inappropriate words, and nondescript words, such as *like, things, whatever,* and *stuff.* Conversely, do not try to impress the interviewer with SAT words that will seem forced.

- Modesty vs. bragging: Don't be afraid to tell your interviewer about your accomplishment, but be wary of showing off. Don't try too hard; just be yourself and tell them what you are passionate about. Before you go, come up with three or four characteristics, interests, or values you want to impart to the interviewer.

- Research the college beforehand: Be sure to do your homework by researching the college where you're interviewing. You want the interviewer to know that you are interested enough in the college to have taken the time to learn about its academic programs, student body, and other points of importance to you.

- Come with your own questions: Always have several questions in mind to ask the interviewer. They will leave time in the interview for you to ask about the college. Don't ask questions you can easily find the answer to on the school website, such as "Do you have an English major?"

- If stumped by a question: It is perfectly acceptable to ask to circle back to a question later in the interview if an answer doesn't come to you right away.

- Have fun: Approach the interview as an opportunity to have an open conversation about who you are and what is important to you. The more relaxed you are, the more you can convey about yourself as an individual.

- Follow-up correspondence: Always ask for a business card, and send a thank-you note or email to the person who interviewed you. This is another indication of your interest in the college.

- Etiquette in a virtual interview: What is different about interviewing online versus in person? Not much. Your preparation should be the same, and your approach to the conversation should be the same. Be aware of your background. Keep it simple and professional so that the interviewer will focus on you, your answers, and your mutual connection (rather than on an animated background of waves crashing on the beach). If you do not use a virtual background, be sure that whatever is behind you is not distracting. We have both talked to students sitting on their bed while pets or family members crossed in and out of view. Treat virtual interviews just like you would a meeting in person—from your dress and posture to your research and questions. The format is different, and that is all.

Sample Questions You May Be Asked

- What is the most significant contribution you have made to your school?

- If I visited your school, what would I find is your role in the school community?

- What would your teachers say are your greatest strengths as a person and as a student?

- What is one thing you would change about your high school?

- What do you like about your high school?

- What are thinking of studying in college?

- What courses have you taken? Why?

- What has been your favorite subject in high school? Why?

- What books did you read last summer? Do you have a favorite and why?

- What three adjectives would your friends use to describe you?

- What are some of your personal and career goals for the future?

- What kind of development do you hope to see in yourself in the next four years?

- What do you enjoy doing in your free time?

- How have you spent your summers?

- How would you describe yourself as a person?

- What events would you say have been crucial to your life thus far? What people?

- Do you have any heroes?

- Are you satisfied with your accomplishments and growth thus far?

- Why are you interested in our school?

- What would you like to contribute to what goes on at this college?

- Have you ever thought of not going to college right away? What would you do instead?

- If you could talk to any one person past or present, who would it be? Why?

- Where and when do you find yourself stimulated intellectually?

- What is one extracurricular activity you are involved in and why?

Sample Questions You Can Ask

- What are the most important campus issues to students at this college?

- What are the greatest strengths of the college?

- What would you change about the college?

- How does the admission office judge whether an applicant is a good fit?

- What is the college's retention rate? Why do students decide to transfer somewhere else?

- How safe is the college's campus?

- What do students do on weekends? Where does most of the social life take place?

- According to students, what is the most difficult course offered on campus?

- How is this college trying to improve itself?

- How close are the students and faculty here?

- How has this college changed in the last five years?

Practice: Get out your phone and voice-record your response to a few of the sample questions you may be asked. Then play back the recording. Few people like the sound of their own voice, but pay attention to your volume, tone, pace, and word choice. *When do you come across as positive and compelling? What stands out as unclear or unconfident?* Pick one or two of the same questions, and record yourself again as you answer them. *Do you hear an improvement in how you come across? What lessons from what you heard can you apply to any question you may be asked in an interview?*

LETTERS OF RECOMMENDATION

Note: The current student-to-counselor ratio in US high schools is nearly 500:1. (This is double the ratio recommended by the National Association for College Admission Counseling.) Admission readers understand that at large high schools a student's time spent one-on-one with counselors or teachers may be limited. If you attend a high school like that, be assured that admission committees will not hold a generic or brief letter of recommendation against you in their review.

On your application, your personal details (hometown, family information, etc.) provide a *sketch* of your background. Classes taken, grades, and test scores *outline* your academic ability. Extracurricular involvement and your essay *provide color by filling in details* about what you enjoy or how you think or what you want to do in the future. Letters of recommendation from counselors and teachers at your school are the *frame* for the picture you have painted; these letters support you by complementing and enhancing your application. You will not be the one writing your letters of recommendation, of course, but it is helpful to understand this component of an application, and you should have a sense of what admission readers are seeking to learn when they read letters of recommendation.

Whose Letters Do Colleges Want to Read?

Colleges *do* want to hear from teachers or counselors or other community members who are excited about what you have to offer. Effective letters of recommendation reinforce character traits and patterns of behavior you have represented elsewhere in your application. Admission readers want to understand the role you play in class, the way you approach problems, your level of self-awareness, and the impact you have made on classmates, teammates, other club members, or fellow employees. Admission readers ask themselves if the recommender's characterization of you aligns with their campus ethos. In chapter 1, you thought through *why* you were going to college. Help your recommenders out by sharing with them your answer to that question and telling them what led you to apply to your chosen schools.

Colleges *do* value an enthusiastic advocate who puts you in the context of your high school, your class, and the other students they have taught during their career. Ideally, admission readers want recommenders who have seen you grow, change, improve, and learn, even if you had struggles and doubts along the way. This means that you need not choose the teacher who gave you the highest grade or the coach who saw you shoot the winning basket of the championship game. Often, in fact, recommendation letters are less persuasive when they make you seem perfect. Admission readers do not expect perfection. Instead, they appreciate a balanced view and narratives of dynamism: strengths, weaknesses, growth, and maturation. They want what's real. They want authenticity. They want to hear from someone who knows when you had to stretch yourself to achieve or overcome something. They like hearing about the challenges you faced that point to your potential for handling what college will throw at you.

Colleges *do* appreciate someone who can add something new.

> Effective letters of recommendation echo character traits and patterns of behavior you have described and documented elsewhere in your application.

"Johnny has a 4.0 GPA and a 34 on the ACT. He is involved in X, Y, and Z activities. He would make a great addition to your campus." While these statements may be true, admission readers have come across this information elsewhere in the application, or someone could make the statement who barely knows you. Compelling letters bring a new angle on an applicant. Sometimes they are surprising and make readers wonder, "Really? I never would have expected that." Helpful recommenders are simply trustworthy, insightful adults in your current community speaking to curious adults in your desired future community.

Whose Letters Do Colleges Not Want to Read?

Colleges *do not* need to hear from someone who taught or coached you in middle school. Recommendation letters are required because they can provide additional insight. Often admission officers receive letters from teachers, coaches, club sponsors, or band directors who are unable to provide recent, relevant, and compelling insight. Do not waste an opportunity by having someone "frame" the self-portrait you painted in your application with outdated or scant knowledge of your character and potential.

Colleges *do not* care about big titles. Every year admission offices receive letters from senators, actors, and athletes. Often these come with pictures, which can be fun. These will get posted on the back of doors or passed around the office. Normally, though, these letters are recycled from year to year and add little of value. If an application asks for a recommendation from someone other than a counselor or teacher, the admission office would rather hear from a neighbor who watched you grow up, whose kids you babysat, and who is proud of you than from someone with a recognizable name or impressive job title.

What Does This Mean for You?

Consider the voices that have emerged in your application. You have listed your family background, your classes, honors, and activities and written an essay that tells a story about who you are. Your school counselor has written a letter of recommendation on behalf of the school that elaborates on your role in, and contributions to, the community. Perhaps you have interviewed with a representative of the institution and provided context for your high school experience in the Additional Information section of the application. When you are choosing teachers to write recommendations in support of your application, determine what has not already been communicated about you in your application and let what's missing guide your choice. Has your perseverance not come to light as you might have hoped? If so, ask a teacher who saw you struggle with a subject and buckle down to overcome the challenge. Students fall into the trap of turning only to the teachers who gave them the best grades. Most students will ask two teachers for recommendations (some colleges require two but others limit submission to one), so balance the voices speaking on your behalf. You might be an aspiring humanities major, but sending recommendations from two English teachers may be redundant. Consider asking a math or science teacher who can talk about the right side of your brain.

Teacher recommendations are just that—from teachers who have worked with you in the classroom (ideally in junior or senior year). Admission officers do not want that teacher to go into your extracurricular involvement. They want to know who you are as a learner, classmate, lab partner, and so on. Choose a teacher who will speak to your creativity, curiosity, and ability to think analytically, synthesize material, and write fluidly.

"What if they don't write me a good recommendation?" This is a question we often hear, and the answer is simple: if you have reason to think a person wouldn't write favorably about you, ask someone else. In fact, it is perfectly acceptable to say to a teacher, "I would really appreciate it if you would write a letter of recommendation on my behalf, and I am curious to know if you think you know me well enough to write a positive one." If they cannot answer yes, they will decline.

You should give your counselor, teacher, or other recommender several weeks' notice before the deadline. Go to them well in advance to ask if they are willing to write a letter for you. Tell them what colleges you're applying to and why. Be honest about what you are hoping they can offer as an advocate, an insider, and a framer of the portrait that is your application.

Try This

This chapter is full of suggested exercises. Spend some time going back through it, and make an activities list, discuss interview questions with a friend or family member, and brainstorm some recommenders. Doing this now will help you avoid a last-minute scramble as deadlines approach.

 Talk about This

1. What are your primary takeaways about how admission readers are considering your activities outside class?

2. What three things would you want to convey in an interview or have a recommender share about you?

3. Does understanding more about what colleges are looking for outside the classroom move you to remove or add any colleges on your list?

 CHECK IN. After reading this chapter, are you still on the same page as a family? If you are not all-in together, what do you need to do, discuss, or learn to get there?

☆ **Extra Credit**

No matter what grade you are in, reviewing your résumé can give you insight into the ways you spend your time. If you don't have a résumé, create one (it doesn't have to be fancy). Consider how colleges will look at it. Scan the QR code in the upper corner to access a worksheet that will help you in reviewing your résumé.

PART IV

CHAPTER 11

Admission Decisions

Why do we never get an answer
When we are knocking at the door
Because the truth is hard to swallow
That's what the war of love is for.
"QUESTION" BY THE MOODY BLUES

Lt. Kaffee: Colonel Jessup, did you order the Code Red?

Col. Jessup: You want answers?

Lt. Kaffee: I think I'm entitled to.

Col. Jessup: You want answers?

Lt. Kaffee: I want the truth!

Col. Jessup: You can't handle the truth!

In this famous scene from the movie *A Few Good Men*, Lieutenant Kaffee (Tom Cruise), a young, somewhat naïve navy lawyer, cross-examines the highly decorated, deeply respected Colonel Jessup (Jack Nicholson). Kaffee is trying to determine whether the colonel ordered a "Code Red," a covert order that allegedly led to the death of an enlisted Marine. As you can tell, Jessup does not believe that Kaffee or any nonofficer can truly comprehend the pressures of his job. Now, college admission is not the Marines, but Kaffee's demand for the truth is a fitting lead-in to this chapter.

HERE IS WHAT YOU KNOW

You now have a more accurate portrait of the higher-education landscape. You know there are thousands of colleges and universities in our nation. You know too that there are great schools abroad—the landscape is indeed global, and the options are vast. You know that most institutions admit more students than they deny and that many institutions conduct transparent, formulaic review to arrive at admission decisions.

You also know that the first principle of college admission is based on economics: supply and demand. That is, the number of applications for the number of spots in a class is what drives the admit rate. If the number of quality applicants goes up, selectivity also goes up, and the admit rate therefore goes down. Additionally, you know that when the quality and number of applicants to a college increases, that college adds factors to its admission review and transitions to holistic review, in which it consider factors beyond grades and test scores.

In part III, we offered you a peek behind the curtain in admission offices. You now understand what colleges are looking for and the conversations that occur in admission committees. That information and insight will help you understand how one school varies from another in its admission priorities and goals. Now you have arrived at the "courtroom" chapter and are seeking the truth of *how* admission decisions in holistic review are actually made and why. What? You thought we already covered that? The question is "Can you handle the truth?"

THE TRUTH ABOUT HOLISTIC REVIEW

First—this is elementary but important—holistic admission review means that it is a human process. Human means subjective. Human, we can all agree, means imperfect. Human means unpredictable.

Second, schools with holistic review make nuanced decisions with limited information in a compressed amount of time. Third, these schools often move quickly past the quantitative factors (test scores and grades) because of the high academic quality of their applicants.

Undeniably, there is something hardwired in all of us that longs for what is right, equal, and just—a perfect process with predictable results. In college admission, *the truth* is that imperfect humans, using limited details on tight timelines, are reviewing qualitative and personal information (your writing, your background, your experiences, your interests, and your strengths) and comparing them, in a relative manner, to those of thousands of others. So, in addition to not being perfect or predictable, holistic admission *is not fair*.

> Holistic admission is absolutely not *fair*, but it seeks to be consistent.

Therefore, it is no surprise that these are refrains we hear every year:

"How can you wait-list my son? He scored 30 points higher on his ACT and took two more AP classes than your average. And we know someone down the street who did not have that and got in."

"Something is wrong with your process if my daughter, who has been through as many medical issues as she has and still has a 3.8 GPA, is not getting in. Talk about not being fair. She deserves this."

"And don't get me started on financial aid—or lack thereof. Talk about injustice."

It may surprise you to hear that our colleagues around the country who annually deny admission (or are unable to provide as much financial aid as they would like to) to thousands of incredibly talented students are shaking their heads at the injustice right along with you. They would not contest your rational reaction. You are not crazy. They know that. They agree that it's *not* fair. In fact, they would be the first to concede that they deny many students with higher SAT/ACT scores or more community service or a stronger choice of curriculum or a better written essay or more participation in clubs and sports than other applicants who were admitted.

Take time to speak with someone who recently applied to selective colleges and received their decisions. Or talk to your school counselor, who annually tracks entire classes of students who receive admission decisions. They will likely relay an anecdote about a student with perfect test scores who was not admitted; a three-sport athlete who also volunteers at the hospital who was deferred, wait-listed, and ultimately denied; or a valedictorian whose grandfather taught at the institution and who did not get in.

If you are looking for fair, you have come to the wrong place. As our colleague, Tim Fields, senior associate dean of admission at Emory University says, "Fair is a place where they judge pigs and sell corndogs." Holistic admission is absolutely not that, but it seeks to be consistent.

INSTITUTIONAL MISSION

If supply and demand is the first principle of college admission, then fulfilling institutional mission is the second—and there are only two. Be it Northwestern University or Northeastern University, the University of Washington or Washington University, Reed College or Wright State University, they all have a motto, as well as a vision and mission statement. Each school was founded and continues to exist for a specific reason, with a recruitment and admission process designed to support that. Therefore, the goal of admission offices practicing holistic review is *not* to be fair; it is *not* to publish a formula for families to calculate the probability of being admitted. Instead, it is to advance their institution's own mission.

Mission Drives Admission

Mission means that the middle-50-percent test scores and grade ranges or averages you see posted on a school's website or in its admission publication are *guides, not guarantees*. They are one part of a bigger story: the institution's "deep purpose." Mission means that applicants' rigor of curriculum, course performance, impact on their community, essays, recommendations from teachers and counselors, interviews, and their unique circumstances and background all matter, but they are not the only factors at play.

If you look at the academic profiles for admission to Amherst College and Caltech, you'll find the two schools are quite similar. But take a look at their missions:

Amherst College

Terras Irradient "Let Them Give Light to the World"

Amherst College educates men and women of exceptional potential from all backgrounds so that they may seek, value, and advance knowledge, engage the world around them, and lead principled lives of consequence.

Amherst brings together the most promising students, whatever their financial need, in order to promote diversity of experience and ideas within a purposefully small residential community. Working with faculty, staff, and administrators dedicated to intellectual freedom and the highest standards of instruction in the liberal arts, Amherst undergraduates assume substantial responsibility for undertaking inquiry and for shaping their education within and beyond the curriculum.

Amherst College is committed to learning through close colloquy and to expanding the realm of knowledge through scholarly research and artistic creation at the highest level. Its graduates link learning with leadership—in service to the College, to their communities, and to the world beyond. (Amherst College n.d.)

California Institute of Technology

The mission of the California Institute of Technology is to expand human knowledge and benefit society through research integrated with education. We investigate the most challenging, fundamental problems in science and technology in a singularly collegial, interdisciplinary atmosphere, while educating outstanding students to become creative members of society. (Caltech 2023)

The difference in schools' missions is why it is possible for a student to be admitted to a school with a higher rank or lower admit rate than another college by which they are denied. The student applying to Amherst (with the same profile, involvement, writing ability, scores, and grades) is going to be reviewed through a different lens than they will be by Caltech. Mission is, in part, what counselors are talking about when they discuss fit or match.

Geography—particularly at selective public universities—is one driver that can dictate admission decisions. The University of North Carolina at Chapel Hill is mandated by the state's legislature to enroll no more than 18 percent of students from outside the state (Tate 2021). This is why the admit rate for UNC–Chapel Hill is typically more than three times higher for in-state students than nonresidents.

University of North Carolina at Chapel Hill

The nation's first public university serves North Carolina, the United States, and the world through teaching, research, and public service. We embrace an unwavering commitment to excellence as one of the world's great research universities.

Our mission is to serve as a center for research, scholarship, and creativity and to teach a diverse community of undergraduate, graduate, and professional students to become the next generation of leaders. Through the efforts of our exceptional faculty and staff, and with generous support from North Carolina's citizens, we invest our knowledge and resources to enhance access to learning and to foster the success and prosperity of each rising generation. We also extend knowledge-based services and other resources of the University to the citizens of North Carolina and their institutions to enhance the quality of life for all people in the State. (University of North Carolina–Chapel Hill n.d.)

> Geography—particularly at selective public universities—is one factor that can dictate admission decisions.

Every year, valedictorians from other states around the country are rejected by UNC–Chapel Hill yet are accepted by Ivy League schools. Does this sound unjust? Not if you understand that *mission drives admission*. And mission can change. A college closes its nursing program; it begins offering majors in engineering; it eliminates its wrestling team; the political climate in its state shifts; it builds a new residence hall and increases the size of its first-year class. Mission changes, and with it admission review is modified to reach new benchmarks.

Georgia Tech as an Example

Founded in 1885, the Georgia School of Technology began offering classes in 1888 with one major—mechanical engineering. At the time, it was an all-male trade school responding to the needs of late nineteenth-century Georgia and the US South. The focus was on preparing young men for industry, leadership, and the design of new machines for a rapidly industrializing state, region, and nation. Were there more "qualified" or "smarter" students at the time who had aspirations of becoming ministers or lawyers or physicians? Unquestionably. Had they applied to Tech with those career ambitions, they likely would not have been admitted. It was not Tech's mission to educate students for those professions.

In 1912, Georgia Tech established a School of Commerce, which ran its business program. In 1952, Tech opened its doors to women for the first time and, in 1961, became the first school in the South to inte-

> **By reading the mission statements of colleges and universities, you can predict their institutional priorities.**

grate classes without a court order. Imagine a family who had two boys. One started Tech in 1950. Three years later, the younger brother applies. He is by all accounts smarter than his older brother but does not get admitted. A shift in mission changed the applicant pool, the admission process, and the competition. Supply and demand drives admit rates. If supply grows, due to a shift in mission, then admission review changes accordingly, based on factors aside from the ones we covered in chapter 8.

Here is Georgia Tech's mission statement today:

Georgia Tech
The Georgia Institute of Technology is a public research university established by the state of Georgia in Atlanta in 1885 and committed to developing leaders who advance technology and improve the human condition. (Georgia Institute of Technology n.d.)

Do you get a sense of Tech's institutional priorities in its mission statement, and can you speculate about what might appear in its evaluative rubric for admission review? It is not hard to imagine conversations by the admission committee about identifying students with a commitment to or potential for "improving the human condition."

By reading an institution's mission statement, you have a window on its institutional priorities and may be able to infer how geography, major, background, and so forth will affect the assessment of applicants. The *truth is*, though, that you cannot fully control whether admission committees agree that you meet their institutional priorities.

An Olympic Example

In the XXXI Summer Olympics, Gabby Douglas (the defending gold medalist) competed in the women's gymnastics all-around qualifying round. After four events (vault, uneven bars, balance beam, and floor exercise), she finished third out of the 24 competitors (top 12 percent). Sounds pretty good, right? However, in this humanly judged competition, she was eliminated, because the rules state that only the top two finishers from each country are able to advance to the next round. In this case, she was third overall (by one-fourth of a point) but also third among Americans. That is right—the top two competitors were Simone Biles and Aly Raisman—two of her US teammates.

Sound familiar? She was competing in an incredibly talented pool, in a specific year, in a competition with particular rules, judged by imperfect humans making slight calculations over multiple factors (events). Fair? No. Perfect? No. Reality? Yes.

Here is the thing though—she signed up for it. Gabby knew this was not a preset bar that all she had to do was jump over. Would she have lost a night's sleep before performing at a local or state-level competition? Absolutely not. She could have stayed out late the night before eating Cheetos and still waltzed in and cruised to first place. But on that stage—with that competition—she understood that advancing was not guaranteed.

CAN YOU HANDLE THE TRUTH?

Gabby Douglas's margin was 12 percent. Only a handful of colleges in our nation have admit rates of 12 percent or less. If you are applying to one of these—and frankly, if you are applying to a school taking less than 50 percent—you need to understand that getting edged out for reasons you may never know is a distinct possibility. There is not going to be a check box on the application that asks you to acknowledge this, but perhaps there should be. You may be among the best in your high school, county, or even state, but that does not guarantee you will be selected from a deep pool of talented, accomplished applicants in a process driven by institutional priorities supporting a particular mission. You may have five relatives who attended the university. You may have been wearing that school's gear since you were in diapers. You may have aced all of your AP tests and the math section of the ACT. But in that year, given where you're from, what you want to study, what the university is emphasizing or deemphasizing in its institutional priorities, and—most importantly—the rest of the competition, you may not get admitted.

HANDLING ADMISSION DECISIONS

We believe you can handle the truth. We believe that, as a family, your focus is now not simply on getting in but on staying together through the college admission experience. We have walked you through how holistic decisions are really made. Now it is time to understand the possible admission decision outcomes—and how to handle them.

Defer

Each year many students are *deferred* from Early Action (EA) or Early Decision (ED) to Regular Decision. Essentially, deferring students is a college's way of hedging its bets. The admission staff admits students that they are 100 percent confident about wanting to enroll; denies the students who are either not academically competitive or not seen to be good matches with institutional priorities; and then they defer the rest. The goal is to gauge the strength and size of the entire applicant pool once Regular Decision applications come in. It is the office's way of managing supply and demand, and it's common to see 20 to 40 percent of EA/ED applicants being deferred to the next round.

What Does This Mean for You?

Being deferred means you have some more work to do. You will need to send in your final fall grades. You may need to write an additional essay or submit a form telling the admission committee more about your senior-year accomplishments and/or extracurricular activities. Deferral is a "hold on" or a "tell us more." The college will be looking at how you have done in a challenging senior schedule or if your upward grade trend continues or if you can juggle more responsibility outside the classroom given your course load. If you are deferred, view it as an opportunity to refocus and get motivated to finish your senior year well. It might even mean retaking standardized tests in order to score closer to the school's admitted-student profile.

It means you may need to submit another application or two. The good news is that many great schools have deadlines in January, after most EA/ED decisions are released. Bottom line—you need to submit applications to a few additional schools with higher admit rates and lower academic profiles than the one that deferred you.

It means holistic review is a real thing. Whether your scores and grades were above, below, or right in the middle of a school's academic profile, a defer decision only proves what you already knew—admission is about more than your numbers. Institutional priorities, shaping a class, and supply and demand drive admission decisions.

It means you need to check your ego and wait. We told you college admission was not designed to be fair; now you are living that reality. Unfortunately, deferral means spending a few more months in limbo. It also means a second chance for you to evaluate whether this school is a good match for you or if another institution may have risen to the top of your list. The admission committee has decided they want to evaluate you in the context of their overall pool. Do not let your ego get in your way. Too many students do not send in fall grades, complete the deferred form, or send other information schools ask for because their pride has taken a hit. Think of the admission experience as your first foray into your college years, and start looking at *maybes* not as annoying but as valuable to your overall admission experience. Having patience, an ability to navigate uncertainty, and confidence in times when you do not have finality is not easy, but it does prepare you well for other situations you will continue to face. Remember—it is called an admission *process* for a reason, because it is not always over in one round. Do not go partway and stop.

It means you need to look forward, not backward. If you are deferred, *do not* look back. *Do not* second-guess whether you should have taken AP Geography in the ninth grade instead of band or blame Mr. Thompson for giving you an 89 instead of a 93, which would have bumped up your GPA by 0.083. Are you going to get admitted in the next round? Maybe. Control what you can control. You only get one senior year in high school. Do well—but more importantly do good. Do not worry about admission offices you will never enter; instead recommit to the rooms you walk into every day. Be a good friend. Be a good sibling.

Be a good teammate. Go thank a teacher or coach who wrote a recommendation for you. Hug your parents.

Wait-list

Otherwise known as admission purgatory, the wait list sucks! Go ahead and add it to your list of "things that suck," along with pink eye, losing to your biggest rival in the final seconds, and someone leaving an empty box of Girl Scout cookies in the pantry. You have already waited for a decision (sometimes having already been deferred), and now you are being asked to wait again.

Why Do Schools Have a Wait List?

The answer for why schools wait-list depends on whom you ask. Deans, admission directors, and enrollment managers will say it is because predicting a 17-year-old's behavior is not an exact science.

> The wait list exists, in part, to allow schools to achieve their institutional priorities.

Parents and students will say it is because enrollment people are not that smart or maybe even a little cruel. The truth is, if colleges could predict how many students each year will accept their offer of admission (yield) and pay their enrollment deposit, then wait lists would not be necessary. Perhaps one day we will live in a world where students apply to only one college; all get admitted, enroll, are happy, earn 4.0 GPAs, retain at 100 percent, graduate in four years, get high-paying and fulfilling jobs after graduation, name their babies after the admission director, and then donate consistently and generously for the rest of their lives. Until that time, we have wait lists (and books of baby names).

Colleges build and use historical yield models to predict the number of students who will say yes to their offer. However, because the number of beds in residence halls, the number of seats in classrooms, and the faculty-to-student or advisor-to-student ratios are set, colleges intentionally plan to come in slightly below their target number. They do this to account for the years when students "over-yield." If you are applying to a school that enrolled more students than it planned to the year prior, it is fair to assume it will be conservative this year and fill an even higher number of spaces from the wait list by design.

The wait list also exists to allow schools to meet institutional priorities. After their deposit deadline has passed, colleges evaluate their class goal and then use their wait list to meet demographic targets not met in the initial round of admission offers. They may want more students from a particular state or region to proliferate their college's brand. They may have just hired a new dean in the business school who is clamoring to grow the program. Maybe they are still trying to find those female chemistry students we talked about in chapter 2. Ultimately, students chosen from the wait list are handpicked to fill a purpose: net tuition revenue, academic profile, academic major, and so on.

What Does This Mean for You?

It means you need to accept your spot. At most schools, the wait list decision is actually an offer. Check what they send you, and read their website closely. Typically, you'll need to take action of some kind to accept or claim your place on the wait list. Alternatively, you may decide to close or withdraw your application from continued consideration.

If you claim your spot, be sure to do anything additional the school requires of you. Is there a supplementary short-answer question you need to answer? Do you need to send in another recommendation letter or schedule an interview? Each school will handle this differently, so read your wait list notification carefully. If the school tells you *not* to do or send something . . . well . . . don't.

It means you need to deposit at another college. The university that has offered you a spot on its wait list should instruct you to take this step, and it is absolutely critical. Because so many students wait until the deadline to confirm their enrollment or put down a deposit, colleges typically do not have a firm sense of whether they need to use their wait list until late April or the beginning of May. This is also why the majority of wait list activity occurs in May and June, and in recent years offers have been extending even farther into the summer. Putting your money down at another college secures your spot in its incoming class and allows you to hedge your bets. Unfortunately, wait list activity is unpredictable, so while we know it may be difficult, our recommendation is to assume you will not be offered a spot and begin to get excited about your other options.

It means you should reach out to your admission counselor (unless you have been instructed not to). If you have met or corresponded with someone from the college's admission office, perhaps when they visited your high school or while you were on their campus, send them an email. Let them know you claimed your spot on the wait list and completed the school's stipulated form or essay. You are indicating continued interest in attending. Wait lists are not ranked, and they are not first-come first-serve. Wait list activity is all about shaping a class, and you want to be at the top of an admission officer's mind. To be clear, we are not telling you to reach out every day. This is a one-and-done proposition. We have had a student send a painted shoe with a message on the sole reading, "just trying to get my foot in the door." Memorable, but ultimately ineffective. Admission offices regularly receive chocolates, cookies, and other treats, along with poems or notes. It is safe to say that a couple hundred grams of sugar and a few couplets are not going to outweigh institutional priorities. There is a line between demonstrating interest and stalking. Do not cross it.

> Have the confidence to embrace uncertainty as an adventure rather than a source of anxiety in your admission experience.

It means you need to wait well. Nobody says waiting is one of their favorite things to do. It is not easy or fun. Waiting can be frustrating and unsettling, and unfortunately we do not have a solution for that. What we can tell you is that life is full of situations like this. Will I get a new job and when? Will a house come on the market that we can afford in the area we want to live in? Will the results of this test come back from the doctor with life-changing implications? This may be the first time you have had to wait for something you really wanted—to have to sit in a period of uncertainty as you await a result or a decision—but it will not be the last. Waiting can be particularly hard when it seems like everyone else is all set and everything is smooth. Trust us: from the outside, many people seem to have it together. Life looks easy for them (especially if you trust their social media feed). Your goal is to embrace uncertainty as an adventure rather than a burden. Do not let being in limbo keep you from enjoying the last part of your senior year. Have fun on spring break. Go to prom. Take the time to thank your coaches and teachers. Read an unassigned book because it interests you. Being content in the present is a challenge at any age. You are just getting some early practice at it.

Deny

For a strong student and high achiever, being denied admission may be one of the first nos you have ever received. We were both denied by colleges. We had girlfriends break up with us. We were turned down for jobs. Your goal is to look at this not as a hard stop but rather as a pivot.

What Does This Mean for You?

It means you are not OK. Go ahead and scream, cry, beat your pillow, cook or eat a lot of something. (Do all of these at once if you're really upset.) Whatever it takes to begin clearing your head. Mad? Sad? Frustrated? Disappointed? All of these feelings are totally valid. Give yourself the time, space, and permission to process them.

It means you will be OK. When you are denied admission, you need to remember that no college (or person or job or city) is perfect. Perfect colleges do not exist, but a perfect mentality does. This *is* going to work out. Here is how we know that: every year—*every year*—we talk to current college students who say they did not end up at their first choice because they were denied, and they are so glad it turned out that way. They cannot imagine being anywhere but the place they landed. In the days immediately after a denial, you may not believe that, but it is true. Fact: you are going to end up somewhere great.

Jim Bock, vice president and dean of admission at Swarthmore College, explains,

> There is no perfect student or perfect school and most students would be successful at multiple institutions. I have always argued that students should have several "first" choices as they navigate the admissions process, and given the breadth and depth of choice and opportunity in this country, a less than desirable outcome from one school is really that school's loss and another school's gain. There is a place, multiple places I believe, for every student. This one decision does not and should not define you. Some might say that's easy for me to say given where I sit today, but I have personal experience. I was deferred, then denied early action at my first choice college over thirty years ago, and it made all of the difference. I added a few schools to my list, including Swarthmore, and it changed my life forever. It's part of why I do what I do today. I was disappointed, but it made me more hungry and made me rethink my options and look past the bad tour or less compelling group session and really focus on what set each school apart from one another.

It means college admission is not fair. As our colleague Pam Ambler from Pace Academy in Atlanta says, "The way that admission decisions *feel* is not how they are *made.*" That is spot-on advice. If someone breaks up with you and says, "It's not you, it's me," they are lying. It *is* you. But for colleges, it is about *them*: institutional mission and supply and demand. You know this.

Gary Clark, executive director of undergraduate admission at the University of California–Los Angeles, gives students this advice: "Remember that there are two names on every diploma. One, the institution's, the other, the student's. While you may picture yourself at one university, remember that there are many that could offer you a wonderful experience. If it doesn't work out at your top choice, and you've developed a strong list of prospective universities, then you rally around one of those other options and get excited about the experience you'll have there." Translation: You may get denied by a school based on where you are from or what you want to study or because the school is trying to grow this or that and you happen to be that and this. It is natural to *feel* disappointed or mad or upset. Just be sure you do not equate this decision to an indictment of your character or a prediction of your future potential.

It means you need to be realistic and move on. If you are denied during an Early Action or Early Decision round, then, like with a deferral, you will need to submit a few more applications to schools with higher admit rates and lower academic profiles (*target* and *likely* schools) than the one that denied you. If you are denied in Regular Decision, finish your senior year strong, because the colleges that ultimately admit you will be looking closely at your final high school transcript to make sure you did not have an academic decline after you received their acceptance.

Technically, you can appeal a denial. The truth is that almost none of these appeals succeed. You can likely find a college's appeal form and process on its website. If you appeal, be sure to read the conditions of a "reasonable appeal." Typically, valid reasons include not having your correct transcript or submitting inaccurate or incomplete grade information. Major medical situations or severe life circumstances that you neglected to explain on your application may also be considered. Because you "really want to attend" or because it was the only place you applied to or because everyone in your family went there—not valid reasons. One of our colleagues puts it this way:

"If you decide to appeal, you need to be prepared to be denied again." Damn. That sounds cold. The truth is like that sometimes. Actually, the truth is like that a lot.

Go back to class, your team, your job, your clubs, your friends, and your family. Take some time to look around at the relationships you have built. Be reminded and grateful for the community you have created. These folks want you with them. They love having you as a part of it all—and other colleges are going to invite you into similar communities.

Parents, What Does This Mean for You?

You love your kids. We started with that in chapter 1. Our topic may be college admission, but our theme is family. When admission decisions like defer, wait-list, and deny come, it hurts. You may also feel mad, sad, frustrated, and disappointed. Again, all of these reactions are totally valid. The difference is that you cannot scream and beat your pillow.

It means you have some work to do before decisions are released. If your student is applying to a selective college, you need to prepare them for no—and also for maybe (by deferral or wait-listing). You understand the statistics. You understand the factors behind admission decisions. You know that Gabby Douglas was one of the world's best gymnasts at the 2016 Olympics and easily could have advanced to the women's all-around finals. The reality is that you cannot control admission decisions. In the weeks leading up to the release of these decisions, we encourage you to spend one of your weekly college meetings talking about the possibility of being denied. Be sure your child hears you say again that these decisions have no correlation with how much you love them and believe in them. Remind them that not getting into a certain college has no bearing on their potential for future success.

It means you have some work to do on the day decisions are released. The good news is that when decisions come out, you just need to do the same thing you have done their entire lives—be available. Like the decisions themselves, you will not know what reactions are coming: door slamming, dead silence, screaming, crying. Any of these are possible. Nobody ever said adulting was easy, and here is another test. Ultimately, it will not be about your words but simply about your being there.

We have heard of families who have planned to go to a movie or to cook a favorite meal or who have bought a tub of decadent ice cream in advance. Sometimes this is exactly what your kid will want or need after a decision comes out, and other times you will need to read the moment and shift to a plan B. In other words, parenting. You got this.

It means you have some work to do after decisions are released. In the days and weeks following, your job is to refocus and encourage. As we said earlier, if your student receives a deny or defer decision in Early Action or Early Decision, it will likely mean submitting a few more applications and sending in final fall semester grades. Help your student stay focused on their classes, as all colleges will be looking at those to make final decisions. Point toward next steps and the possibilities of what is to come rather than bemoaning or questioning a decision that has already been made and issued. Keep their sights on the bigger picture and emphasize that this is their one and only senior year of high school. Continue to be their biggest cheerleader. Remind them that they are going to have some great college options and that you are excited to see how it all plays out.

> Parents, after your student receives a denial, remind them that they will have some great college options and that you are excited to see how it all plays out.

Admit

What, you think we forgot? Absolutely not. We were just saving the good news for last. You would think that there is not much here to explain, but we get calls from students every year who say, "So I logged into my portal, and it says that I have been accepted. Does that mean I'm in?" I guess some folks still like to hear it the old-fashioned way. We can do that. *Congratulations!*

What Does This Mean for You?

It means you need to celebrate. Celebrate every admit. Go out to dinner, buy something you have been wanting for a while, or just go get a double scoop of ice cream—whatever makes you happy. Be proud! Take some time to look back on all of the hard work it has taken to get to this point, and be thankful there is a campus community out there that recognizes your hard work and also thinks you could come to their campus and make it better. That's pretty awesome, right?

It means you need to be cool. Keep in mind two things: (1) That decision could have easily broken the other way for you, especially if it was from a highly selective college. We are not suggesting that you are not amazing, but holistic admission is unpredictable, as we have discussed. (2) Some incredibly qualified and talented students did *not* get in, and they are disappointed and hurting. Act like you have been there before. Keep it classy. There is a big difference between "Wow. I was accepted to Michigan. So honored to have the chance to go there" and "Got into Michigan today. They would have been crazy not to take me" (a.k.a. the *opposite* of being cool). The schools that admit you are excited for you to join their campus community because you have already been a positive influencer in yours. Be cognizant of your classmates, friends, and others who get tough news. A little humility goes a long way.

It means you need to read the entire letter. The first paragraph will inevitably begin with congratulatory language and will transition to encouraging you to enroll. Inevitably, perhaps in a bolded or underlined section, it will outline expectations for your continued demonstration of both strong academic performance and good citizenship. The school is basically saying, "Don't screw this up." They expect you to stay focused on your classes and to inform them if you change your class schedule from what you initially listed on your application. The college expects you not to be suspended, expelled, or arrested. As you read this in the admission letter, it may sound funny or ridiculous. Trust us, though; that cautionary language is in there because of prior student academic performance or misbehavior. You have worked hard to earn this offer of admission. Stay on target. Don't blow it.

It means you have a decision to make. You likely waited a long time for some of your admission decisions, and now you are on the clock. By the deadline, you will need to put down your enrollment deposit *at only one school.* The amount varies by school and will be explained in your acceptance letter and subsequent emails or correspondence. In chapter 12, we go over some ways to weigh your admit options. For now, go back to celebrating!

Parents, What Does This Mean for You?

Just as you had to manage your reaction if your student was denied, you need to be mindful of the signals you send upon their acceptance. If your student was admitted Early Decision, then you can safely celebrate with abandon. If they are awaiting decisions from multiple schools, however, be careful about how you play your cards when decisions land. Your student has nearly two decades of experience detecting your "tells." After years of you feigning admiration for the lumpy pottery project they brought home from school or of you clapping too quickly after a lousy recital or game, they know how to read you. When you respond to one acceptance with "Oh, that's great, honey" and another with a leap of joy, you're making a value judgment. You may also be complicating their decision of where they attend. Don't do this! And definitely don't dish out one scoop of ice cream for one acceptance and two for another or order a school's sweatshirt online while they're still reading the decision letter.

💡 *Try This*

Take the Admission Decision Pledge

All: I, [state your name], being of sound (though overly caffeinated) mind and (sleep deprived) body, do hereby swear that I will *not* presume anything in the admission process.

Students: At the advice of these sage authors, I will *not* expect my test scores, though in the top quartile, to guarantee my admittance when I look at middle-50-percent ranges. Likewise, I will *not* look at middle-50-percent ranges of hitherto admitted classes and expect my scores, though in the bottom quartile, to be overlooked in favor of my amazing essay or the many glowing letters of recommendation sent on my behalf.

Parents: Henceforth, I vow not to use an elastic *we* when referring to my student's future college hopes and dreams. I hereby avouch not to feign the voice of an adolescent to obtain the password of an application account or an admission decision in advance. I promise *not* to begrudge the joy of my friends when their children receive acceptances or scholarships.

All: I understand, as heretofore explained, that holistic review is neither fair nor perfect, nor will I likely agree with or be capable of predicting decisions, despite the complex algorithms I employ or the fortune tellers I visit.

Parents: Furthermore, I agree that I will *not* view an admission decision as a referendum on or a cumulative assessment of my parental faculties.

Students: Furthermore, I agree that I will *not* view an admission decision as an indictment of my character, a judgment on my preparation, or a prediction of my future opportunities and happiness.

Disclaimer: Slightly misused Olde English verbiage does not negate the spirit or effectiveness of this pledge.

Talk about This

1. How do the mission statements of the colleges you are considering align with your *why*: that is, your goals, values, and hopes?

2. How can your family prepare for the different decisions you may receive?

3. What truth about college admission decisions encourages you and what truth concerns you the most?

CHECK IN. After reading this chapter, are you still on the same page as a family? If you're not all-in together, what do you need to do, discuss, or learn to get there?

⭐ **Extra Credit**

Look up the mission statements for each college on your list. Copy and paste them into one document. Then read through them and highlight the words and phrases that resonate with you. Do you notice words or themes that are similar across schools? Is any value missing from the statements that's important to you?

CHAPTER 12

Making Your College Choice

Burn the ships, cut the ties / Send a flare into the night
Say a prayer, turn the tide.
"BURN THE SHIPS" BY KING AND COUNTRY

It is all about the vibe . . . oh, and the money.
HIGH SCHOOL SENIOR

May your choices reflect your hopes not your fears.
NELSON MANDELA

Once you make a decision, the universe conspires to make it happen.
RALPH WALDO EMERSON

Despite a decade of parenting, I (Brennan) made a rookie mistake. I took my son into our local candy shop, and with the aroma of fresh chocolate and sugar taunting his senses, I allowed him to choose a treat. He was paralyzed. "I don't know how to decide," he said—his initial excitement quickly besieged by choice.

I immediately recognized the puzzled look on his face, as it resembled those of the high school seniors I counsel each year. After months of anticipation, as you have waited for colleges to make their decisions, suddenly the acceptances roll in, and the tables are turned. We are confident that if you follow our guidance, you will have acceptances from several schools where you could see yourself thriving.

Like a kid in a candy shop, you will have to choose. For many students, this is the most significant decision they have made to date, and it is a complicated one. Selecting a college involves choosing a new home, reestablishing friends and community, and making a major financial decision, all rolled into one. Too often, students and families experience the type of anxiety that author and psychologist Barry Schwartz (2004) points out in his book *The Paradox of Choice: Why More Is Less*. In the spring, after students have submitted their admission deposit, or at summer orientation or even as the fall semester begins, we commonly hear students express lingering doubt about their selection of a college. Our goal in this chapter is to provide you with the information you'll need to appreciate the chance of having a choice, to consider thoughtfully your options, and ultimately to make a (wedge-free) family selection with confidence.

So, how do you finally choose one college?

YOU *GET TO* DO THIS

Unless you apply under a binding decision plan (outlined in chapter 7), you will have until the National Candidate Reply Date of May 1 to make your choice. If you are admitted under Early Decision, you will need to close any outstanding applications. We recommend you do this immediately so that the other schools to which you've applied do not waste their time considering your application. It frees up space for other applicants and also means fewer emails for you—so a win-win.

For most students, however, the spring is about weighing options, comparing choices, and considering offers. Before we delve into how to do this, quickly look back over the words in that last sentence— *options*, *choices*, and *offers*. If you are reading this chapter before the spring of senior year, you may question whether that will really be the case for you. Trust us: if you have followed the suggestions in this book, you will be admitted to a college that is a great match for you, a place where you can learn, grow, and achieve your goals. If instead you are reading this chapter during the time of decision-making, good job!

We told you this would happen. What a great spot to be in. Remember that having options was what this was all about. Ironically, we often hear students describe this choice as a burden rather than a gift. We hope you will not view it as "I *have to* decide" but rather as "I *get to* decide." You *get to* think through the place where you'll thrive and create a network. You *get to* talk through your options with your family, who love you, are proud of you, and are excited about this next chapter of your life. You *get to* do this while finishing high school with peers who know and care for you and among teachers who are excited for you and want to see you continue to succeed. You *get to* do this. What a privilege!

> The spring of senior year is a time to weigh options, compare choices, and consider offers.

WHAT TO EXPECT WITH ACCEPTANCE

What can you expect from colleges that accept you? An utter blitzkrieg (look it up). Phone calls (to every number listed on your application), emails, texts, letters, owls, and random alumni knocking at your door. In chapter 2, we told you how important *search* is to colleges. Well, *yield* is search's evil twin that takes communication and hard-selling to a whole new level. Get ready. Marketing from schools goes into overdrive once you're admitted, because the more admits a college can convert into deposits, the fewer applicants the college will need to admit from its wait list. From the standpoint of rankings and prestige, a higher yield is to the college's advantage because it keeps its admit rate lower.

You had to wait for months for an admission decision, and now the tables are turned. Colleges said, "Send us your application, but don't call or email us because we are 'in committee.'" Now they are singing a different tune. We are not suggesting that you set your email to auto-response, telling them to check back in late April. Instead, we are just telling you to expect a full-court press.

Schools are going to invite you to admitted student days or open houses. Some of these events may be offered virtually, and if your schedule or resources do not allow you to go to campus, you should absolutely take advantage of this virtual programming. But in most cases, schools will want to get you on campus, and ideally you will have the opportunity to visit in person as an admitted student. During these programs, you can count on hearing from amazing students, top faculty, successful alumni, and the president or other high-level administrators. Generally, smaller schools will give you an opportunity to interact with current students, sit in on a class, eat in a dining hall, tour campus, explore your area of academic interest, and see a first-year residence hall. Larger public universities may not be able to offer as personalized an experience, but their admitted student programs frequently allot time for you to speak with representatives from academic advising, housing, dining, orientation, and other first-year support offices set up at tables in a fair-like portion of the day.

In recent years, colleges have invested thousands of dollars to create memorable experiences and virtual programming for admitted students that are designed to connect them to one another. Programs often feature team competitions, scavenger hunts, off-campus excursions, and service projects meant to help students meet one another, enjoy their time on campus, and get a feel for what the community will be like as a student.

It is also common for colleges to host receptions geared toward connecting you with alumni, parents of current students, and other admitted students living in your area. Sometimes these are casual; in other cases there will be a speaker in a formal program. These are low-cost, small-time-commitment opportunities where you can ask your questions and hear (typically, in a less scripted manner) from people in your community talk about their experiences on campus and the impact those have had on their life since graduating. We highly encourage you to attend these events, ask questions, and connect with local alumni. Focus especially on the other admitted students. Would you be excited to spend the next four years hanging out and learning with these people?

You are going to receive letters, emails, and calls from people with job titles unfamiliar to you: dean, chair, provost, registrar, bursar. Once you are admitted, the admission office essentially hands off your information to the rest of the campus. The admission officers know that, in many ways, you are done with them, and it is now the full campus's job to recruit you. Expect to be contacted by faculty from your desired academic major, the athletic association, student groups, the orientation office, the outdoor recreation department, and at least one person named Matt or Katie. It can feel overwhelming at times.

Remember that you have until May 1 to make your choice. Your job is to keep asking your questions to as many people as possible during this time; the school has made it easier now for you to do that. Next, we turn to what you need to do after being admitted and before making a final decision.

CELEBRATE YOUR CHOICES

We closed the last chapter with this instruction, but it bears repeating: *celebrate every acceptance.* You worked hard to have each option, so enjoy the good news when it arrives. Again, the celebration does not have to be elaborate. We are not suggesting a big party or weekend trip. Just promise us that you'll take the time to do something fun as a family.

TAKE A CLOSER LOOK

Whether it has been six months since you visited campus, a year, or it's your first time, your outlook as an admitted student is totally different from what it was as a prospect or applicant. At this point, you have a more defined sense of what you need and want in your college experience. You also have (as predicted) other admission offers and will be making direct comparisons at this stage.

It takes time and money to travel to campuses, so do not just go along for the ride. To return to our car-buying metaphor, this is the time to "kick the wheels" and test-drive a school; this is not the time to sit in the passenger's seat while the salesperson steers you through the experience. Prepare ahead of time to ask the critical questions that have led you to this point and that you really want to have answered before making a commitment.

What questions linger, and who can answer them for you? What about the school do you feel confident about, and what do you still need to see or do while on campus? What are your priorities for your college experience, and what evidence do you need to confirm those can be met at this school?

Remember, at this point, colleges are in promote-and-convert mode. Use that to your advantage by pressing them. It is fine to be honest about the other school(s) to which you have been admitted and ask them to delineate the differences in their academic programs, campus culture, student outcomes, and return on investment. You will feel far more confident when you leave a campus if you hear stated in plain terms what makes the school different from others and the best choice for you.

Maybe you need to learn more about career services and internship opportunities, or perhaps you are curious about research positions for undergraduates. If you have a learning difference, you probably want to know details about student support, tutoring, and accommodations. You may want to find out about specific affinity groups on campus and the culture around inclusion and diversity. Plan to visit the academic department you are interested in and talk with professors, advisors, and students about their area of concentration and scholarly work. Matthew DeGreeff, dean of college counseling and student enrichment at Middlesex School, says to students, "Ask schools, 'When I have to do hard things well—in terms of academics, social, artistic, and/or athletics—who will be there to guide me and support me?'"

> Hear as many perspectives as possible while visiting a campus.

Remember that you are the customer, and you are investing your time and money in making this important decision, so dig below the surface. The reaction of campus community members will be telling. Is the campus generally welcoming? Do people go out of their way to greet you, congratulate you, and make you feel like you belong there? Are answers consistent across faculty, administrators, and students? If you find great variance, you will need to determine whether that's an indication of limitless possibilities or limited possibilities and uneven experiences. Don't take any one person's opinion as the gospel truth. No individual is an expert on all things about a college or university. Your goal is to gather as many perspectives as possible. Debra Johns, associate director of admissions at Yale University, advises, "Look at *anything* provided by students. Pay attention to the tone on admitted student websites. Does it resonate with you or not? Ask, 'Can I see myself growing, stretching and evolving here? Will this be an incredible journey? Will I be challenged on every single level at some point during my four years?'"

As you spend time on a campus, ask yourself the following questions, and consider the advice of college admission professionals who have guided thousands of admitted students through this experience.

Will You Feel Comfortable?

You should be asking whether you feel at home when walking the campus of schools you are considering. Your goal is to find a place where you can challenge yourself to learn, grow, and thrive. Do not undervalue the basics. Talk to current college students, and they will tell you—especially if you have any food allergies, dietary restrictions, or preferences—food matters. Likewise, try to visit the first-year residence halls, even if they are not part of the formal tour. Where you rest and sleep is critical to both your mental and physical health, so pay attention. Do not discount the importance of having a space where you can recharge, study, and socialize.

Food

- Does the meal plan allow for flexibility, or is it limited in choice?

- Are you required to purchase the school's meal plan in your first year only or throughout your entire time living on campus?

- Are there kitchenettes where you can cook for yourself?

- Are there ample gluten-free, kosher, or nondairy options?

- Are there grocery stores and restaurants nearby that provide other food options?

Housing

- Are there substance-free housing options if that's a priority for you?

- Are single-gender floors or residence halls available?

- Are there gender-inclusive housing or bathroom options?

- Can first-year students have single rooms, or are shared rooms, suites, triples, or apartment-style setups the norm?

Will You Feel Safe?

The question of safety is more likely to be at the top of your parents' list than your own, but you need to feel like you can take risks and learn without fear, ridicule, or harm. Colleges will often point to the security call stations situated around campus as an indication of a safe environment. Do not settle for this baseline standard. Find out what security concerns exist on campus and what the most recent issues have been. The campus newspaper, open campus forums, and social media are good sources of information about police presence, security issues and prevention strategies, student perceptions of safety, and the frequency and specifics of incidents. Many schools have apps for students that let them indicate their location, request a ride, or send an alert.

Seek out a range of perspectives—current students, recent graduates, local residents, faculty, staff—to gain a clear picture of the environment on campus. The Clery Act mandates that colleges provide a report of campus crime, so be a smart consumer in obtaining this information. From sexual assault statistics to theft to hazing, you will be able to research the safety climate on campus. Beyond your physical safety, is the academic culture one in which you will be challenged intellectually and have the ability to express your opinions in an open, honest, respectful, and encouraging atmosphere? Reflect on your high school experience to determine what you are and are not looking for inside and outside the classroom.

Physical Safety

- How does the school respond to natural disasters, public emergencies, and health concerns?

- What systems are in place for campus alerts or emergency notification? How are parents made aware of crime or other incidents that occur on campus?

- What is the highest-profile crime reported on campus in the past year? How does that compare to other schools you are considering, other colleges in the area, and your hometown?

- How safe is the area surrounding campus?

- What is the relationship like between the college and the town?

- What are the campus statistics for dating violence, domestic violence, sexual assault, and stalking?

- What procedures exist for institutional discipline in cases of dating violence, domestic violence, sexual assault, stalking, and other crimes?

- Does campus security provide a safe escort service after dark; if so, how accessible is it and how often is it used?

> In choosing a college, you want to determine whether you are excited about becoming a part of its campus community.

Intellectual Safety

- What is the academic climate like on campus?

- Does the institution support freedom of expression (inside and outside the classroom)?

- Are students and faculty open to diverse opinions? Do they "talk across the aisle" politically?

- Has the campus hosted controversial speakers, and what was the community's response?

- What is the academic culture around "trigger warnings"?

Will You Belong?

Do you feel a sense of community, connection, and belonging on campus? If colleges have done their job in telling their unique story, and if you have done your research and listened, it will be evident that each campus has its own distinct culture, ethos, and dynamic. A key part of making your college choice is about finding *your* people. Do you have a sense of belonging on campus? Is it a school where you can be yourself?

Sense of Belonging

- What types of people challenge, support, stretch, and encourage you?

- What sort of individuals do you like to be around? Are they well represented on campus?

- Is the school inclusive and welcoming of difference?

- Are you looking for a college experience that mirrors your current community and high school or one that takes you outside your comfort zone by exposing you to a new culture?

- Do you want a college that has a lot of school spirit?

- Are students engaged in and out of class?

- What do students do on weekends?

- Is it a "suitcase campus," where students tend to go their separate ways when classes are done?

- How connected are alumni? Is there a strong network that persists beyond the campus gates?

- If you are honest, do you really see yourself there?

It's not life or death. Don't get caught up in prestige or what you are going to study, as the likelihood is you will change your mind and discover new academic interests. You are not going to study 24/7. Make sure whatever are your passions/interests/activities that at least a few of them are available and open to you regardless of your proposed major or activity. —Spike Gummere, special assistant to the president, Lake Forest College

---

Can You Be Successful?

In his book *David and Goliath: Underdogs, Misfits, and the Art of Battling Giants*, Malcolm Gladwell (2013) explores unlikely outcomes and the dangers of comparing oneself to others. He details the story of a young woman who attended Brown University rather than the University of Maryland. She struggled in chemistry—her chosen field—because of her feelings of inadequacy that may not have plagued her elsewhere. The choices we make determine the direction and quality of our lives. Which of your college options is the best match for you in the short and long term?

Chances for Success

- In the past, what experiences and environments have provided you with encouragement and inspiration to grow?

- Will the faculty and fellow students offer the freedom you need to be proud of your accomplishments and to discover and enhance your abilities?

- In college, do you want to be a "big fish in a small pond" or a "small fish in a big pond"?

- Do you sense this is a place where you'll worry about not measuring up or a place that will inspire you to find confidence in your potential to excel?

"Will I grow?"—rather than looking for a college that suits exactly who you are, I think it ideal to choose a college where there's at least some sense that you'll have to grow into it. Since I would hold that you shouldn't leave college being the same person you were when you started, I think you can't find the growth if you go to a campus that feels perfect in every way. —Jim Rawlins, associate vice chancellor of enrollment management, University of California–San Diego.

Can I identify three specific ways I'm excited to make community and make my mark here? —Kelly Talbert, director of admissions, Boise State University

What am I good at? Do not focus too much on prestige and what will "appear" to be the best choice rather than on which option will allow the student to discover their talents. —Patrick Winter, executive director for recruitment and admission, Kansas State University

Can You Thrive?

The temptation, at any age, is to focus on the short term, the immediate. This is completely understandable because we are constantly barraged with advertisements, sales pitches, and social media that implore us to opt for the quick fix or the today-only sale. On his leadership podcast, Andy Stanley (2018) discusses the concept of "self-leadership." He outlines the dichotomy between the immediate and the ultimate. The immediate, he says, is what is right in front of us. It is about wants, image, and so on. In contrast, the ultimate centers on values. Who are you? Who do you want to be? What are your values, and, importantly, do you resonate with and gain inspiration from the values of those around you? These are big questions and a challenge to answer at any age. But they are critical to helping you choose your college.

Potential to Thrive

- Put simply, which college will allow you to be your best self?

- As you consider college options, what resources and supports exist on each campus to help you reach your goals?

- Are you interested in double majoring or pursuing a minor? If so, how flexible is the curriculum?

- Do you want the freedom to delve immediately into your major, or do you want a school that requires breadth of study for the sake of exploration?

- How accessible are opportunities for creativity?

- What are your desires for your college experience, and will your choice provide a framework for you to achieve them?

Students and families need to be asking about outcomes and how the school the student attends will help them achieve goals they never thought possible. Students seem to be missing the idea that college is about exploring new areas they do not have any experience in and finding what they want to do and create for themselves after attending. Schools that have a history of transforming students into creative thinkers are rich learning environments, and families should be asking how a student is supported through a kind of learning that encourages creativity and pushes the limits of a student's experience. —George Zimmerman, assistant vice president of enrollment management, West Virginia University

RUN THE NUMBERS

In the television show *Lost* (bar none, the best American television show of all time), Hurley (Jorge Garcia) has a series of flashbacks that depict him winning millions of dollars in a lottery using the numbers 4.8.15.16.23.42. Immediately afterward he begins to witness his friends, family, and coworkers suffering horrible misfortunes. Ultimately he ends up in a mental asylum where another patient explains with horror, "The numbers are bad! You gotta get away from them!" Well, the numbers you heard as a prospective student are not bad now; in fact, they are fundamentally more important to you as an admitted student. They mean more, and they are critical in the equation of making your choice. So do not run from them—embrace them.

Reexamine the starting salaries of graduates from the schools you have been admitted to, specifically in the major you plan to study. Look also at the average debt and repayment timeline of graduates. (The websites of College Scorecard, Third Way, Payscale, and Degree Choices have great resources for this.) Find out what employers come to campus to hire students for internships or co-ops and that recruit graduating students for jobs. Evaluate the return on investment that *Forbes*, *Kiplinger*, *Money*, and other publications publish. These publications typically take starting salaries, mid-career earnings, and overall costs into consideration in their methodology, but be sure you understand the formulas they used to arrive at their ratings.

When you receive offers of financial aid, we hope you will review chapter 4. Be diligent in comparing the offers you get. We recommend that you create a spreadsheet for this purpose. How much is a school offering in merit- or need-based scholarship, which you will not need to pay back? Is the award renewable or good only for one year? Does your aid package assume you'll have a work-study job? What does a school offer in loans, which you'll have to repay? Does it include a Parent PLUS Loan? Revisit your financial conditions, limitations, and expectations.

Unless you applied under an Early Decision plan, you will have in hand all financial aid packages to compare by the last week of March or first week of April. This gives you around a month to make your choice. Do not rush it. Frequently families do not completely understand the financial aid packages (which may have different formats and terminology), so do not hesitate to call the financial aid office or request an online meeting so that you can speak with a representative about your package and its implications for you while in school and after graduation. When you are on the call or if you visit in person, be sure to ask about years subsequent to the first one. Are there departmental grants or scholarships you may qualify for after your first year? Do aid packages for first-year students typically look more generous than those of upper-class students? What might change for your family financially if one of your siblings begins or finishes college while you are still in college? The numbers are not bad, but they can be tricky. No question is off limits, so keep pressing until you are confident that you understand exactly what your real cost will be to attend.

Ask each college the often overlooked "What is your retention rate to the second year?" and "What is the *four*-year graduation rate?" —Mike Sexton, former vice president for enrollment management, Santa Clara University

---

TRUST YOUR GUT

Ultimately, only you can make this decision. It is said that the road of life is paved with flattened squirrels that could not make a decision. Don't be one of those squirrels. It may sound trite for us to say it, but it is true: you know you. Be confident and trust your gut. Closing other doors is never easy. This is one of many times you will have this type of choice to make; it will come as well with relationships, jobs, graduate school, or moving someplace new. Sometimes, the hardest part about being talented and having options is that there really is no one *right* answer. Perhaps Steve Jobs (2005) said it best in his Stanford commencement address: "Your time is limited, so don't waste it living someone else's life. Don't be trapped by dogma—which is living with the results of other people's thinking. Don't let the noise of others' opinions drown out your own inner voice. And most important, have the courage to follow your heart and intuition. They somehow already know what you truly want to become. Everything else is secondary."

Here are some more thoughts from admission professionals to consider if you are sweating the choice you must make.

Close your eyes. When I say go, what college campus are you standing on? You are making a decision for one year. You will make the best decision for yourself at this time with the information you have now. If after you attend a school and the information you know changes, you can always make another decision. Try not to place the pressure of "this one decision will affect the rest of my life" on yourself. Life is a series of choices and decisions. —Sally O'Rourke, former director of college counseling, Mercersburg Academy

> In the end, you need to trust your gut when deciding which college to attend.

Ask each college, "What is the most important character aspect of this school?" It helps separate schools beyond programs, aid packages, and rankings and allows the school to have its own "personality" among others in the same genre of school. —Whitney Soule, vice provost and dean of admission, University of Pennsylvania

Choosing a college is often more of an emotional decision than it is a rational one. This is why I recommend students honestly and objectively consider what they really want from their college experience and how the colleges they are considering match their expectations. College is a big investment of time and money, so you want to make the right decision for the right reasons. —Scott Verzyl, vice president for enrollment management and dean of undergraduate admissions, University of South Carolina

Choosing your college is like buying a pair of jeans. You bring many into the dressing room and choose the pair that feels the best, and is within your budget, out of the available options. They may fit well but are far from perfect when brand new. It's only after wearing them, and washing them over time, that they become truly comfortable. That's like college—over time, you make new friends, choose interesting and challenging classes, get involved in your new community and declare a major. All of these experiences, over time, help the college fit even better.

There is no one perfect fit; there will be good and bad classroom experiences, defining friendships and emotional hardships, unexpected and inspiring opportunities at all the schools you consider. Compromise is inevitable and no college/university is tailor made for you. The things that might make you uncomfortable at first may bring the most personal growth and help launch you into a fulfilling life. —Ann Marie Strauss, director of college counseling, Bryn Mawr School

Follow your heart, considering your head and your wallet. —Miguel Wasielewski, executive director of admissions, University of Texas at Austin

Start with thinking hard (and honestly) about what matters most to you, what situations, circumstances, etc., make you smile most often and then look at your school options and consider where you are likely to smile more often and for the most reasons. Ask each college, "What are the top two or three reasons that students choose to leave your school?" —Eric Monheim, director of college counseling, St. Mark's School

College is about meaningful engagement with others who don't share your worldview. Think of yourself as a rubber band. Choose the school that stretches you the most without breaking you. Ask which college's core values most closely resemble yours. —Heath Einstein, dean of admission, Texas Christian University

Think carefully about choosing a college mainly because of the big, fun athletic program, especially football—because that only covers four, maybe five Saturdays (home games) out of the entire school year. Sure, those four or five days will be fun, but you need to think about how you will feel about your choice of college on a rainy Tuesday afternoon in February when the campus is quiet. —Catherine Odum, director of college guidance, Charlotte Country Day School

Look for a place where the energy will get you to engage in several areas. Ask each college, "What are some of the opportunities here that are not to be missed?" —Sheppard Shanley, former senior associate director of admission, Northwestern University

BURN THE SHIPS!

In 1519 Hernán Cortés sailed to what became Veracruz, Mexico, at the direction of the king and queen of Spain, to find gold, silver, and a new place to settle. When he and his crew anchored offshore, his crew talked incessantly about returning home. They were thinking about other places and imagining the life they left behind. As they came ashore, Cortés ordered, "Burn the ships!" so that they would not look back and would instead commit themselves to a new land and life.

Once you put down your enrollment deposit, that is your job as well. At this point, you need to be all-in—buy the T-shirt, put the window decal on the car, be confident in your decision. Start following student groups at the school on social media, donate the shirts you got from other schools (you don't have to be like Cortés and burn them), withdraw any outstanding applications at other colleges, and start planning on going to orientation that summer. Be thankful for having had the opportunity to choose, refuse to let buyer's remorse gnaw at you, and move forward confidently.

Guard yourself from the temptation to think the grass is greener elsewhere. Begin your conversations with others and within yourself with an attitude of gratitude for the opportunities you have rather than a spirit of entitlement or loss. —Michael Schell, associate superintendent of enrollment management and marketing, Catholic Schools Office

DEADLINE MEANS DEADLINE

Admission professionals are typically personable and good-natured. But when it comes to deadlines, do not test their generosity. They are concerned with making an incoming class, after all. Imagine this scenario: You do not put down your deposit by 11:59 p.m. on the deadline of May 1, and the admission director for the school arrives on the morning of May 2 and finds that the number of admits who have paid their deposit exceeds the school's class-size target. That director is going to shut off the capacity for anyone else to make a deposit. Deadline means *dead*line. Make your decision and put your money down.

⋅ờ⋅ *Try This*

1. Narrow your choices down to one to four schools.

2. Visit each one, ideally in person during an accepted-student event or on your own. If you are unable to make it to campus, participate in the school's accepted-student program online.

3. After your visits, write down the pros and cons of each college. Create a category for each feature that matters the most to you (academics, social life, athletics, food, etc.). Is one college's list of pros longer than that of the other(s)?

4. Role-play by choosing a college and then spending the next three days telling yourself that is where you're going to attend. Wear the college's shirt, hat, or hoodie. Hang its pennant in your room. For those few days, try to put the other options out of your mind, and be aware of your reactions to your decision. Are you excited, relieved, regretful, anxious, hopeful? Jot down your reactions. When those three days are up, repeat the exercise with the other colleges you are still considering.

💬 Talk about This

1. What are the main factors holding you back from making a decision?

2. Is there information you still need to gather before you can decide? If so, what do you need to know and how will you get answers?

3. Think of another big decision that you or a member of your family had to make. How was that decision made? What can you apply from that experience to the decision you are making now?

 **CHECK IN.** After reading this chapter, are you still on the same page as a family? If you are not all-in together, what do you need to do, discuss, or learn to get there?

☆ Extra Credit

Watch the video of Steve Jobs delivering his 15-minute commencement address at Stanford University in 2005. He makes a series of important points that will give you perspective for making a confident choice.

As we covered in chapter 4, return on investment, or ROI, can be a big factor in your decision of where to go to college. Follow the QR code in the upper corner to a worksheet that will help you explore your potential ROI from colleges.

CHAPTER 13

Closing Letters

Get up everybody and sing / Everyone can see we're together
As we walk on by / And we fly just like birds of a feather.
"WE ARE FAMILY" BY SISTER SLEDGE

A COLLEGE COUNSELOR'S LETTER TO STUDENTS

He who has a why to live for can bear almost any how.
—Friedrich Wilhelm Nietzsche

In this final chapter of the book, I (Brennan) have two homework assignments for students. (Rick has a send-off letter to parents that follows.) Don't worry; this won't involve worksheets, and you will not be graded. In fact, if you have learned anything in these pages, it should be that searching for and applying to college is not a test or project that you can, or should try to, ace. Even better news: the due date for these assignments is flexible.

The first assignment is possibly the most important thing you will do during your college admission experience. The second is some required reading, and I will provide you with CliffsNotes to highlight the take-home messages. All you really need is an open mind and a continued willingness to stay grounded in family and future in your approach to college admission. Are you ready?

DO THIS

First some background: When I was in my early thirties, my mother (then in her late fifties) was diagnosed with early-onset Alzheimer's disease and frontal-lobe dementia. This began a five-year deterioration of her memory. Did she remember all of the special moments from my childhood? Did she remember driving me and my brothers from activity to activity? Did she remember the battles we had over homework? Did she know how selfless she had been since the day I was born? Did she remember our visits to colleges and the laughs we shared as I dreamed about my future and she hesitantly anticipated my departure? Did she know how grateful I was? Did she know how much I loved her? I assumed she did, but how often did I intentionally say it beyond signing off from a phone call or when departing for a trip?

OK, now the action: When you finish reading this paragraph, put the book down and go find your parents. Look them in the eyes, and tell them that you need them to know that *you love them* and *you appreciate them*. (You can add a hug for emphasis.) It is that simple: "I love you" and "Thank you." Don't laugh it off with sarcasm as you tell them. Don't text it to them. Don't dismiss this exercise because your love and appreciation is "a given" or "no-brainer." Choose to express yourself and acknowledge the awesome power they have given you. OK . . . now go. I will be waiting.

Welcome back. It felt good, right? Even if it seems needless to say, you are *where* you are, and in many ways *who* you are, because of them. This expression of love and gratitude affirms our recommended approach to college admission. This experience is about relationships, communication, and choice. To prioritize investing in people will not only determine how successful your college search and application experience will be, but it will also have implications for your college career and life well beyond it. You may be the one applying, but college admission is a team effort that requires communicating honestly and frequently in order to stay unified. Do not try to go this alone. Express your love and gratitude early and often.

READ THIS

Every great course has a robust syllabus of readings to guide your learning experience. The following books provide important lessons and questions that will make your college search more meaningful. I know you're busy. Who has time to read more than what is already assigned in school? Don't worry; I am going to make this easy by providing a synopsis and boiling down their messages. For extra credit, check out "Suggested Further Reading" and "Web Resources" at the end of the book.

Start with Why: How Great Leaders Inspire Everyone to Take Action by Simon Sinek

Synopsis: As the title suggests, Sinek stresses the importance of understanding why we do what we do. If you don't have the time to read the book, at least listen to his wildly popular TED Talk to hear how he weaves together the examples of Dr. Martin Luther King Jr., the Wright brothers, and Steve Jobs. The tie that binds these individuals is their ability to focus less on the outcome and more on articulating the reason behind their actions.

    Key Quote: "Knowing your WHY is not the only way to be successful, but it is the only way to maintain lasting success and have a greater blend of innovation and flexibility. When a WHY goes fuzzy, it becomes much more difficult to maintain the growth, loyalty, and inspiration that helped drive the original success."

    Take-Home Message: We have driven Sinek's message into the ground throughout the book: you must first connect with your *why*. You are probably sick of hearing it, but it is at the core of our philosophy. Admission to college is not a passive experience; it is about engagement, and I am challenging you to lean in. My hope is that you will have the confidence not simply to submit to the expectations of those around you. And that extends well beyond college admission.

Use this as an opportunity to ask yourself *why*—and then enjoy seeing the *where* and *what* follow.

This is the ideal time to really consider who you are and explore your vision for the future. I see too many students buy into the myth that college admission is merely something to "get through," a stressful experience of jumping through hoops. Sure, it takes planning, work, and compromise, and there will be parts of this journey that will be more enjoyable (maybe college visits) than others (perhaps standardized testing). However, if you stay true to yourself and keep your hopes for the future front and center, it will be less of a chore and more of an adventure.

Applying to college is not just about submitting applications and waiting for a reply. It is about envisioning the years to come and the experiences you hope to have. We have provided throughout this book many questions for you to ask yourself. Here are a few to consider in closing: What are you excited about? What are you scared of? What do you want to be different in your next chapter of life? What is something new you hope to try? Whom do you want to meet? What do you want to learn that you haven't yet had the opportunity to explore? Think big, and let your college search and application support these dreams.

> The college admission experience is the ideal time to consider who you are and explore your vision for the future.

Where You Go Is Not Who You'll Be: An Antidote to the College Admission Mania by Frank Bruni

Synopsis: Again, the title says it all. In this important study of college outcomes, Bruni asks us all to take a collective deep breath and realize that admission to any given school does not guarantee success, happiness, or meaning in life. Using stories and statistics about well-known people, he lays out a case for applying to and attending schools of all shapes and sizes.

Key Quote: "The nature of a student's college experience—the work that he or she puts into it, the skills he or she picks up, the self-examination that's undertaken, the resourcefulness that's honed—matters more than the name of the institution attended."

Take-Home Message: Are you a quantitative or data-driven person? Do you need assurance that life will still work out if you are denied by your top-choice college and have to "settle" for a school farther down your list? Bruni's book demonstrates the point we have repeatedly made—there is no perfect or dream college. Your goal instead is to have a perfect approach to finding a good college for you. (Oh, and don't worry; your parents are told below to read Bruni too.)

The Road to Character by David Brooks

Synopsis: Through a study of great leaders and activists, Brooks invites us to consider the aspects of character that really matter. This *New York Times* columnist is adept at capturing the human condition. Brooks refers to "eulogy virtues"—those things you are and will always be known for, the contributions you make to others and the joy you bring to life. These qualities, far more than any list of your achievements or awards (what he calls "résumé virtues"), are what distinguish you.

Key Quote: "People with character may be loud or quiet, but they do tend to have a certain level of self-respect. Self-respect is not the same as self-confidence or self-esteem. Self-respect is not based on IQ or any of the mental or physical gifts that help you get into a competitive college. It is not comparative. It is not earned by being better than other people at something. It is earned by being better than you used to be, by being dependable in times of testing, straight in times of temptation. It emerges in one who is morally dependable. Self-respect is produced by inner triumphs, not external ones."

Take-Home Message: So much of preparing for college admission can seem like résumé building. "What activities *should* I do?" "What classes do I *need to* take?" "Which essay topic *must* I choose?" It is easy to focus on the selection part of college admission and to view it as a judgment on you as a person. Having worked with hundreds and hundreds of college applicants, I continually hear students ask themselves, "Will I measure up? Will I stand out? Will I get in? Will I be successful?" The answer, unequivocally, is yes. I will say that again: *yes.*

No matter where you end up, you are going to be an invaluable addition to that campus community. My hope is that you'll not waver from that belief.

IF YOU REMEMBER ANYTHING . . .

When I was first starting out in education, a colleague suggested that when planning my classes for the year, I consider what "beach knowledge" I wanted my students to recall. That is, when my students are sitting on the beach in July, what do I want them to remember from my class. So, now that you have completed the homework above, I present the beach knowledge I want you to take with you. My hope is that you will add to this list and take it to heart.

College admission is . . .

- a personal journey: this is your search, so own it.

- an invitation to explore identity and purpose: this will not happen overnight.

- imperfect: it is a human process, so expect "user error."

- a celebration of your hard work.

- about engagement: so lean in.

- fun: the minute it becomes a chore, stop and check yourself; enjoy the ride.

- an investment in you: both short and long term.

- about unity, not vanity: don't sacrifice relationships for status.

- a privilege: so take advantage of the opportunities you have.

- full of choice: be open and consider all of your options.

College admission is *not* . . .

- a value judgment on whether you are "good enough."

- life or death.

- fair.

- about status: aim high but for the right reasons.

- a game or prize.

- the final exam for high school: you only do high school once, so live in it.

- one size fits all.

- to be taken at face value: dig deep and ask probing questions.

- a reason to create an unreasonable schedule: prioritize balance.

- a passive experience: you are in control, so assert it.

- a search for perfection: there is not one "right" college.

- a test: like life, this is the real thing, so be in it.

Here is what I know: you are bound for success. You are bound for an exciting college experience filled with opportunities to learn, connect, and grow. *Where* all of that will happen is a mystery—and like all good mysteries, it should be filled with twists, turns, discovery, new places, and interesting people. My hope is that you find joy in uncovering the clues that will lead you and that ultimately you will arrive on a college campus confident and excited to embrace opportunity.

AN ADMISSION DEAN'S LETTER TO PARENTS

I (Rick) will never forget the day my wife, Amy, and I told my parents that she was pregnant with our first child. We were at our favorite restaurant in town, and when the bill came, I leaned across the table to grab it. My dad, as expected, simultaneously reached for his wallet. "Don't worry, Grandpa. I got it," I said, as I slid the sonogram over to him and my mom.

After some hugs and tears, they conveyed their congratulations, and we shared our excitement and confessed our nervousness. As usual, my mom's words were succinct and poignant: "There is no 100 percent right way. Just make sure your kids always know you love them and that you are proud of them. Everything else will take care of itself." Since that time, my wife and I have received plenty of parenting advice (largely unsolicited) about everything from swaddling to school choice, diapers to discipline, and car seats to summer camps. To this day, however, my mom's words remain the most instructive.

So, I'm going to take a page from her book and keep my advice (and hopes) for your family's college admission experience simple.

Change Your Filter

I grew up in Decatur, Georgia. At the time, it was . . . fine. Lots of auto shops, a few good burger places, and the typical churches, recreation centers, schools, and city services of most towns. My street was divided—half the houses were in the city limits of Decatur, and half were in the county of DeKalb. As kids, we did not think much of it, other than that the city sign made a good target for an array of launched objects. Adults agreed (not about the sign) that there was basically no distinguishable difference in quality between county and city. When I went to college in North Carolina, nobody there had heard of Decatur, so I would say I grew up a few miles east of downtown Atlanta.

> Look beyond what you see.

Today, Decatur is a different story. The affordable three-bedroom, two-bath houses that once filled Decatur are largely gone. It is tough to find anything on the real estate market for less than $500,000, and new construction commonly exceeds seven figures. People living just outside the city line now vehemently petition for annexation; the gas stations have been converted into gastropubs (and will now gladly charge you $15 for "frites"); boutiques line the streets; the school system is among the best in the state; and the quality of life is continually touted in trendy national magazines. Even the city sign is nicer.

Bottom line: Decatur has become a true destination. You simply cannot apply the same filter you did 20 years ago or even 5 years ago for that matter.

As you go through the college admission experience, I hope you will "look beyond what you see" and *change your filter*. Basically everything about college admission has changed—the way students search for schools, the format and content of applications, the cost of college, the volume and competition of applicant pools, and, importantly, the brand and reputation of many universities.

Old Filter

> "The University of X? Where the kids from our school went if they could not get in anywhere else here?"

"If you drove slowly down Main Street with your window open, they'd throw a diploma in."

"On Tuesdays people were already tailgating for Saturday's game."

New Filter

I am not going to lie, Decatur used to be a little sketchy. I remember looking askance at the lollipops that bank tellers would hand out. So when your student brings you a brochure from the University of X, I'm hoping you will consider it with fresh eyes. You may find that its town is now perennially written up as a great place for food, family, and culture; the university has invested heavily in student support and programs; the students are winning international competitions for research and prestigious scholarships and fellowships. Change your filter. U of X may just be a great match. Don't diminish your student's excitement with your preconceived notions. The truth is we can all be cognitive misers at times. Model for your kid what you have asked them to do in the past when it comes to broccoli or a new school: keep an open mind. As you know, good high school students, good college applicants, and good college students test assumptions, research, and continually rethink. Show them the way.

Old Filter

"He has a 1460. He'll get in for sure."

"They gave me a summer provisional admit offer, and I was able to stay if I did well."

"I wrote a two-word essay: 'Go' followed by the mascot's name, which I misspelled, and they still let me in."

New Filter

I hear you; 1460 is a high test score. You should be proud. And you are right: 20 or more years ago there was room for "creative admission" practices at colleges that now admit less than one of every three applicants and carry wait lists with as many applicants as applied the year you started college. There was a time when, even at highly selective schools, it was about the numbers, so good grades and solid test scores would likely lead to admission. Thankfully, there still are great colleges running numeric formulas to make their decisions.

If your child chooses, however, to apply to schools that receive far more applications than they have spaces in their next class, I hope you will change your filter and not make any assumptions. Holistic admission means that test scores and GPA are only two pieces in a larger conversation that includes an applicant's impact and influence and that college's institutional priorities.

Old Filter

"Tuition was less than $1,000 per quarter."

"I paid my next semester's bill with the money I saved from my internship."

"I was able to pay off all of my student loans within five years of graduating."

New Filter

In today's real estate market you are as likely to find a new house in Decatur listed for $200,000 as one for $200 (read: no chance). As you begin to research college costs, you'll likely have some eye-popping, heart-stopping, head-shaking moments. Don't let tuition or overall cost of attendance alone keep you from visiting a school or encouraging your student to apply if you all determine that it's a good match academically, geographically, and culturally.

I hope you will be humble enough to share your financial situation early and openly with your student. Walk them through your limitations, conditions, and expectations as we discussed in chapter 3, and use the example of Maya from chapter 4 to guide you in preparing for the conversation. If you are willing to share your financial information with your student, you will be amazed by how well they'll absorb and apply it. Take the time to have honest discussions about finances, check out colleges' Net Price Calculators, and read up on different financial aid packages and programs. One of the biggest gifts you can give your student in the admission experience is educating them about financial choices and the implications of carrying debt after they graduate.

You will be able to find many affordable financial matches. I hope you will lead your family student to select one of these, rather than overextending financially and unnecessarily incurring burdensome debt.

A Special Note to Alumni

"I have been donating consistently for the last 20 years."

"There should be spots held for families who have multiple-generation connections."

"Don't y'all care at all about preserving tradition? We've been bringing our kids there since they were in diapers."

If you loved your college experience, changing the filter of your own alma mater is sometimes the toughest adjustment. It is understandable why you'd want your child to visit and apply to your alma mater, but I hope you will remain objective as they consider whether it is a good match for their goals.

One of the biggest tragedies I see in the admission experience is the reaction of alumni when their kid gets denied by their alma mater. They take it as a personal affront and let it taint their own experience and love for the school. Commit early to preventing that from becoming part of your story. Before you write your alma mater out of your will, cancel your season tickets, donate sweatshirts to Goodwill, or remove a tattoo, remember that the way admission decisions *feel* is not how they are *made*.

I hope you will have the vision to help your student start with asking *why* they want to go to college, have the patience to listen to their answers, and have the wisdom to bring them back to those guiding responses along the way. Allow their goals and hopes to guide, not an arbitrary list of schools, the opinions of others, the culture of your high school community, a rankings publication, or outdated stereotypes.

Control What You Can Control

You cannot control admission decisions. You cannot control institutional priorities or merit scholarships or financial aid packages. You cannot control the competition in any given applicant pool. What you can control is how you conduct yourself and the example you set for those around you.

I hope you will be an example in your community. At times the gossip about admission will be unhealthy and unproductive. I hope you will recognize these moments and either remove yourself from the conversation or else redirect it. When a friend's son gets admitted to college, share in their joy. When your daughter's teammate is dejected about being denied, encourage her with what you know—that she is going to have other incredible choices. Tell her with confidence and excitement that good news is coming.

I hope you will be an example on social media. You are going to see some misinformed opinions, negative banter, catty comments, and bald-faced lies. My hope is you won't engage in that dialogue online, and take opportunities in person to recenter your friends, neighbors, or relatives. Strongly consider not posting anything about your child's college search or admission experience, unless you think it could benefit others. Use your platform to be positive and reassuring. Provide healthy, desperately needed perspective to online discussions when they go off the rails and fan the flames of anxiety.

I hope you will be an example for your family. Back away when you are on a college visit, and let your student ask the questions to the tour guide or admission counselor. In a short year or two, your student will be on a college campus. They will need to be able to navigate and advocate for themselves with professors and in interviews for an internship or a job. Look at this as an opportunity to prepare them for success in that next chapter.

I hope that as a parent in this process, you will remember that you are more of a coach than a player. You are a parent—not an applicant. That is so much easier said than done. So feel free to go for a walk or a drive when you hear yourself say things like "*We* are taking the SAT next weekend" or "*Our* first choice is Vanderbilt." Ask yourself if those pronouns are just a reflection of your love and 17 years of intertwined lives or if they are a subtle indication that you should step back and let your student demonstrate what you know they are capable of. Parenting is a delicate dance, but it is one you know well. Be honest with yourself, and you will know when to take the lead and when not to. You got this!

Trust your student's ability to express themselves effectively in their writing on college applications. Use your weekly meetings to ask questions about essays and make helpful edits or suggestions rather than rewriting or inserting words like *prodigious* or *convivial*.

You are going to see inequities. You will see students get in with lower test scores than your own child has. The kid down the street or the star athlete or the son of a donor (insert unthinkable prototype here) is going to receive acceptances or scholarships that your student does not. You are going to read or watch videos, pictures, social media posts, or comments online about neighbors or classmates who, by every measure you can observe, do not seem "as good as" or "as qualified as" your student.

Each year, after decision letters go out, admission officers receive fuming phone calls and vitriolic emails, threats, accusations of bias and conspiracy, and expletive-laden rants. These *never* come from students. I hope that when you are tempted to "get in my car and drive down there," you will take a deep breath and (when necessary) bite your lip. When you get upset, remember that those emotions are just a manifestation of your love for your child. They need to hear that you love them, so keep telling them.

I hope you will encourage your child to enjoy their high school years. Remind them to keep perspective when a test does not go well or a final grade is lower than what they wanted. If they want to quit a team or an activity because they are miserable, support their decision. Hug them often. Enjoy this special and all-too-short chapter of life.

It Is All Going to Work Out

My hope is that you will not get stuck in an echo chamber when your student is in high school and especially when they are looking at colleges. Find ways to break out of that. Take some time to look at the Fortune 500 or Fortune 100 list of companies and their CEOs. Most of them graduated from schools that are *not* categorized as highly selective. Read Frank Bruni's book *Where You Go Is Not Who You'll Be*. Listen to the many stories that your own friends and colleagues will tell about their own college experiences. They will tell you that they did not get into their top choice or could not afford to attend a certain school; now, though, 20 or 30 years after graduating, they would not have it any other way.

The bottom line is that parents of high school students should talk about college admission to fewer parents of other high school students and to more parents with kids in college. Ask those parents to reflect on their admission experience. Inevitably, you will hear them say they wish they had not stressed as much about everything. They will tell you about their daughter who was not admitted to her first-choice school, ended up elsewhere, and is thriving now. Enthusiastically, they will relate how their son did not receive the merit scholarship he had hoped for, selected another option from his choices, and now has an incredible internship and a girlfriend (whom they actually like).

> Keep it simple— love your kids well.

I understand that, as a parent, the college admission experience seems complicated because it is filled with myriad deadlines. It seems confusing because the press and how-to guides regularly provide incomplete, and frequently inaccurate, data. It seems consuming because friends and colleagues are quick to share their "inside" information and stories (or the alleged stories of relatives) on social media. It seems confounding because those same friends and colleagues have divergent opinions that they are quick to share with you at school, the grocery store, or in the stadium bleachers. It seems complex because colleges and universities all have different processes, review different factors, and operate on different timelines.

After watching the admission cycle repeat itself for two decades, I am convinced that people are focused on "getting in" when they should simply be committed to staying together. My hope is that you will keep it simple—love your kids well. They need to hear it, so do not stop telling them, "I trust you. And I am proud of you."

Soon (sooner than you probably want to believe) you will be helping your child move in at college and taking the requisite family picture next to some iconic campus building or statue. I witness these photo ops every year, and I can tell you there are three possible scenarios:

1. Everyone cries: mom, dad, student (sometimes even the younger sibling or passerby flagged down to take the picture).

2. Parents cry, and the student scans the walkway to see how many people are coming that direction.

3. Nobody cries, but there are some deep breaths, bitten lips, and blinking.

For parents in the third group, on the drive back home, after having carried all the bags, boxes, and devices into the dormitory, there are tears. Make no mistake—on that day every parent cries.

As a parent, these are complicated, bittersweet tears. They are a mixture of joy and loss, tears filled with both love and pain, tears of pride and regret, tears that distinctly remember small kids on bikes or wearing backpacks that hung down to their knees, and tears that hope for a life impossible to fully imagine. They are tears for words spoken and unspoken. These tears bemoan the end of a chapter and celebrate the start of a new one.

We cannot tell you *where* your family will be standing on that day, but the fact that you have read this book gives us all the confidence in the world that your move-in day is coming. Our hope is that you will be committed to *how* your family arrives on campus—truly together. To quote a very wise woman: "There is no 100 percent right way. Just make sure your kids always know you love them and that you are proud of them. Everything else will take care of itself."

☆ **Extra Credit**

Okay, your turn. Set aside some time to write letters to one another. Students, write to each parent or supporter. Parents, write to your child and to each other, if you have a partner or another adult with whom you've shared this experience. Express your gratitude for what has happened up until this point, and highlight your hopes for you all in the future. You may choose to give the letters now or at some point in the future. We hope you will write more letters like this in life because the power of gratitude is undeniable. While we on are the topic of expressing thanks, we genuinely appreciate your reading our book. And know that we enjoyed writing it for you.

Acknowledgments

We would like to express our immense gratitude to those who have taught and supported us in writing this book. First and foremost, our families, from whom we have learned that the power of unity, connection, and unconditional love is the foundation for a healthy, balanced, and fulfilling life. Our children—Andrew, Elizabeth, Rebecca, and Samuel—are constant reminders of the importance of purposeless play and the joy that can be found in living in the moment. We also feel fortunate to work at institutions that support both the professional and personal growth of faculty and staff, as well as encouraging engagement in the field of education well beyond campus. We are grateful for our Rhode Island friends for bringing us together and reminding us that it is "all about the kids" and to Denis Gainty, whose example of love for his children inspired us in writing this book. Finally, we owe huge thanks to Greg Britton and the team at Johns Hopkins University Press for believing in this project, recognizing the potential, and helping us stay true to our message of hope and unity.

BRENNAN

Deep thanks to my family—Timothy, Marjorie, Daron, Justin, Meredy, Katherine, Jessa, Lauren, Duncan, Brad, Jodi, Sam, and Rebecca Barnard—whose unconditional love and support have allowed me to pursue my calling as an educator and who have constantly made me want to be a better person. You have instilled in me the value of togetherness and commitment to others. To the many faculty members at Westtown School, Franklin & Marshall College, and the University of Vermont for teaching me how to express myself and for giving me the foundation on which to build a meaningful life. To Ken and Claire Grant, Paul and Laurie Hurd, and the Hyde School community for launching my career and helping me realize that my vocation is to work with young people at this important time of transition. To the Khan Lab School, Derryfield School, and an amazing group of colleagues, past and present, for their friendship and inspiration and for providing the time and resources to pursue my passion for writing. I am especially grateful to Bruce Berk, Sue Flagg, Jill Teeters, and Amanda Gagne for their patient editing and insightful feedback over the years. Thanks to my colleagues at Making Caring Common at the

Harvard Graduate School of Education and my partners at College Guidance Network for their support and flexibility. To the amazing educators in ACCIS, NACAC, and the Character Collaborative, whose dedication to students and their families is inspiring. To the thousands of students and families with whom I have worked, who have taught me volumes about human nature, fear, hope, and unity. To Matthew Struckmeyer for his tireless wordsmithing and ability to cut to the heart of my message. To Sarah Rebick, Mike Schell, Chris Sacco, John Rigney, Dan Sacco, Bill Cote, Anna Follensbee, Tim and Pam Neville, Alisa Barnard, Matt Hyde, Andy Strickler, Susan Tree, Kim Dow, David Joiner, David Holmes, Lizzie Ormiston, Lloyd Thacker, Ben Temple, Kortni Campbell, Kasey Ormiston, Nancy Aronie, Alan Haas, Allison Matlack, Susan Kennedy, Mike Morris, Jennie Freeman, Shereem Herndon-Brown, Eric Mayer, Brent Powell, Danny Taffe, Tim Pratt, Amy Rogers, Whitney Soule, and many, many others whose friendship, guidance, and love fills my life. Finally, to Rick Clark, whose thoughtfulness, support, depth, and collaboration have made this journey meaningful, joyful, and memorable.

RICK

To my incredibly, ridiculously, amazingly patient and loving wife, Amy, who models every day the person I want to be someday. My kids, Andrew and Elizabeth, for the poignant reminder that the most important things in life are simple—and for bringing me ineffable joy, purpose, and pride. I'm beyond thankful for my parents and sister for instilling confidence and demonstrating unconditional love. To the leadership of Georgia Tech for giving me the space to innovate, create, and risk in the name of "Progress and Service." Inexpressible appreciation and respect for my longtime colleagues for their constant encouragement and support, especially Matt McLendon, Mary Tipton Woolley, Katie Faussemagne, George P. Burdell, Deborah Smith, Becky Tankersley, and the unbelievably talented, passionate, and committed teams I've had the chance to serve alongside. Go Jackets! WSTE. Leadership Georgia 2018 (Best Class Ever) for reminding me "we get to do this." To the All Souls congregation for years of care and community. Cheers to Clambake Nation ("Hi, Neighbor!"). A huge shoutout and mad props to the NACAC/SACAC family for inspiring me to speak, write, and lead in the name of students, access, educational progress, and equity. To Brennan for his collaboration, trust, and invaluable perspective and kindness. Lastly, to my brothers—TJ, Crewser, and the McCauley Street boys—who share a bond unbroken by time or place. Much love.

Suggested Further Reading

10% Happier: How I Tamed the Voice in My Head, Reduced Stress without Losing My Edge, and Found Self-Help That Actually Works—a True Story by Dan Harris (2014)

Acceptance: A Legendary Guidance Counselor Helps Seven Kids Find the Right Colleges—and Find Themselves by David L. Marcus (2010)

Age of Opportunity: Lessons from the New Science of Adolescence by Laurence Steinberg (2015)

Anxious Kids, Anxious Parents: 7 Ways to Stop the Worry Cycle and Raise Courageous and Independent Children by Lynn Lyons and Reid Wilson (2013)

At What Cost? Defending Adolescent Development in Fiercely Competitive Schools by David L. Gleason (2017)

The Black Family's Guide to College Admissions: A Conversation about Education, Parenting, and Race by Timothy L. Fields and Shereem Herndon-Brown (2022)

Brainstorm: The Power and Purpose of the Teenage Brain by Daniel J. Siegel (2014)

College: What It Was, Is, and Should Be by Andrew Delbanco (2014)

College of the Overwhelmed: The Campus Mental Health Crisis and What to Do about It by Richard Kadison and Theresa Foy DiGeronimo (2004)

Colleges That Change Lives: 40 Schools That Will Change the Way You Think about Colleges by Loren Pope (2012)

Creating a Class: College Admissions and the Education of Elites by Mitchell Stevens (2007)

The Curse of the Good Girl: Raising Authentic Girls with Courage and Confidence by Rachel Simmons (2010)

David and Goliath: Underdogs, Misfits, and the Art of Battling Giants by Malcolm Gladwell (2015)

The End of American Childhood by Paula S. Fass (2016)

Excellent Sheep: The Miseducation of the American Elite and the Way to a Meaningful Life by William Deresiewicz (2015)

Far from the Tree: Parents, Children, and the Search for Identity by Andrew Solomon (2012)

Fiske Guide to Colleges by Edward B. Fiske (annual)

The Gift of Failure: How the Best Parents Learn to Let Go So Their Children Can Succeed by Jessica Lahey (2016)

Give and Take: Why Helping Others Drives Our Success by Adam Grant (2013)

Grit: The Power of Passion and Perseverance by Angela Duckworth (2016)

A Hope in the Unseen: An American Odyssey from the Inner City to the Ivy League by Ron Suskind (1999)

How Children Succeed: Grit, Curiosity, and the Power of Character by Paul Tough (2012)

How to Raise an Adult: Break Free of the Overparenting Trap and Prepare Your Kid for Success by Julie Lythcott-Haims (2015)

Letting Go: A Parents' Guide to Understanding the College Years, 6th ed., by Karen Levin Coburn (2016)

Let Your Life Speak: Listening for the Voice of Vocation by Parker Palmer (1999)

Mindfulness for the Next Generation: Helping Emerging Adults Manage Stress and Lead Healthier Lives by Holly Rogers and Margaret Maytan (2012)

The Naked Roommate: And 107 Other Issues You Might Run Into in College by Harlan Cohen (2017)

Our Kids: The American Dream in Crisis by Robert D. Putnam (2015)

The Overachievers: The Secret Lives of Driven Kids by Alexandra Robbins (2006)

The Paradox of Choice: Why More Is Less by Barry Schwartz (2004)

The Parents We Mean to Be: How Well-Intentioned Adults Undermine Children's Moral and Emotional Development by Richard Weissbourd (2010)

Pressured Parents, Stressed-Out Kids by Wendy S. Grolnick and Kathy Seal (2008)

The Price You Pay for College: An Entirely New Road Map for the Biggest Financial Decision Your Family Will Ever Make by Ron Lieber (2021)

The Road to Character by David Brooks (2016)

Start with Why: How Great Leaders Inspire Everyone to Take Action by Simon Sinek (2009)

The Teenage Brain: A Neuroscientist's Survival Guide to Raising Adolescents and Young Adults by Frances E. Jensen with Amy Ellis Nutt (2015)

There Is Life after College: What Parents and Students Should Know about Navigating School to Prepare for the Jobs of Tomorrow by Jeffrey J. Selingo (2017)

Tribe: On Homecoming and Belonging by Sebastian Junger (2016)

Ungifted: Intelligence Redefined; The Truth about Talent, Practice, Creativity, and the Many Paths to Greatness by Scott Barry Kaufman (2015)

Where You Go Is Not Who You'll Be: An Antidote to the College Admissions Mania by Frank Bruni (2016)

Who Gets In and Why: A Year inside College Admissions by Jeffrey J. Selingo (2020)

Web Resources

COLLEGE SEARCH TOOLS

BigFuture: bigfuture.collegeboard.org

College Data: www.collegedata.com

CollegeRaptor: www.collegeraptor.com

College View: www.collegeview.com

Princeton Review: www.princetonreview.com

Unigo: www.unigo.com

VIRTUAL COLLEGE TOURS

CampusTours: www.campustours.com

The College Tour: www.thecollegetour.com

YouVisit: www.youvisit.com

STANDARDIZED TESTING

ACT: www.act.org

ACT Academy test prep: act.org/academy

FairTest: www.fairtest.org

Khan Academy SAT test prep: www.khanacademy.org

Peer-to-Peer free test prep: schoolhouse.world

SAT: collegereadiness.collegeboard.org

FINANCIAL AID AND SCHOLARSHIPS

Department of Education, US: studentaid.ed.gov

Fastweb: www.fastweb.com

Finaid: www.finaid.org

Going Merry: www.goingmerry.com

MyinTuition: www.myintuition.org

NACAC financial aid resources: www.nacacnet.org

NextStudent: www.nextstudent.com

RaiseMe: www.raise.me

Sallie Mae: www.salliemae.com

Scholarshiphelp.org: www.scholarshiphelp.org

Scholarships.com: www.scholarships.com

Studentawardsearch.com: www.studentawardsearch.com

TuitionFit: www.tuitionfit.org

GENERAL

ACT: www.act.org

Campus Safety / Crime Stats: ope.ed.gov/campussafety

Coalition Application: www.coalitionforcollegeaccess.org

College Board: www.collegeboard.com

College Guidance Network: www.collegeguidancenetwork.com

Colleges That Change Lives: www.ctcl.com

Common Application: www.commonapp.org

Education Conservancy: www.educationconservancy.org

Less Stress High School: www.lesshighschoolstress.com

National Association for College Admission Counseling (NACAC): www.nacacnet.org

National Collegiate Athletic Association (NCAA): www.ncaa.org

PODCASTS

The Admission Directors Lunchcast

Admissions Beat

Application to Admission

College Admissions Decoded

College Charge

College Essay Guy

The Truth about College Admission

Understanding the Choices

Your College-Bound Kid

Glossary

Early Action (EA): A nonbinding admission plan with a deadline typically between mid-October and late November. EA decisions are normally released in December or January.

Early Decision (ED): A binding agreement where a student will commit to enrolling if admitted. Many colleges offer two rounds of early decision: ED1, usually in early November, and ED2, in early January. A few colleges allow applicants to apply ED on a rolling basis, meaning that at any time during the admission cycle, an applicant can decide to enter into a binding agreement with the consideration of their application.

priority applications: Also called "VIP applications," "snap apps," "fast apps," and other names, they are streamlined applications (prepopulating biographical information) designed to encourage students to apply early. In many cases, schools using these applications waive application fees and essay requirements.

priority deadlines: A decision plan (often with a deadline of November 1 or December 1) allowing a student to be considered in the school's first round of review. This plan is often found at large public schools, such as the University of Texas at Austin. Some colleges have priority deadlines for specific merit scholarships.

Regular Decision (RD): The standard admission plan with a deadline usually in early January or February and notification in late March.

Restrictive Early Action (REA) / Single Choice Early Action (SCEA): A hybrid admission plan allowing students to apply and receive decisions early under a nonbinding application. In doing so, applicants agree not to apply to another school under a binding ED plan at the same time.

rolling admission: Ongoing review of applications in the order of submission. Admission offers are extended on a rolling basis until the available spots in a class are filled, at which time most schools will still accept applications for their wait list.

TESTING

ACT: A standardized test used in college admission that has four sections: reading, writing, science, and math. Each subscore for a section has a maximum score of 36 points, and the highest total composite score a student can earn is a 36. The composite score is the average of the four subscores, rounded to a whole number.

CEEB Code: A College Entrance Examination Board Code is assigned to every high school and college. This code is included on a high school's profile and can be obtained from a school's guidance office or through searching online.

IELTS: The International English Language Testing System is a test of English as a foreign language that uses a nine-band scale to identify levels of proficiency, from nonuser (band score 1) to expert (band score 9).

SAT: A standardized test used in college admission with two sections: evidence-based reading and writing, and math. Each subscore has a maximum of 800 points for a total possible score of 1600.

superscoring: Combining individual subscores from the sections of tests taken at different test administrations to create the highest combined score.

test-free: Such a school does not consider standardized test scores when making admission decisions and will not view scores if an applicant submits them.

test-optional: Such a school does not require standardized test scores for admission. Note, though, that some schools require an additional essay or other information from a student who does not submit scores.

TOEFL: The Test of English as a Foreign Language measures reading, listening, speaking, and writing skills necessary to performing academic tasks. Each section of the test has a maximum score of 30.

FINANCIAL AID

cost of attendance: This is the total cost a student will pay for a year of college, including tuition and fees, room and board, as well as average costs for books, supplies, transportation, and personal expenses. Reporting this is a federal requirement for colleges and universities. An offer of financial aid cannot exceed the cost of attendance.

CSS Profile: The College Scholarship Service Financial Aid Form is required by many (mostly private) colleges in addition to the FAFSA.

demonstrated need: The cost of attendance minus the expected family contribution equals a student's demonstrated need.

Student Aid Index (formerly expected family contribution, or EFC): This is the amount of money that the federal and institutional financial aid formulas determine a family can afford to pay for a student to attend.

FAFSA: The Free Application for Federal Student Aid is a requirement for any form of federal financial aid, as well as state aid in most cases. It is also used by many colleges and universities to determine eligibility for institutional (school based) aid.

Federal Direct Loan: This is a federal loan for students (formerly known as the Stafford Loan).

Federal Work-Study Program (FWSP): This is a form of financial aid awarded to a student who demonstrates financial need through their FAFSA. Typically, it entails the student having an on-campus job.

grant: Money awarded to a student in "gift aid." These awards come at no cost to the student and do not have to be paid back in the future. Often the term *scholarship* is used interchangeably to refer to the same thing.

merit scholarship: A financial award based on a student's achievement or potential (academic, athletic, artistic, etc.). Typically, it is awarded by the college/university or a private organization. A merit scholarship is not need-based "gift aid" and does not need to be paid back.

need-aware admission: A process of reviewing applicants for admission in which the student's ability to pay *is* taken into consideration.

need-based financial aid: A combination of federal, state, and institutional grants/scholarships, loans, and other financial assistance offered to a student based on their family's ability to pay for the student's education, as determined by the FAFSA (and the CSS Profile, for schools that use it).

need-blind admission: A process of reviewing applicants for admission in which a student's ability to pay *is not* taken into consideration.

net price: The amount of money a student will pay out of pocket after financial aid is awarded.

Net Price Calculator: A federally mandated tool that each school has on its financial aid website. This resource allows families to estimate a financial aid package for which they might be eligible.

Pell Grant: A federal grant based on "exceptional financial need" that does not have to be repaid.

PLUS Loan: A low-interest government loan for the parents of a student attending college.

subsidized direct loan: A federal loan available to students with financial need. The amount available to borrow is determined by the student's year in school and may only go to meet demonstrated need.

tuition discounting: The process by which a college offsets its published tuition "sticker" price with institutional grant/scholarship aid. A school's *discount rate* is the percentage that the school's total institutional grant aid represents relative to its gross revenue from tuition and fees.

unmet need: Also referred to as *gap*, it is the difference between a student's financial aid award (gift aid, work-study, need-based loans) and a student's demonstrated financial need. This occurs when colleges are unable to meet the full demonstrated need of all admitted students.

unsubsidized direct loan: Federal loan available to students regardless of financial need. The amount available to borrow is determined by year in school.

DECISIONS

acceptance/admit: An offer of admission to a college or university.

conditional acceptance: An offer of admission to a college or university that is contingent on certain steps an applicant must take or criteria they must fulfill in order to ultimately enroll.

deferral: A delayed admission decision for candidates who apply through early application plans. Often an updated transcript and/or an update on involvement is required or recommended when a student is deferred.

denial: An application for admission to a college or university that is declined.

guaranteed transfer: An applicant is denied admission as a first-year student but is offered the option to transfer to the college (frequently as a second-year student) provided that the student earns a specified GPA at another institution.

spring/January acceptance: An offer of admission to a college or university with a second-semester start date. Often these offers include the opportunity to enroll in a college-sponsored program off campus (usually abroad) to earn credit during the first semester.

wait list: Neither an acceptance nor a denial, to be wait-listed means that an applicant is potentially admissible but that the college will keep the student on hold in the applicant pool for later consideration based on its enrollment numbers. The student must claim a spot on the college's wait list for later consideration—often after the National Deposit Deadline Day of May 1.

OTHER TERMS

admit rate: The percentage of applicants to a school who are offered admission.

Coalition Application: A universal application for admission through Scoir that is used by more than 140 public and private colleges and universities.

Common Application: A universal undergraduate application for admission that is used by more than 800 public and private colleges and universities.

demonstrated interest: An applicant's enthusiasm for or engagement with a college as shown through visits, communication, and other contact with the admission office. Some schools track these interactions and factor them in admission decisions.

double deposit: Putting deposits down with two colleges to delay having to commit to one.

gap year: A yearlong break between high school and college allowing a student to travel, work, or explore a passion (language, sport, culture).

high school profile: A document developed by a high school to provide colleges with context for that school's curriculum, middle-50-percent test scores, grading policies, community, demographics, college enrollment, and other relevant information.

holistic admission: A method for reviewing applicants that accounts for a student's quality and achievement both inside and outside the classroom.

institutional priority: A goal set by a college that may influence its admission decisions. Such a priority could be geographic, demographic, or curricular.

legacy: An applicant with a family connection to the college. The definition and evaluation of legacy varies by school.

melt: The number or percentage of students who pay their enrollment deposit but do not ultimately enroll.

rigor: The degree of challenge demonstrated by the courses a student took within a high school's curriculum. Rigor is often relative to the courses available or to the overall applicant pool locally or statewide.

search: A process by which colleges contact large numbers of students to elicit their interest in the institution.

yield: The percentage of students admitted to a school who choose to enroll there.

References

Chapter 1. *Why* Are You Going to College?

Matthews, J. 2010. "No Easy Solution to the Mysteries of College Admissions." *Washington Post*. http://www.washingtonpost.com/wp-dyn/content/article /2010/05/23/AR2010052303569.html?noredirect=on.

Chapter 2. Remapping the Admission Landscape

Arkansas Division of Higher Education. n.d. "Institutions in AR." Arkansas.gov. https://sams.adhe.edu/Institutions.

Fast Facts. 2021. "International Students." Institute of International Education. https://opendoorsdata.org/wp-content/uploads/2021/11/OD21_Fast-Facts -2021.pdf.

IPEDS Data Retrieval Center. 2020–2022. US Department of Education, Institute of Education Sciences, National Center for Education Statistics. https://nces.ed.gov/ipeds/use-the-data.

National Center for Education Statistics, US Department of Education. 2022. *Digest of Education Statistics, 2020* (NCES 2022009). Table 317.20. https://nces .ed.gov/programs/digest/current_tables.asp.

Ruffalo Noel Levitz. 2022. *2022 Cost of Recruiting an Undergraduate Student Report*. Cedar Rapids, IA: Ruffalo Noel Levitz. https://learn.ruffalonl.com/rs/395-EOG -977/images/RNL_2022_CostRecruiting_Report.pdf.

Statista. 2021, 2022. "Number of Community Colleges in the United States in 2022, by Type"; "Number of Higher Education Institutions in the United States in the Academic Year of 2020/21, by State." https://www.statista.com /topics/3468/community-colleges-in-the-united-states/; https://www.statista .com/statistics/306880/us-higher-education-institutions-by-state/?locale=en.

U.S. News and World Report. n.d. "Top 100—Lowest Acceptance Rates (2021)." https://www.usnews.com/best-colleges/rankings/lowest-acceptance-rate.

Chapter 3. Wedges of College Admission

Federal Student Aid. 2022. https://studentaid.gov/understand-aid/types/loans /plus.

Gray, K. 2022. "Salary Projections for Class of 2022: Bachelor's Grads a Mixed Bag." National Association of Colleges and Employers. https://www.naceweb .org/job-market/compensation/salary-projections-for-class-of-2022-bachelors -grads-a-mixed-bag/.

Hanson, M. 2022. "College Savings Statistics." Education Data Initiative. https://educationdata.org/college-savings-statistics.

Hanson, M. 2022. "Scholarship Statistics." Education Data Initiative. https://educationdata.org/scholarship-statistics.

Hanson M. 2023. "Student Loan Debt Statistics," Education Data Initiative. https://educationdata.org/student-loan-debt-statistics.

Helhoski, A., and E. Haverstock. 2023. "What's the Average Parent PLUS Loan Debt?" Nerd Wallet. https://www.nerdwallet.com/article/loans/student-loans /whats-the-average-parent-plus-loan-debt.

Lutostanski, S. 2018. "The Compelling Case for Being an 'Intentionally Lazy' Parent." *Washington Post.* https://www.washingtonpost.com/news/parenting/wp/2018/04/10/the-compelling-case-for-intentional-laziness-parenting/.

Chapter 4. Paying for College

Association of Public and Land-grant Universities. n.d. "How Does a College Degree Improve Graduates' Employment and Earnings Potential?" https://www.aplu.org/our-work/4-policy-and-advocacy/publicuvalues/employment-earnings.html.

Causey, J., A. Gardner, H. Kim, S. Lee, A. Pevitz, M. Ryu, A. Scheetz, and D. Shapiro. 2022. *COVID-19 Transfer, Mobility, and Progress.* Herndon, VA: National Student Clearinghouse Research Center.

Federal Student Aid. n.d. "The U.S. Department of Education Offers Low-Interest Loans to Eligible Students to Help Cover the Cost of College or Career School." https://studentaid.gov/understand-aid/types/loans/subsidized-unsubsidized#how-much.

Hanson, M. 2023. "Pell Grant Statistics." Education Data Initiative. https://educationdata.org/pell-grant-statistics.

Lieber, R. 2022. "The College Pricing Game" (episode). *The Daily* (podcast). https://www.nytimes.com/2022/09/14/podcasts/the-daily/college-student-debt.html.

Shepard, D., and D. Filipovic. 2023. "2023 Student Loan Debt Statistics." LendingTree. https://www.lendingtree.com/student/student-loan-debt-statistics/.

Chapter 5. Creating a College List

Gladwell, M. 2021. "Lord of the Rankings" (season 6, episode 2). *Revisionist History* (podcast).

Morse, R., and E. Brooks. 2022. "How U.S. News Calculated the 2022–2023 Best Colleges Rankings." *U.S. News and World Report.* https://www.usnews.com/education/best-colleges/articles/how-us-news-calculated-the-rankings.

National Center for Education Statistics, US Department of Education. 2017. *Beginning College Students Who Change Their Majors within 3 Years of Enrollment.* NCES 2018-434. https://nces.ed.gov/pubs2018/2018434.pdf.

Selingo, J. 2020. *Who Gets In and Why.* New York: Scribner.

Sinek, S. 2009. *Start with Why: How Great Leaders Inspire Everyone to Take Action.* New York: Portfolio.

Chapter 7. Admission Plans, Deadlines, and Application Review

Board of Regents, State of Iowa. 2022. "Regent Admission Index." https://www.iowaregents.edu/institutions/higher-education-links/regent-admission-index/.

Coalition for College. n.d. "Our Vision and Mission." https://www.coalitionforcollegeaccess.org/.

Common Application. n.d. "About." https://www.commonapp.org/about-us.

Dix, W. 2016. "Rethinking the Meaning of Colleges' Low Acceptance Rates." *Forbes*. https://www.forbes.com/sites/willarddix/2016/05/24/rethinking-the -meaning-of-colleges-low-acceptance-rates/#26edbdb41dd0.

Georgia Tech, Institute Research and Planning. 2003. *Georgia Tech Factbook (2003)*. https://irp.gatech.edu/fact-book.

Georgia Tech, Institute Research and Planning. 2013. *Georgia Tech Factbook (2013)*. https://irp.gatech.edu/fact-book.

Chapter 11. Admission Decisions

Amherst College. n.d. "Mission of Amherst College." https://www.amherst.edu /amherst-story/facts/mission.

Caltech. 2023. "Caltech Tech at a Glance." https://www.caltech.edu/about/at-a -glance.

Georgia Institute of Technology. n.d. "Strategic Plan." https://strategicplan .gatech.edu/vision.

Tate, A. 2021. "The Cap on Out-of-State Student Enrollment at North Carolina Universities Could Be Increasing—but Only for HBCUs." Media Hub. https://mediahub.unc.edu/the-cap-on-out-of-state-student-enrollment-at -north-carolina-universities-could-be-increasing-but-only-for-hbcus/.

University of North Carolina–Chapel Hill. n.d. "Mission and Values." https:// www.unc.edu/about/mission/.

Chapter 12. Making Your College Choice

Gladwell, M. 2013. *David and Goliath: Underdogs, Misfits, and the Art of Battling Giants*. Boston: Little, Brown and Company.

Jobs, S. 2005. "'You've Got to Find What You Love,' Jobs Says." Stanford University Commencement Address. *Stanford News*. https://news.stanford.edu /2005/06/14/jobs-061505/.

Schwartz, B. 2004. *The Paradox of Choice: Why Less Is More*. New York: Harper Perennial.

Stanley, A. 2018. "Self-Leadership, Part I"; "Self-Leadership, Part II" (June, July episodes). *Leadership* (podcast). https://andystanley.com/podcast/.

Index